Is the Supreme Court the Guardian of the Constitution?

T0273251

THE RIGHTS EXPLOSION

Robert A. Licht, series editor

THE FRAMERS AND FUNDAMENTAL RIGHTS

IS THE SUPREME COURT THE GUARDIAN OF THE CONSTITUTION?

OLD RIGHTS AND NEW

Is the Supreme Court the Guardian of the Constitution?

Edited by Robert A. Licht

The AEI Press

Publisher for the American Enterprise Institute
WASHINGTON, D.C.

1993

This book was funded in part by a grant from the National Endowment for the Humanities.

Distributed to the Trade by National Book Network, 15200 NBN Way, Blue Ridge Summit, PA 17214. To order call toll free 1-800-462-6420 or 1-717-794-3800. For all other inquiries please contact the AEI Press, 1150 Seventeenth Street, N.W., Washington, D.C. 20036 or call 1-800-862-5801.

Chapter 7 appeared in slightly different form as chapter 3, "The Supreme Court as Republican Schoolmaster," in *1967 The Supreme Court Review*, ed. Philip B. Kurland, pp. 127–80. © 1967 by The University of Chicago. All rights reserved.

Library of Congress Cataloging-in-Publication Data

Is the Supreme Court the guardian of the Constitution? / edited by Robert A. Licht
    p. c.m.—(AEI studies)
    Includes bibliographical references and index.
    ISBN 0-8447-3813-1 (c). — ISBN 0-8447-3812-3 (p)
    1. United States. Supreme Court. 2. Judicial review—United States. I. Licht, Robert A. II. Series.
KF8742.I82   1993
347.73'26—dc20
[347.30735]   92-34511
                                                                         CIP

1 3 5 7 9 10 8 6 4 2

ISBN 978-0-8447-3812-3

The AEI Press
Publisher for the American Enterprise Institute
1150 17th Street, N.W., Washington, D.C. 20036

Contents

Editor and Authors

ROBERT A. LICHT is resident scholar and director of constitution studies at the American Enterprise Institute. He taught philosophy at Bucknell University and liberal arts at St. John's College in Annapolis. Mr. Licht has been a visiting scholar at the Kennedy Institute for Ethics and a National Endowment for the Humanities fellow at AEI. He is the author of "On the Three Parties in America" and "Reflections on Martin Diamond's 'Ethics and Politics: The American Way'" and the coeditor of *Foreign Policy and the Constitution* and *The Spirit of the Constitution*. He is the editor of *The Framers and Fundamental Rights* and *Old Rights and New*.

GEORGE ANASTAPLO holds AB, JD, and PhD degrees from the University of Chicago. He is professor of law, Loyola University of Chicago; lecturer in the liberal arts, the University of Chicago; and professor emeritus of political science and of philosophy, Rosary College. Mr. Anastaplo's most recent books are *The Constitution of 1787: A Commentary* (Johns Hopkins University Press, 1989) and *The American Moralist: On Law, Ethics, and Government* (Ohio University Press, 1992).

WALTER BERNS is John M. Olin University Professor at Georgetown University and adjunct scholar at the American Enterprise Institute. He serves on the Judicial Fellows Commission, has been a member of the Council of Scholars in the Library of Congress and of the National Council on the Humanities and has served as the alternate U.S. representative to the U.S. Commission on Human Rights. Mr. Berns's most recent book is *Taking the Constitution Seriously*.

JOSEPH M. BESSETTE holds the Alice Tweed Tuohy Chair of Government and Ethics at Claremont McKenna College. He has served as acting director and deputy director of the Bureau of Justice Statistics in the U.S. Department of Justice and as director of planning, training, and management of the Cook County (Illinois) State's Attorney's Office. Mr. Bessette has taught at the University of Virginia, Catholic University of America, University of Chicago, and Georgetown University. In addition to other writings on American government and politics, he is coeditor and contributor to *The Presidency in the Constitutional Order* (1981) and coauthor of *American Government: Origins, Institutions, and Public Policy.*

EVA T. H. BRANN is dean of St. John's College, Annapolis, where she has been a tutor since 1957. She is a member of the Maryland Advisory Committee on the U.S. Commission on Civil Rights. Ms. Brann has written articles on the Declaration of Independence, Madison's "A Memorial and Remonstrance," and the Gettysburg Address. Her books include *Late Geometric and Protoattic Pottery: The Athenian Agora* (1962), *Paradoxes of Education in a Republic* (1979), and *The World of the Imagination: Sum and Substance* (1991).

LOUIS FISHER is senior specialist in the separation of powers at the Congressional Research Service of the Library of Congress, where he has worked since 1970. He received his doctorate in political science from the New School for Social Research. Mr. Fisher has taught at a number of universities. He teaches part time at the Catholic University law school. Mr. Fisher has written more than 150 articles for law reviews, political science journals, and other publications. His books include *American Constitutional Law* (1990), *Constitutional Conflicts between Congress and the President* (1991), *The Politics of Shared Power* (1993), *Political Dynamics of Constitutional Law* (1992), and *Constitutional Dialogues* (1988). He has testified before congresssional committees on constitutional issues such as the legislative veto, the item veto, the pocket veto, the balanced budget amendment, and executive privilege.

RALPH LERNER is professor in the Committee on Social Thought and the College of the University of Chicago. Apart from his work in medieval Jewish and Islamic political philosophy, he has specialized in American political thought from the Revolution to the Civil War. He coedited (with Philip B. Kurland) *The Founders' Constitution* (five volumes, 1987) and wrote *The Thinking Revolutionary: Principle and Practice in the New Republic* (1987).

HERMAN SCHWARTZ has been professor of law at the American University School of Law since 1982. He is a specialist in constitutional law and human rights. His recent activities have dealt with constitutional and penal law revision in Eastern Europe, particularly Czechoslovakia, Bulgaria, and Poland; the U.S. Supreme Court; judicial appointments; civil rights and civil liberties in the United States; civil liberties in Israel; prison problems in foreign countries and in the United States; and church-state problems. Mr. Schwartz is the author of *Packing the Courts:*

The Conservative Campaign to Rewrite the Constitution (1988), a study of Ronald Reagan's judicial appointments, and the editor of and a contributor to *The Berger Years* (1987). He has written numerous articles on constitutional law and the courts for scholarly and other journals.

GORDON S. WOOD is university professor and professor of history at Brown University and has been a visiting professor at All Souls College, Oxford. He is the author of *The Creation of the American Republic, 1776–1787* (1969) and *The Radicalism of the American Revolution*.

1

Introduction

Robert A. Licht

At the time of the framing and ratification of the Constitution, Alexander Hamilton asserted with assurance that the judges of the Supreme Court were to be the "faithful guardians of the Constitution."[1] Early in the history of the Republic, with the infamous *Dred Scott* decision, this assertion became questionable. Since then much has changed: in our Constitution because of the Civil War amendments; in the idea of constitutional interpretation and jurisprudence;[2] and in the intellectual climate of the nation.[3] Although these changes have brought the Court increased prominence in our affairs, the passage of time has not smoothed over but rather has sharpened the distrust of the Court as the institution allegedly designated by the framers to secure the Constitution. Nowhere has this become more evident in recent years than in the Court's role in the so-called rights explosion.

This is the third and final volume in a series devoted to the topic of the rights explosion. It required no prophetic inspiration, when planning the series, to see that the final volume must address the constitutional function and role of the Court: the role the Court had assumed for itself on this issue must bring into question its legitimate function.[4] Now, however, the internal crisis of legitimacy resulting from the Court's preoccupation with "fundamental" rights has regrettably become public in the majority opinion and the dissent of Justice Antonin Scalia in *Planned Parenthood of Southeast Pennsylvania v. Casey*—the aftermath of the paradigmatic case of the rights explosion, *Roe v. Wade.*

The spectacle is both so extraordinary in itself and so closely tied to the themes of this volume that some of the Court's arguments on

1

the question of legitimacy may be useful here. The majority opinion in *Planned Parenthood* asserts that

> our analysis would not be complete . . . without explaining why overruling *Roe's* central holding would not only reach an unjustifiable result under principles of *stare decisis*, but would seriously weaken the Court's capacity to exercise the judicial power and to function as the Supreme Court of a Nation dedicated to the rule of law.[5]

What is at stake is nothing less than the Court's legitimacy:

> The Court's power lies . . . in its legitimacy, a product of substance and perception that shows itself in the people's acceptance of the Judiciary as fit to determine what the Nation's law means and to declare what it demands.

The "underlying substance" of legitimacy is the Court's reliance on "principle" in its decisions; the Court cannot compromise "with social and political pressures":

> Because not every conscientious claim of principled justification will be accepted as such, the justification claimed must be beyond dispute. The Court must take care to speak and act in ways that allow people to accept its decisions on the terms the Court claims for them, as grounded truly in principle, not as compromises with social and political pressures. . . . Thus the Court's legitimacy depends on making legally principled decisions under circumstances in which their principled character is sufficiently plausible to be accepted by the Nation.[6]

But when the Court overrules its own decisions, it conveys intellectual weakness and vacillation to the public: "There is a limit to the amount of error that can plausibly be imputed to prior courts. . . . The legitimacy of the Court would fade with the frequency of its vacillation."[7]

Moreover, "to overrule under fire in the absence of the most compelling reason . . . would subvert the Court's legitimacy beyond any serious question."

The Court calls on the public to submit to unpopular decisions but recognizes that there are costs for both the winners and the losers when they accept and support such a decision; this cost requires that the Court be even more "steadfast":

> Some cost will be paid by anyone who approves or implements a constitutional decision where it is unpopular, or who refuses to undermine the decision or to force its reversal. . . . An extra price will be paid by those who themselves disapprove

of the decision's results . . . but who nevertheless struggle to accept it, because they respect the rule of law. To all those who will be so tested by following, the Court implicitly undertakes to remain steadfast, lest in the end a price be paid for nothing.[8]

Finally,

[The American people's] belief in themselves as . . . a people [who aspire to live according to the rule of law] is not readily separable from their understanding of the Court invested with the authority to decide their constitutional cases and speak before all others for their constitutional ideals. If the Court's legitimacy should be undermined, then, so would the country be in its very ability to see itself through its constitutional ideals.[9]

Acid and scornful was Justice Antonin Scalia's dissent from that line of reasoning:

The imperial judiciary lives. It is instructive to compare this Nietzschean vision of us unelected, life-tenured judges—leading a Volk who will be "tested by following," and whose very "belief in themselves" is mystically bound up in their "understanding" of a Court that "speak[s] before all others for their constitutional ideas"—with the somewhat more modest role envisioned . . . by the Founders.

Here he refers to *Federalist* 78, that "the judiciary . . . may be truly said to have neither FORCE nor WILL but merely judgment." He goes on to quote Lincoln's First Inaugural:

Or . . . compare this . . . with the more democratic views of a more humble man: "[T]he candid citizen must confess that if the policy of the Government upon vital questions affecting the whole people is to be irrevocably fixed by decisions of the Supreme Court . . . the people will have ceased to be their own rulers, having to that extent practically resigned their Government into the hands of that eminent tribunal."

Scalia is "appalled" that the Court would stand fast on an erroneous decision in the name of legitimacy:

I cannot agree with, indeed I am appalled by, the Court's suggestion that the decision whether to stand by an erroneous constitutional decision must be strongly influenced—*against* overruling, no less—by the substantial and continuing public opposition the decision has generated. . . . In my history-book, the Court was covered with dishonor and deprived of legit-

3

imacy by *Dred Scott* . . . an erroneous (and widely opposed) opinion that it did not abandon.[10]

He warns of the consequences of the Court's "almost czarist arrogance" in the face of public opposition:

> The American people love democracy and . . . are not fools. As long as . . . we Justices were doing essentially lawyers' work up here—reading text and discerning our society's traditional understanding of that text—the public pretty much left us alone. . . . But if in reality our process of constitutional adjudication consists primarily in making *value judgments* . . . then a free and intelligent people's attitude toward us can be expected to be (*ought* to be) quite different. The people know that their value judgments are quite as good as those taught in any law school—maybe better.[11]

Finally,

> By foreclosing all democratic outlet for the deep passions this issue arouses, by banishing the issue from the political forum that gives all participants, even the losers, the satisfaction of a fair hearing and an honest fight, by continuing the imposition of a rigid national rule instead of allowing for regional differences, the Court merely prolongs and intensifies the anguish.[12]

As regrettable as this public display may be, perhaps there is a certain inevitability in the Court's periodically having to confront the grounds of its own authority and its inherent constitutional vulnerability. For, as several of the authors of this volume suggest, it is paradoxical that the Court—an institution having "neither FORCE nor WILL but merely judgment"—in a republican regime founded explicitly on popular sovereignty and elective representation, might be thought, or believe itself to have, the greatest, exclusive, and final constitutional authority.

Gordon S. Wood on Judicial Review in the Era of the Founding

"Only in the twentieth century," writes Gordon Wood in chapter 9, "has the Supreme Court become the all-encompassing guardian of the Constitution." This root authority of the Court derives from the power of judicial review, and this power may in fact be traced to the beginnings of the Republic:

> Not only did the Founding Fathers radically transform the character of the judiciary in America and give it a significance

it had never had before in Anglo-American culture, but they gave American judges the legal weapons that eventually made judicial review possible.

In colonial America, judges were "appendages . . . of royal authority" and were identified with the executive. But at the time of the Revolution, the state constitutions took away from the executive the power of appointing judges. While this change brought the courts "under the dominion of the legislatures," it also brought them under the influence of legal reformers like Beccaria. By weeding out archaic laws and technicalities, and codifying parts of the common law, the legislatures hoped to reduce judicial discretion. Rather, the "unstable . . . and log-rolling democratic legislatures" instead defeated "the purpose of simplicity and clarity." Judicial discretion perforce increased.

Opinion now turned against the legislatures as "the greatest threat to minority rights and individual liberties." The judiciary was favorably viewed as a "primary means of restraining . . . rampaging popular assemblies." In the 1780s a "remarkable transformation" took place, whose history "has never been written," namely, "the emergence of what Americans called an 'independent judiciary.'"

While the notion that an independent judiciary could nullify legislative acts did not sit easily, nevertheless, the phenomenon of judicial review developed in the the wake of "fundamental changes taking place in Americans' ideas of government and law."

For Americans, the idea of legislative sovereignty began to be supplanted by the idea of popular sovereignty. For this reason, it became possible to argue that a "Supreme Judiciary" might void the acts of legislatures. Hamilton, writing in *Federalist* 78, called the Court "an intermediate body between the people and the legislative." Even so, this view of the judiciary did not by itself create "what came to be called judicial review."

The idea of judicial review required as well the development of the concept of "fundamental law." Although the notion was common in eighteenth-century American and English law, it had "little day-to-day practical importance." It was the "written constitutions of 1776–1777" that "gave revolutionary Americans a handle with which to grasp" this idea. But the next step, that fundamental, written law had a special role in negating legislative acts, was "not yet clear," and resistance to the notion was considerable: "While Jefferson and Madison thought that judges might act as guardians of popular rights," Wood says, "they never believed that judges had any special or unique power to interpret the Constitution."

Indeed, according to Madison, *all* branches of government had a

5

"concurrent right to expound the constitution." In this view, "fundamental law" was "so different in kind from ordinary law" that its exercise was thought to be an "awesomely delicate political exercise." The fact then that a constitution was a fundamental written law could not, by itself, overcome the prejudice against judicial review.

According to Wood, the key to understanding how judicial review came to be accepted is that the fundamental law came to run in the ordinary court system: "The fact that our written fundamental constitutions, our public laws, are interpreted and construed in a routine fashion . . . is at the heart of our peculiar practice of judicial review."

That is, judicial review is the consequence of the "legalization of fundamental law." The English common law tradition, whereby judges followed "well worked-out rules . . . in construing the law" and were given an "extraordinary amount of room for statutory and common law interpretation and construction," eventuated in bringing the "higher law of the Constitution within the rubric of ordinary law . . . as if it were no different from a lowly statute." Thus was the Constitution "domesticated."

This required the removal from politics of the "entire process of adjudication." The judiciary "now tended to avoid the most explosive and partisan political issues." At the same time, however, judges attempted to define "other important issues as . . . within their exclusive jurisdiction." Thus were lines drawn "around what was political or legislative and what was legal or judicial." Especially judicial in nature were questions concerning "the vested rights of individuals." Such questions could no longer be thought of as primarily the province of popularly elected legislatures: "Americans could no longer count on their popularly elected legislatures to solve many of the problems of their lives. . . . It is hard to imagine a more severe indictment of popular democracy."

And so was born what Tocqueville was the first to observe, the American invention of a legal aristocracy: "The courts of justice are the visible organs by which the legal profession is enabled to control the democracy."

Ralph Lerner on the Court as Republican Schoolmaster

A legal aristocracy, if problematic in itself in a democracy, may nevertheless confer a benefit, indeed supply a want in the American regime. Ralph Lerner, in the seventh chapter, "The Supreme Court as Republican Schoolmaster," argues that the Court and the legal profession constitute an aristocracy peculiar to the American Republic, one that, in the founding era at least, assumed for itself a task not explicit in the Constitution but indispensable to its survival: the duty of perpetuating the Republic by forming and shaping a citizenry. In this, they reflected the concerns of "thinking revolutionaries": "For thinking revolutionaries it was axiomatic that securing the republic depended on first forming a certain kind of citizenry."

Although each part of government—legislative, executive, and judicial—must share in this task, the role of the Court was particularly ambiguous, since "the picture of a sitting judge as propagandist, haranguer, or part-time philosopher would warm few hearts, then or now."

But a wider conception of the role of the judge in a democracy is also available. Tocqueville saw that a democratic people might benefit from the "quasi-aristocratic habits" of lawyers and judges. Judges must be well educated, good citizens but also statesmen, sensitive to, dependent upon, and shaping and leading public opinion.

Senate Bill 1, the Judiciary Act of 1789, required the Supreme Court to ride circuit "over the length and breadth of the land." The Court took advantage of the opportunity and used one of its responsibilities, the charge to the grand jury, as a means "to proselytize for the new government and to inculcate habits and teachings most necessary . . . for . . . self-government." The judges understood that the "political charge" to the grand jury "was a deviation"; yet they justified themselves, in the words of John Jay, on the grounds that "occasions of promoting good-will, and good-temper, and the progress of useful truths among our fellow-citizens should not be omitted."

The foremost theme of the "political charge" was "the close connection between self-restraint and true liberty." The republican citizen, in the view of the justices, would be "plainspoken, self-possessed, manly in a quiet" way, and "jealous of his rights but aware of his duties and the self-esteem of others." He would submit "cheerfully" to constitutional majorities, "which is the very basis of all republican governments."

Although such political charges might be considered "impudent meddling," the "probity and caution" of justices like Jay saved them: "Jay enacted in the courtroom the very spirit and teaching that he would inculcate in others." The practice came to an end because of the famously intemperate Justice Samuel Chase's abuse of the political charge. Four decades later, Roger Taney could opine to a grand jury that discussing principles on such occasions "would be a waste of time."

Nevertheless, the practice reveals "the fundamental reasoning for an institution designed to play a broad and permanent part in the life of the nation." The preaching of the justices presumed "a kind of superiority." Did the framers conceive of the Court "as acting and speaking on principles of public-spiritedness and civic devotion"? Could the judges "transcend considerations of enlightened self-interest"? These are questions relating to the character—the virtue—of the citizen in the best sense; they are central to understanding how a republican regime might perpetuate itself.

The Anti-Federalists had complained of "a profound disharmony in the new system." Patrick Henry and Noah Webster had asserted that self-love and self-interest were more dependable principles than virtue. John Marshall had replied that, in the American system, private and public interest were so blended that most men would have a stake in society. Madison as well said that it was a great republican principle "that the people will have virtue and intelligence to seek men of virtue and wisdom." Nevertheless, the question of the Anti-Federalists persisted: how could a regime of liberty endure without addressing the problem of "sustaining popular virtue"?

The discussion of *The Federalist* on this point "is muted and surprisingly incomplete." The authors of *The Federalist*, Lerner argues, "relied on quasi-aristocratic leaders and teachers, like the national judiciary, to sustain and to guide the kind of public their regime presupposed." But in the stress of the fight for ratification, they preferred to make it appear that the regime was actually a "self-sustaining system" and not dependent on virtue, on men like themselves. That is, the founding of a popular regime depended on men "both great and not wholly popular." In the end "a sense of duty" beyond self-interest is "indispensable" and "no branch of government was more likely to shelter and to provide a political platform for that presupposed sense of duty . . . than the judiciary."

The judges, Publius declared, would be "too far removed from the people to share in their prepossessions." Their "nonpopular" character would qualify them to be "an intermediate body between the people and the legislature." Their special training, moreover, would set them apart. Publius's view of the Court, according to Lerner, is that, indeed, it would be closer to the will of the people and "peculiarly fit to discover in the Constitution what the will of the people was." The Court requires a degree of "courage and magnanimity" to serve the people "at the peril of their displeasure," in the words of Publius. Supreme Court justices, Publius makes it clear, might become "teachers of republicanism" who would use "the text of the Constitution . . . in a judicial spirit of moderation and fairness," in Lerner's words.

The judiciary serves as "an instrument of national supremacy" and carries "the authority of the Constitution and the laws to the people," while remaining essentially powerless to take over the government. The judiciary is almost completely separate from dependence on popular sovereignty. Because, in Publius's words, "the interests of the people are at variance with their inclinations," the Court is uniquely situated to assert those interests. In this sense, the judiciary acts "as a special guardian of the principles of the Constitution" precisely because "it can remove itself from its popular source of power." The very separation of the judges increases their ability to perform their "higher function" as the "faithful sustainers and guardians of the regime."

Eva T. H. Brann on Education, the Supreme Court, and the Constitution

For Lerner, the Court and the legal profession repair in part a lacuna of the American regime, one that sets it apart from the ancient tradition of republics: its failure to address directly its own perpetuation through the formation of a republican citizenry. Lerner suggests that, while in the formative years of the American republic the Court took a direct role in educating the citizenry through the charge to the grand jury, in the end, and for most of its history, its aristocratic remoteness and its principled opposition to popular inclinations, together with the fact that it is continuously before the public, "riding circuit" as it were, best serve the needs of perpetuation. Surely, however, the framers could have taken the more direct route of direct public education.

Eva Brann, in the fifth chapter, "Education, the Supreme Court, and the Constitution," interrogates the Constitution's silence on this subject and collaterally examines how the Court, in the service of the Constitution, has influenced the development of education, private and public.

The topic of education and the Constitution may be considered in two ways. We may ask how education is included in the Constitution and, conversely, "the way the document appears in education." More broadly, we may ask what is "the influence of the Constitution on the constitution of American life." Brann first considers the narrow sense.

The Constitution "contains not a word" about education, although the framers were clearly concerned with it. Both James Madison and Charles Pinckney submitted plans, Madison to set up a national university and Pinckney "to establish seminaries for the promotion of the arts and sciences." As Brann notes, "What is . . . remarkable about these . . . plans, from a contemporary point of view, is that no author showed the slightest concern for any constitutional problem."

Moreover, "each of the first six presidents" favored the establishment of a national university. But popular support for such a plan was weak, primarily because of concerns about curriculum, particularly the place within it of religious instruction:

> The suspicion of antireligion would have been magnified for a nonsectarian national university—and nonsectarian it must surely have become, quite aside form the predilections of the founders, once the Bill of Rights was passed.

The state constitutions, however, made a place for education, both secular and religious. Brann writes, "The legitimate business of making people better does not belong to the federal government, and therefore it belongs to the states." This is "a large part of the answer" to the question of why the Constitution is silent on the subject.

The role of the Supreme Court reflects the fact that education is "not a federal power under the Constitution." In the early days of the Republic, the *Dartmouth College* case decided in favor of the independence of small colleges. It was not until after World War II that the Court became involved to any substantial degree in education questions, and this mostly in regard to "rights and liberties in educational settings." The concern with curriculum is never about "what must be taught but rather what may or may not." Generally, these cases concern the limits of a state's control over curriculum in publicly supported schools. In the words of Justice McReynolds, "The state may do much . . . to improve the quality of its citizens . . . but the individual has certain fundamental rights which must be respected." In the end, therefore, both the states and the federal government are limited in their ability "to make [their] . . . citizens good." Brann continues:

> The content of education has been twice safeguarded under the Constitution. The curricula of public schools are subject only to the restrictions arising from fundamental, individual rights, and private schools are free to teach what people will pay to learn.

Turning to the subject of the Constitution in education, Brann looks at the work of three authors: Thomas Jefferson, Horace Mann, and John Dewey.

Jefferson argued that the proper purpose of a university is "to form . . . statesmen, legislators and judges" and its curriculum properly would include John Locke's *Second Essay*, the Declaration, and *The Federalist*. "We may infer," writes Brann, "that the Constitution was certainly to be read, but read under the aegis of *The Federalist*."

Horace Mann argued explicitly that the Constitution must be part of a public school education: "The common basis of our political faith, shall be taught to all." Mann's goals were incorporated into public education, in part, by "civics" courses. But civics has been replaced by "social science," and this owes much to the influence of John Dewey.

Dewey called for "the socialization of mind"—rather than for the inculcation of "knowledge of, and reflection on, the definitive political frame of our social life." This mode is not "a knowledgeable reverence for a political framework—the conservatism of the republican revolution. It is rather a continuing critique of the social system." As a result, in the public schools, "knowledge of the founding documents has all but collapsed."

Brann inquires into what the requirements must be for a restoration of a public education that can shape an American civic character and proposes a six-part program for that purpose. First, Americans must place politics before society, since the Constitution "attributes no power or duty to society. Responsibilities and rights belong entirely to political bodies or individuals." Second, "liberty [must] always [be] actual, equality mostly potential." Third, "the people [are] to judge"; that is, the people must have "the political willingness to accept majoritarian mandates while preserving a lively trust in the Constitution's arrangements for protecting minorities." Fourth, people must see that "fundamental law" is "the embodiment of rights," that is, that the Bill of Rights elevates "the Constitution above merely positive law." Fifth, citizens must understand "the federal or layered disposition," that is, that we live a life of "split-level loyalties": national, state, and local. Finally, citizens must accept "the separation of civic and religious life. . . . This high tact and discretion is a peculiarly American mode; it is the antithesis of totalitarianism."

Herman Schwartz on the Court and Public Policy

In the absence of a citizenry civically educated and constitutionally knowledgeable, the disjunction between the judiciary and the people can only grow. Gordon Wood sees this gap as problematic for a popular democracy; Lerner sees a nonpopular, knowledge-based legal aristocracy prepared to oppose popular inclinations as a necessary support for a republican regime. In Herman Schwartz's chapter, we can see what is generally understood in the nation's law schools as the proper work of a knowledge-based legal aristocracy, remote from the people because of its arcane knowledge, but working in their behalf for what it understands to be the highest goals of the nation.

Schwartz takes as his subject the relation of the Court to public policy, an idea central to appreciating its powers. The Court's role in public policy raises a fundamental question: "How much power should this unaccountable, countermajoritarian institution exercise?" Schwartz looks at two areas of concern: property rights and the Court's role in statutory construction.

He prefaces his discussion, however, with a more general inquiry into the meaning of "public policy" in a legal context.

From the legal side, there is a tradition that separates law and politics. But this view of the law as an "arcane science" above "politics and partisanship" was put to rest by the school of legal realism and, more recently, by critical legal studies. Rather, "the real distinction is not between public policy and law," Schwartz says, "but between different kinds of public policy." Some is strictly legislative, and some falls within the purview of the courts, and "the hard question is which kinds are for which branch."

Nevertheless, the myth of a sharp distinction between law and public policy continues to play a role, most notably in the nomination process for Supreme Court appointments. Although "neutral value-free factors" are held up as the proper criteria, "if one thing is clear to everyone . . . nominations are almost always intended to implement the president's vision of . . . what is best for the public good."

We can see where the distinction between law and public policy is proper and where it functions as a smoke screen in two other areas as well: the so-called political questions and the area of "standing law." Political questions are those issues the Court "will not even hear," often matters of foreign policy, and the Court has been "fairly straight about its reasons." But the issue of "standing" has often served as a mask, and standing rules "have been used to exclude cases involving civil rights, civil liberties, and other social causes." The Court has argued that it cannot be "continuing monitors of the wisdom and soundness of executive action." But this reasoning has, in effect, reduced the "standing" issue to the "political questions" doctrine, since the Court has denied relief to plaintiffs where, in Justice Stevens's words, "the strength of the plaintiff's interest . . . has nothing to do with whether the relief . . . would 'intrude upon'" the other branches of government.

Where then do we draw the line between law and public policy? Schwartz turns first to property rights. Until recently, this was an area of "primary concern" for the Court. The goal of the Court was "to protect vested property." Using the contract and due process clauses of the Constitution lifted "the issue out of 'politics' into the realm of higher law, which is beyond policy." Although this era ended with the Great Depression, there is now a movement, identified with the University of Chicago Law School, to restore property rights to their former prominence.

But there are good reasons not to revive this kind of judicial activism. In Schwartz's view, "the law of property is . . . a human construct" and reflects society's interests and desires. Inevitably, the

Court must favor "one economic group while disadvantaging another." When is this appropriate? Today, "most economic rights seeking constitutional protection are likely to be those of the haves against the have-nots." The Court must thus become "explicitly allied" with those who have power and wealth and become an agent of class conflict and economic factionalism. The Court's authority would be greatly damaged, as indeed it has been in the past and for the same reasons. It is thus preferable for the Court to be activist in behalf of First Amendment rights instead of economic rights.

The other area where the law–public policy issue has been prominent is statutory interpretation. For the past sixty or so years, there has not been much dispute that statutory law must rely on original legislative intent (whereas, in Schwartz's opinion this is "almost impossible" in *constitutional* interpretation). Now this approach has been challenged by Justice Scalia and Judge Alex Kozinski. They have called for "rationalizing the law" and "making a harmonious whole out of the system of laws." Legislative intent, they argue, should be ignored in pursuit of these goals. Rather, statutes "should be read in keeping with . . . the meaning that is 'most in accord with context and ordinary usage . . . [and] with the surrounding body of law.'" For Schwartz, the Scalia approach "intrudes the judge's own vision of public policy over that of the legislature." But "nowhere in the Constitution is a commission given to judges to assert their own views of the meaning of statutes." Would it be cynical to observe, Schwartz asks, whether it is

> no more than coincidence that the application of this approach, which weakens legislative power, appears when conservatives have come to dominate the bench and the White House, and liberalism's sole recourse is to the Congress?

George Anastaplo on the Supreme Court as a Court of Law

We see in Schwartz a conception of the work of the Supreme Court from within the legal aristocracy: confident that its work, correctly understood, is properly "public policy" and "political"; vigilant and active on civil rights, reticent on economic rights; bold in constitutional interpretation in behalf of civil rights and liberties; and deferential to legislative intent in statutory interpretation.

In chapter 2, "The Supreme Court Is Indeed a Court," by George Anastaplo, we see a rather different, perhaps more modest view, from within the aristocracy, of the Court's powers. For Anastaplo, whether the Supreme Court is guardian of the Constitution embraces three separate questions. Was the Court ever intended to be the *primary* guardian? Was it intended to be *one of several?* Or has it become the primary, although it was not originally intended to be?

"It is unlikely," writes Anastaplo, "that any informed American in the 1780s considered the civil liberties of the people in jeopardy . . . because there was no national supreme court." Security of rights depended on a tradition that long antedated the Bill of Rights. Indeed, the reliance on a bill of rights, in the view of some, may have inhibited the development of rights as they "had developed since Magna Carta."

The Constitution itself "offers no indication that the national courts, including the Supreme Court, should be any different . . . from what other courts are like." That is, courts "resolve legal disputes between individuals." In resolving disputes, the courts were to exercise common law jurisdiction, a practice "since time immemorial." And the highest court was expected "to provide supervision . . . with respect to what inferior courts did in their common law determinations." Further, the national courts, under the supremacy clause, were expected "to construe the laws of the United States" and to ensure that state court judges "paid due deference to the Constitution."

But it is also possible to say, from the text of the Constitution, what the Supreme Court "was not intended to do." There is no indication that it was "to assess acts of Congress for their constitutionality." Because of the lack of precedent, this was not likely to have been "created by implication." Before the Civil War, "only two acts of Congress were declared unconstitutional." For those seven decades, "no one missed the Supreme Court as guardian." Indeed, when the Court did exercise judicial review, in *Dred Scott,* it "almost proved the gravedigger of the Constitution." The most effective guardians in the first century of the Constitution "were the Congress and the president." All this shows that "guarding the Constitution is not an activity that the courts are equipped . . . to perform directly." The courts guarded the Constitution "by doing justice . . . in the cases properly before them." Where the Court is constitutionally expected to act as guardian, that is, supervising state activities, so too are Congress and the president.

When, in the nineteenth century, the Court took on the role of guardian, the results, as in the *Civil Rights Cases,* were unfortunate. The Court's notable success in *Brown v. Board of Education* had to take "heroic measures to correct its own misguided guardianship of another era." So too are the "Fourteenth Amendment cases of recent decades," which represent "efforts by the Supreme Court to return the country to the state of affairs that might have prevailed had the Congress and president been permitted to conduct themselves . . . as guardians of the Constitution."

If rights have been one of the main areas in which the Court could be expected to serve as guardian, the other is the *powers* of government. According to the framers, the rights of the states were to be protected "through the members of the Senate." After popular election of senators, however, "does it make more sense to look instead to the courts?" Does not popular sovereignty, "as the ultimate political authority behind the Constitution" make reliance on the Supreme Court "inappropriate"?

As with the powers of the states, so too are the powers of the Congress and the executive. The Congress and the executive have, after all, taken oaths to support the Constitution, and "it is not prudent" for them to turn to the Court. Courts rely on precedent, but precedent cannot be binding on the political branches: they are answerable to the people—the Court is not.

An activist Court runs the risk of being thought too political. Because it is so difficult to distinguish "constitutional" from "political," "is it not better to rely for constitutional judgments" on Congress or the people? The Court can be shielded from political passions "only if it is not depended on to be a guardian of the Constitution with respect to the activities" of the legislative and executive branches. It would be far preferable for the Court to be "involved in the development of the common law."

When the Court takes an active role in shaping the Constitution, "the only part of the 'original intention' of the framers that matters is . . . the establishment of the Supreme Court." Thus "which constitution" shall the Supreme Court guard if the justices "should be regarded as *the* guardians of the Constitution"?

Joseph M. Bessette on Legislative Tyranny

Anastaplo's dissent from the law professoriate's understanding of the Court's function raises the question of the design of the Constitution, that is, the question of "original intent" in one of its significations. Although this phrase is much abused, and the notion is disparaged when used in reference to constitutional jurisprudence, it is of the utmost importance for understanding both the political science of the framers and the distortions of the original Constitution over the course of the history of the republic.

Joseph Bessette, in the fourth chapter, "Guarding the Constitution from Legislative Tyranny," looks at the question of the Court's function from the perspective of constitutional design: "Was the Supreme Court *designed* or *intended* to be the guardian of the Constitution?" What is the Constitution that is guarded? A focus on rights is too narrow, although it has a good deal to say about them: the Constitution is "primarily a document constituting the organs of the new national government." The record of the debates makes it clear that the Constitution "ideally would combine stability and energy with liberty and republican form."

But what is the threat to this design? The evidence from *The Federalist* is "legislative tyranny," Bessette writes. The separation of powers was designed to thwart the accumulation of all power, "legislative, executive and judiciary, in the same hands [which] . . . may justly be pronounced the very definition of tyranny," according to Publius. Bessette asks, "From what quarter, then, was the drive toward consolidation of power likely to originate?" From the legislative, Publius believed. He could cite as evidence the abuses of the popular assemblies of the states, particularly Virginia and Pennsylvania.

Was this tendency of legislatures merely symptomatic of revolutionary times, or is it a danger implicit in the very structure of constitutional democracy? For several reasons, Publius clearly believed that the danger was structural. Bessette writes that the most telling, in his view, is that "the representative nature of legislative office . . . creates an alliance between the legislature and the people that fuels conflicts with the other branches." The alliance between a frustrated public and a legislature that believes it represents the "will of the people" "is especially a problem for the executive or the courts when they oppose some deeply felt legislative desire." This is "the most likely mechanism" threatening American constitutionalism.

The constitutional safeguards, the system of "checks and balances," against this are well known. But what is the "contribution of the Supreme Court to this institutional solution" for legislative tyranny? The mechanisms of independence are built into the judiciary: life tenure, secure salaries, and personal motives ensure resistance to legislative encroachment: "Moreover, if Congress acts against the Court in a way that violates a specific constitutional provision . . . the Court is obligated, according to Publius, to declare the offending statute void." It is in this specific but limited sense that the Court is a "faithful guardian of the Constitution."

Is there a sense, however, in which the Court properly embraces an "overarching guardianship for the constitutional order as a whole"? Both Publius and American history, Bessette argues, would deny this. The Court is essentially weak against the elected branches, which possess a number of powerful weapons against the judiciary. Rather, the principal preserver of the Constitution is its design. The question of guardianship in some embracing sense must be altered: "What role, if any, was the Supreme Court to play in assisting the other branches in resisting legislative tyranny?"

The Court, however, is irrelevant in regard to bicameralism, which thwarts legislative tyranny. So too the independent executive sets up an "institutional dynamic" between the branches, "not a legal one." But could not the Court act as a "neutral arbiter" in disputes between the branches? It is the president, however, who has the greatest stake in protecting the powers of his office *if* he will but assert the constitutional prerogatives of that office. Perhaps Andrew Jackson might have defended at every turn the independent counsel provisions of the Ethics in Government Act, but "one can hardly imagine the firestorm of criticism that would descend upon a modern president who . . . adopted the Jacksonian approach on a matter upon which the Court had spoken so clearly (if incorrectly)."

There are two principal reasons for the decline of the presidency. The president is limited to two terms in office and thus, in the second term, is greatly interested in securing his place in history. He is therefore more susceptible to popular opinion. The other reason "is the now widespread acceptance of the view that the Court is indeed the principal guardian of the Constitution, the final arbiter of the true meaning of the fundamental law, and thus the impartial umpire of all disputes over separation of powers." This, however, is a departure from the intentions of the framers, and from the facts of American history, in which the Court "has not been responsible . . . for preserving the integrity of the Constitution's institutional design."

Louis Fisher on the Various Guardians of the Constitution

Anastaplo raises the function of the Court as a court but within the design of the Constitution as a whole. Bessette pursues the theme of the political design of the Constitution and why the Court's powers are necessarily and inherently limited within that scheme. Louis Fisher's chapter, "One of the Guardians Some of the Time," reviews the actual, historical practice of constitutional interpretation within the Constitution considered as a political whole. He argues that history does not bear out the belief that "the ultimate safeguard of our liberties is the Supreme Court."

The Constitution itself offers a narrow basis for judicial review of the actions of state governments in the supremacy clause (Article VI). Similarly, the history of Article III, section 2, "points to judicial review of a specific type: over state actions." So, too, the record of the debates confirms the framers' view of the Court's responsibility over state action.

But the claim that the Constitution, or the framers, intended judicial review to extend to the national government "is opaque." Madison's views are themselves contradictory. In regard to the Bill of Rights, he said that "independent tribunals of justice will consider themselves . . . the guardians of those rights." He also said, however, that no "department draws from the Constitution greater power than another."

The early history of the Supreme Court is similarly ambivalent; it failed to protect individual rights against the Alien and Sedition Acts, a task that fell "to the president and Congress." Indeed, Jefferson believed that if the Court could decide constitutionality in the legislative and executive areas that "would make the judiciary a despotic branch." Even the famous decision in *Marbury v. Madison* (1803), although seeming to establish the Court's ultimate constitutional authority, is, in fact, "more modest in scope." The responsibility of the Court "to say what the law is" means "that the Court is responsible for stating what it thinks a statute means, after which Congress may enact another law to override the Court." Marshall was fully aware that Congress had the power to impeach sitting justices, and after *Marbury*, "he consistently upheld the power of Congress."

Just as the reputation of the Marshall Court exceeds its actual accomplishments, so too the Court's record as the ultimate defender of our liberties does not bear critical scrutiny. The *Dred Scott* decision shows "how constitutional rights are created and settled outside the judiciary." Even before the Civil War amendments overturned that decision, Congress had prohibited slavery by legislation in 1862. No deference was shown to the Court's opinion in *Dred Scott* on that occasion.

The Court's record of guarding rights after the Civil War "was not much better." The *Civil Rights Cases* of 1883 "struck down legislation passed by Congress in 1875 giving blacks equal access to public accommodations." Similarly, in 1875 the Court denied to women the right to practice law, and Congress, in 1879, legislated that right. Henry W. Edgerton's 1937 study of the Court's actual history of protecting individual liberties through judicial review "could not find one that protected the civil liberties of speech, press, and assembly."

The responsibility for protecting individual liberties is, in fact, shared. When Justice Frankfurter, in 1940, upheld a Pennsylvania compulsory flag salute law, popular reaction "was almost unanimously hostile." "By 1942, three members of Frankfurter's majority publicly apologized for their vote," and in 1943 the Court reversed. But the credit "belongs to all the individuals and associations in the country who objected . . . to Frankfurter's opinion."

A similar example may be found in the Japanese-American cases of 1943 and 1944. They "illustrate the danger of depending too much on the judiciary to safeguard the Constitution." Earl Warren, when attorney general of California, defended the internment of Japanese-Americans but as chief justice "regretted those policies," Fisher relates. Warren wrote that "it is still the Legislature and the elected Executive who have the primary responsibility for fashioning and executing policy consistent with the Constitution" and "the day-to-day job of upholding the Constitution . . . rests . . . on the shoulders of every citizen."

Subsequent history of the Court only confirms "that judicial review is not used uniformly to safeguard constitutional rights." The political branches have repeatedly "been forced to reverse Court decisions." The Court is "only one participant in the complex process of guarding constitutional rights."

Walter Berns on the Framers and Judicial Review

Walter Berns in chapter 3 brings us back to the framers and their opinion of judicial review. Where Gordon Wood argues that, in spite of the objections to judicial review on the part of the framers, it nevertheless became part of the ordinary process of law, Berns explores the framers' principled objection to it. In his ironically titled article, "Preserving a Living Constitution," he shows that the framers' fears have been vindicated by the further evolution of judicial review.

The central question of constitutional interpretation was whether it was to be based on "the natural and obvious meaning of the words" or "according to the spirit and intention of it." Hamilton, writing in *Federalist* 81, took pains to deny the reliance on spirit and intention. But within a decade of his writing, Supreme Court Justice Samuel Chase could assert that judicial interpretation is based on the "first principles of the social compact." James Iredell objected that "the Court cannot pronounce [a law] to be void, merely because it is, in their judgement, contrary to the principles of natural justice." Thus were set, from the beginning, the terms of the conflict: were the principles of judicial interpretation to be according to the "spirit" and "natural justice" or according to the letter?

"Put simply," writes Berns, "the idea that judges are entitled to rest their decisions on the principle of 'natural justice'—or any of its modern synonyms—is incompatible with the framers' idea of a written constitution." For the link between legitimacy and the Constitution is *consent*, which is founded on the security of a written constitution.

19

Although the Constitution is a "fundamental law," "it is not a 'higher law' in the traditional sense." It derives from human will, the will of the people, who may, in the words of *The Federalist*, change it "by some solemn and authoritative act," and "no presumption, or even knowledge of their sentiments, can warrant their representatives in a departure from it prior to such an act."

But what was denied by the framers to the representatives of the people, "is now claimed by our judges." John Marshall is often cited as the authority to "adapt" the Constitution. But Marshall has been misquoted. He did not say that the Constitution was to be adapted, but rather, Berns continues, that "the legislative powers granted by the Constitution" were adaptable to meet the "various crises of human affairs." Judicial activism arises from the failure of the Congress to use its powers. This failure has "not only opened the door for the Court but made it *necessary* for the Court to assume a political role." The courts have used the equal protection and due process clauses for "tasks for which they were not intended and are ill suited." Legislative powers were intended and are well suited to these tasks. The legislature, for example, might have invalidated the poll tax; its failure forced the Court to find some principle "either in the text or in the interstices" of the Constitution. As Justice Black in his dissent observed, the Court invoked the "natural-law-due-process formula," which is "a cloak for what it thinks governmental policy should be."

Berns observes, however, that "natural law rests on presuppositions [a divine principle] that no contemporary judge . . . would accept." The same is true of the natural rights of the Declaration of Independence (which rest on "Nature or Nature's God"). The abandonment of the perspective of the framers and of the faith of the Declaration has led to the explicit rejection of constitutionalism in such writers as Sanford Levinson, who has declared the death of constitutionalism as "the central event of our time, just as the death of God was that of the past century (and for much the same reason)." Berns writes:

> Nature's God endowed us with rights and, through the agency
> of the founders, provided us with a Constitution that, to
> secure these rights, put constraints on the popular will. With
> his death, those constraints are deprived of all moral authority.

Law, in Levinson's words, "is stripped of any moral anchoring," and this belief now prevails in the nation's law schools.

"But if constitutionalism is dead, so is the prospect for judicial review." Levinson, according to Berns, can think of no reason why "the people and their elected representatives [should] defer to judgments rendered by an unelected judiciary." Michael Perry tries to avoid this dilemma by asserting, Berns writes, that "the judges speak for the people by appealing to their aspirations." The justices must depend on their own "beliefs" as a lens for observing the "aspirations" of the people. As Berns observes, "The difference between this and a reliance on personal preferences is not readily discernible." But Perry turns the question around: why should today's public officials be morally obligated to defer to the beliefs either of the long-dead and mostly WASP men who ratified the original Constitution? It is "counterintuitive" to insist that they should.

The problem on which Berns focuses is *legitimacy:* if Perry, and others of the same views, can offer no better ground for judicial reasoning than "intuition," then the fundamental principle of republicanism is at risk. "Whether we can expect legislatures to defer to courts depends ultimately on the right of the people to adopt a constitution for themselves *and* for their posterity," Berns says. A republican constitution binds the succeeding generations until, by constitutional means, it is annulled or changed: "Judges may claim the obedience of other public officials because, and only because, they represent the people in their constituting capacity."

A "living constitution," on examination, depends on the "static" constitution for its authority. Otherwise, the Constitution has only a "formal existence," in the words of Fred Baumann. One day, Berns prophesies, the people will awake to the idea that the Supreme Court is merely political and will realize that, unlike their elected representatives, the members of the Court cannot be removed by popular will: if so, "the 'living constitution' is not calculated to enjoy a long life."

Conclusion

Both Berns and Justice Scalia assume a citizenry zealous for its republicanism as well as its rights. More precisely, such a citizenry must understand that the security of rights requires republicanism and for this reason would be prepared to take back its sovereignty from the Court. But such a citizenry must be nurtured and cannot simply be assumed. Where the people cannot recognize the difference between the Constitution and constitutional law and are baffled by constitutional law, and where they may no longer, in Ralph Lerner's words, understand "the close connection between self-restraint and true liberty"— which the Court at one time thought essential to teach—where the people have also become distrustful of the elective institutions of government, neither respect for the rule of law nor zeal for republican self-government can be ensured.

2

The Supreme Court
Is Indeed a Court

George Anastaplo

SOCRATES: *Each of us is naturally not quite like anyone else, but rather differs in his nature; different men are apt for the accomplishment of different jobs. Isn't that your opinion?*
ADEIMANTUS: *It is.*
SOCRATES: *And what about this? Who would do a finer job, one man practicing many arts, or one man one art?*
ADEIMANTUS: *One man, one art.*

PLATO, *Republic*

Prologue

A general question that is debated today asks, Is the United States Supreme Court the guardian of the Constitution? In its most challenging form this question may be, Was the Supreme Court ever intended to be the primary, if not the sole, guardian of the Constitution?

It is significantly different to ask whether the Supreme Court was intended to be one of several guardians of the Constitution. Also significantly different is the question whether the Supreme Court has become, or has had to become, the primary guardian of the Constitution, although it was not originally intended to be.

Rights of the People

Guardianship of the Constitution by the Supreme Court or by anyone else would be principally directed to preservation of the original allocation of powers by the Constitution and to protection of the personal rights guaranteed by the Constitution. I begin with a consideration of the rights of the people recognized by constitutional provisions. How does the Supreme Court serve to protect those rights?

It is unlikely that any informed American in the 1780s considered the civil liberties of the people in jeopardy in the United States because there was no national supreme court.[1] Put another way, it is hardly likely that anyone felt, once the Supreme Court and other national courts had been established, that the rights of the people were for the first time safe in this country. Rather, it is likely that people continued to exercise, and would continue to expect to be able to exercise, those rights as they and their ancestors had done for decades if not centuries on both sides of the Atlantic.

The security of those rights probably did not even depend on the existence or powers of a national constitution, much less on the powers of any court established pursuant to that constitution. The people had, certainly since 1776, confidently exercised the rights they believed were their due, invoking various of them in the Declaration of Independence. It is unlikely that the informed citizen felt more secure in this respect when he learned that the Bill of Rights had been ratified in December 1791. What the addition of the Bill of Rights immediately accomplished remains uncertain.

Some had argued that reducing the rights of the people to writing, to say nothing of subsequently relying upon the Supreme Court to protect those rights, inhibited the continuing development of rights in the way they had developed since Magna Carta. The Ninth Amendment attempts to counteract such inhibition, but we do persist in considering those rights that have been reduced to writing to be the only ones available—at least if the Supreme Court is entitled to intervene to correct what legislatures might do. Otherwise, it is widely feared, the Supreme Court will be out of control, presuming to conduct itself as a legislature. It is generally agreed that courts should not conduct themselves as legislatures do.

Still, it is not generally appreciated how much the recourse to bills of rights in this country has obscured the origins and perhaps the nature and purpose of the traditional rights of the American people.[2] One consequence of the recourse to bills of rights has been the reliance upon the Fourteenth Amendment to secure a general recognition of these rights. A related but more questionable development has been the considerable reliance upon judicial review of acts of Congress since the Civil War.[3]

The Judicial Article

The question whether the Supreme Court was intended to act as the primary, if not the sole, guardian of the Constitution is illuminated by considering what the Constitution itself indicates about what the Supreme Court is to be and to do.

The courts provided for in the Constitution seem to be substantially like the judiciary referred to in the Declaration of Independence. Are not the courts provided for in the Constitution expected to do what courts have always been expected to do in Anglo-American legal systems?[4]

Courts cannot be expected to establish themselves, to define their jurisdiction and powers, or to provide for their number, location, support, and operations. The Constitution itself provides some guidance here and leaves it to Congress to supply whatever else is needed from time to time. The Constitution offers no indication that the national courts, including the United States Supreme Court, should be different in any essential respect from what other courts are like—except for the assignment of the chief justice of the United States to the duty of presiding in the Senate over any trial of impeachment for the president of the United States.

The Judicial Article is the shortest of the articles defining the three branches of the national government. Even so, Article III is long enough to reveal that the courts provided for there had nothing special about them as courts. The Congress and the president had to be provided for at greater length, because both of them were *then* different in significant respects from their counterparts in Great Britain and in most of the states.

The national courts, conversely, were to be fairly conventional. They had only to be identified and established, with much about them left to Congress to spell out. The provision in the Constitution of life tenure for judges made it far more likely that they would conduct themselves as their English counterparts did, correcting whatever deterioration in the standing of judges had taken place because of the turmoil surrounding the Revolution. It also helped that the judges would not be selected by the executive alone.

The Constitution does not indicate that the courts provided for should not do what courts usually do. No provision is made in the Constitution for anyone else to do what judges had long been depended upon to do. The primary duty of courts of general jurisdiction is to resolve legal disputes between individuals.[5]

Little discussion took place in the Federal Convention, so far as we can tell from the surviving records, about what national courts would do. There, too, it seems to have been assumed that the prospective national courts would do what courts had "always" done. What they had always done was to see that justice prevailed in the controversies properly—that is, lawfully—before them.

It is evident, both in the Constitution of 1787 and in the Bill of Rights, that the national courts were to exercise a common law jurisdiction. The typical Anglo-American court had been exercising a common law jurisdiction "since time immemorial." No reason is given, either in the convention debates we do have or in the Constitution, why the courts provided for by the Constitution should not continue to do so.

Also since time immemorial, the highest court of general jurisdiction in the realm was expected by the English and the Americans alike to provide supervision, or at least guidance, with respect to what inferior courts did in their common law determinations. This made it more likely that the common law would remain, and would appear to remain, what it should be: common and just. It is not generally appreciated how much both the common law and the traditional rights of the American people, such as those enshrined in national and state bills of rights, were developed in large part by common law judges. Those judges were grounded both in the principles of British constitutionalism and in the natural-right principles of the Western world.

The Supreme Court was widely understood to have some supervisory duty with respect to the development of the common law in the United States, subject to technical restrictions about the basis of jurisdiction for the cases it would itself hear. This is attested to by decades of expectations and experience, reinforced by the provisions made for the judiciary in the First Congress.[6] All this was consistent with, if not called for by, the prevailing notions in 1787 as to what law is and how it is determined.

Subject to supervision by the Supreme Court, the national courts were also expected to construe the laws of the United States and, pursuant to the supremacy clause, to do whatever was necessary to ensure in cases properly before those courts that the states and especially state court judges paid due deference to the Constitution, treaties, and statutes of the United States. Authoritative development, interpretations, and applications of those national instruments would be provided by all branches of the national government at one time or another.

Limitations of the Supreme Court

Having considered what the Constitution indicates the Supreme Court
should be and do, we must also consider what the Supreme Court
was *not* intended to do, so far as we can tell from the text of the
Constitution of 1787.

There is not the slightest indication in the Constitution that the
Supreme Court is expected to assess acts of Congress for their constitutionality. Compare what is said in the Supremacy Clause, subordi-
nating the laws *of the states* to the Constitution, treaties, and laws of
the United States. The lack of significant precedent for judicial review
in Anglo-American constitutional history makes it highly unlikely that
judicial review of acts of Congress was intended to be created by
implication alone. This seems especially apparent considering how
emphatically such authorities as William Blackstone opposed any
suggestion of what we now know as judicial review.[7]

If the framers had intended judicial review of acts of Congress,
then it is highly likely they would have provided guidance for the
exercise of this power in the same detail with which they provided
for exercise of the veto power of the president. That veto power is
different in critical respects from the practice to which Americans had
been generally accustomed.[8] In addition the framers would probably
have provided more protection for the Supreme Court than they did,
including explicit assurances about its appellate jurisdiction, if they
had intended to have acts of Congress routinely assessed for their
constitutionality by the Court. I refer here only to what is evident in
the Constitution itself, leaving aside the markedly unsuccessful and
hence revealing attempts by some delegates in the Federal Convention
to provide for routine judicial participation in the preparation or
assessment of bills and acts of Congress.

That judicial review was not depended on either to ensure respect
for allocations of powers or to protect the rights of individuals is
further suggested by the fact that only two acts of Congress were
declared unconstitutional before the Civil War. Evidently no one missed
the Supreme Court as guardian of the Constitution during those seven
decades.[9] Rather, that Court almost proved the gravedigger of the
Constitution in the *Dred Scott* case, the major exercise of judicial review
that the Supreme Court did venture upon during that period.[10]

It became evident during the first century under the Constitution
that its most reliable guardians, aside from the people themselves,
were the Congress and the president. This guardianship culminated
in what both branches did to save the Constitution and the Union
during the Civil War—sometimes having to ignore, if not defy, the

U.S. Supreme Court. Guarding the Constitution is not an activity that the courts are equipped or expected to perform directly. The courts, including the Supreme Court, *are* depended upon to contribute to the guarding of the Constitution by doing justice when opportunities arise in the cases properly before them. Of course, in *construing* relevant statutes in a case, a court is entitled to believe that the legislators who made those statutes probably intended to act in conformity with the Constitution as commonly understood.[11]

Supervision of State Activities

The Supreme Court *was* expected, along with the rest of the national government, to correct state activities not in conformity with the Constitution, treaties, and laws of the United States. But the Constitution appears not to expect more along this line from the courts than it does from Congress and the president. The other branches are as much the guardians of the Constitution as the Supreme Court,[12] Congress being the branch of the national government left ultimately in control. Congress and the president are expected to sort out their constitutional differences without much help from the Supreme Court, but subject to the authority of the people.

This is not to deny that the Supreme Court has performed good service in the cause of American constitutionalism in such cases as *Brown v. Board of Education.*[13] But the efforts of the Supreme Court in such cases might never have been needed, or needed in the form or to the extent they were, if the Court had conducted itself as it should have in the last quarter of the nineteenth century.

By such legislation as the Civil Rights Act of 1875 Congress had attempted to deal with various forms of discrimination in the South, including conduct that was not "state action" in the full sense of that term even today. But the Supreme Court, purporting to serve as the guardian of the Constitution, had stymied these congressional efforts.[14] It also had stymied efforts by aggrieved litigants to make state laws conform to the Fourteenth Amendment.[15]

In such cases as *Brown* the Court resorted to heroic measures to correct its own misguided guardianship of another era. The Fourteenth Amendment cases of recent decades represent repeated efforts by the Supreme Court to return the country to the state of affairs that might have prevailed had the Congress and president been permitted by the courts to conduct themselves in the post–Civil War years as guardians of the Constitution.

Another series of cases in recent decades, that dealing with the use of the commerce clause on behalf of the general welfare, found the Supreme Court restoring to Congress the extent of the commerce power that for a century it had been prevented from exercising—by the Supreme Court.[16] No serious problem would ever have developed had the Supreme Court been as generous in its recognition of the commerce power as it has been of the parallel war power.

It is difficult to imagine the Constitution that the Supreme Court believed itself to be guarding in one ill-conceived opinion after another about the commerce clause or the Fourteenth Amendment. The Supreme Court succeeded instead in making concerned citizens wonder if a necessary conflict must exist between sensible government and constitutional propriety.

The Appropriate Source of Powers

Who the guardians of the Constitution should be and what form guardianship should take depends on who is considered the source of the allocation of powers in the Constitution.

Justice Felix Frankfurter spoke in a 1952 dissenting opinion of "the great number of subjects of public interest, jurisdiction of which the states have never parted with."[17] He implied there, as he and others have elsewhere, that the states were somehow the source of the powers available to the national government. It is this kind of "history" that leads to the insistence that the Tenth Amendment is being violated by congressional exercise of various powers. A related question here is when the United States should be understood to have begun.

It is likely that the framers of the Constitution of 1787 intended that legitimate state prerogatives would be immediately protected by the states through the members of the Senate selected by the state legislatures. Now that senators are chosen by popular elections, does it make more sense to look instead to the courts to vindicate states' rights? Would it not be odd, however, to have the duties and powers of the Supreme Court changed significantly because of changes that happen to have been made in the mode of selecting senators? Besides, the complaints that states are likely to have here are not limited to the conduct of Congress. Are not the national executive and courts as likely as the national legislature to impinge upon the states' prerogatives? Would the courts of the national government have been depended on to police the judicial as well as the executive activities here of the national government?[18]

The history on which the typical states' rights approach seems to depend should itself be challenged. What evidence suggests that the powers claimed or exercised by the national government have been "parted with" by the states? After all, the allocation of powers in the Constitution was made *not* by the states but by the people. The people have retained the ability, through their access both to freedom of speech and to the ballot, to control the powers claimed and exercised by their Congress and their president. In extreme cases, moreover, the people hold in reserve the right of revolution, to make sure that their governments conduct themselves as they should. No serious effort was made by Americans in 1776 to go to a court to correct what the British legislature and executive were doing to them. Some of the things done to them *were* condemned by Americans as unconstitutional.

Does not an insistence upon the people as the ultimate political authority behind the Constitution make reliance upon the Supreme Court for guardian duties inappropriate? If the people were once sensible enough to "ordain and establish" the Constitution, and if they have always been relied upon to assess and amend that Constitution when necessary, then why do they need the Supreme Court or any other body to determine for them when their Constitution is being violated by a national government that they control?[19] Indeed, why should the people rely, for the ultimate guardianship of the Constitution, upon the one official body over which they have the least direct control?

We should notice as well that there have always been major issues bearing on constitutionality that are difficult if not impossible to get before a court.[20] This too suggests that it is not prudent to permit members of Congress and the president—who have also taken oaths to support the Constitution—to depend on the courts to determine the constitutionality of congressional and executive measures. To look to the Supreme Court as *the* guardian of the Constitution means in effect that the Constitution will not be looked to and looked after as it should be. Conservatives should be more concerned about executive usurpation and less concerned about "legislative tyranny," just as liberals should be more concerned about judicial usurpation, less about official threats to privacy and "freedom of expression."

Historical Precedents

Another reminder is appropriate here. Whenever Congress and the Supreme Court have differed on a great constitutional issue, has not the Congress usually been correct? Consider the *Dred Scott* and *Civil Rights Cases* of the nineteenth century and the child labor and New Deal Cases of the twentieth century.[21]

Courts are temperamentally inclined to make more of precedents than are legislatures. It *is* important that precedents be respected when courts deal with the circumstances and rights of litigants who rely on the law as they had reasonably expected it to be. To rely on precedent as much in constitutional interpretation as we should in private litigation, however, is to cripple a community in those critical times when the available powers of a government have to be used to a greater extent than or in ways different from what have been customary. A fresh look at such powers in the Constitution, reinforced by the necessary and proper clause, is more likely to be taken by those who are routinely held politically responsible for the consequences of what is or is not done.

It is hardly prudent to rely upon guardians who are themselves immune from being either penalized or rewarded by the citizens affected by the policies such guardians are promulgating. A properly educated people, well-versed in constitutional principles, is necessary.

Consequences of the *Dred Scott* Decision

Those who look to the Supreme Court as the principal guardian of the Constitution have the dreadful embarrassment of *Dred Scott* to reckon with. What was the Supreme Court supposed to be guarding on that occasion? The rights of property? Even the precedents were against what the Court did, considering what national governments had done since 1787 to regulate the introduction of slavery into the territories of the United States.

One consequence of the *Dred Scott* decision was that no government in the United States, national or local, could control what happened to slavery in the territories. This proved to be profoundly disturbing in its ramifications, something that could be reliably corrected only by a constitutional amendment—if not only by a civil war. How prudent is it, then, to rely for guard duty upon those whose devastating mistakes can be so difficult to correct? Faith in constitutional processes can be subverted by such folly as the Supreme Court has exhibited on occasion.

Complicating matters further is the tendency to consider any unwise or unjust exercise of power by a legislature or an executive to be automatically unconstitutional. But the Constitution of 1787 grants to the national government broad powers with respect to war, peace, taxes, the national economy, and the monetary system of the country. The people, not the courts, must be depended on to make it likely that the national government properly uses only so much of its broad powers as may be needed from time to time.

Policy Considerations and Constitutional Interpretation

It may be virtually impossible, in practice, to distinguish "constitutional" from "political" elements in an assessment of particular applications of many constitutional provisions. Because it is difficult to separate these two elements, is it not better to rely for constitutional judgments upon those bodies—whether Congress or the people—who can properly take both elements into account when deciding what may be done?[22]

Courts, conversely, are likely to seem unduly activist if they permit policy considerations to influence their constitutional interpretations. But it may not be reasonable to expect to decide great issues of state without taking into account profound political considerations and consequences—matters that life tenure may prevent most judges from being sufficiently sensitive to.

Even when a judge has conscientiously tried to interpret the Constitution without regard to his political preferences, it may be difficult for disappointed litigants to believe that political considerations played no part in judicial determinations. It is also difficult for politicians to believe that political considerations are not taken into account when decisions are made that obviously have massive political consequences. Some might even consider it irresponsible for a judge to ignore such consequences. It is therefore to be expected that the community will assume that a judge's political orientation is likely to affect his decisions about the larger constitutional issues. The more that constitutional issues are decided by judges, therefore, the more the selection of judges will be scrutinized and politicized.

The Supreme Court can be effectively shielded from political passions and permitted to do what it alone can do only if it is not depended upon to be a guardian of the Constitution with respect to the activities of the other two branches of the national government. The Supreme Court can most reliably act as guardian when it is seen to do well what judges have always done: decide, according to the established law of the land, the controversies that litigants properly bring before it. I have argued, therefore, that the Supreme Court should be less involved in the judicial review of acts of Congress and more involved in the development of the common law than it has been for some time.[23]

Activities of the States

This is not to deny that the Supreme Court is empowered, like Congress and the president, to assess various activities of the states for their constitutionality. But it would probably be better for Congress rather than the Supreme Court to take the lead in examining and correcting some of the activities of the states.

Consider, for example, the many Fourteenth Amendment–based challenges to state activities we have seen in recent decades. The Supreme Court is expected to limit itself to strictly constitutional issues in assessing what a state has done, unless a relevant congressional statute or national treaty is involved. But Congress, in preparing a statute, need not limit itself to constitutional issues, nor the president in negotiating a treaty. Section 5 of the Fourteenth Amendment, for example, permits Congress, unlike the courts, to consider policy factors in deciding what it wants done—including what it wants done about what states or the people of a state have done with respect to the concerns addressed by the amendment.

The post–Civil War Congresses did make efforts with respect to civil rights matters in the states—and decades after the Supreme Court had thwarted these congressional efforts, the Court eventually had to deal with the consequences. Of course, Congress itself sometimes fails to do what it could do better than the Supreme Court. This is seen in the reapportionment cases, which the courts have had to address in a piecemeal fashion and which Congress could have dealt with more efficiently—and with more accommodations to local variations and with less reliance upon numerical formulas.[24]

The Supreme Court as guardian of the Constitution does not create problems only when it hampers the Congress or the president. It can also be troublesome when it interferes with so-called state usurpations of the powers of the national government. Consider, for example, the burdens-on-interstate-commerce cases: "The [Supreme] Court has not always been articulate, nor the Justices always in agreement, about the governing values in the hundreds of cases in which state laws have been challenged as contravening the commerce clause."[25]

What need is there for the Supreme Court to police, in a multitude of cases, whatever the states may do in trying to regulate that part of "interstate commerce" that comes within their reach? Here, as elsewhere, Congress is capable of looking out for the country's interests, allowing states to exercise as much of the congressional commerce power as Congress pleases.[26]

Epilogue

It is often said that the Supreme Court was established as the guardian of the Constitution because ours is a written constitution, unlike the constitutions of many other countries at the time the court first undertook this guard duty. But is it not evident that "the Constitution" that is looked to and protected by the Supreme Court has been written not by the framers in 1787 and the Congresses that have devised constitutional amendments but in large part by the Supreme Court itself? This is complicated by talk of "a living Constitution," which can mean that the only part of "the original intention" of the framers that matters is that which is reflected in the establishment of the Supreme Court—even though *that* original intent did not anticipate judicial review of acts of Congress.

In short, which constitution is the United States Supreme Court likely to guard if the Court should be regarded as *the* guardian of the Constitution?

3

Preserving a Living Constitution

Walter Berns

That federal judges might do what it is now claimed they have a right to do was foreseen by the Anti-Federalist Brutus, who gave it as one of the reasons why the Constitution should not be ratified. The Court, he said,

> will be authorised to decide upon the meaning of the consti-
> tution, and that, not only according to the natural and
> ob[vious] meaning of the words, but also according to the
> spirit and intention of it. . . . [The judiciary will] be exalted
> above all other power in the government, and subject to no
> controul.[1]

Alexander Hamilton, writing in *Federalist* 81, did his best to dispel this fear. There is not, he said, "a syllable in the plan under consideration which *directly* empowers the national courts to construe the laws according to the spirit of the Constitution, or which gives them any greater latitude in this respect than may be claimed by the courts of every state." Within a decade, however, Brutus's fears proved to be justified.

First Invocation
of Extraconstitutional Principles

The first invocation of extraconstitutional principles came in *Calder v. Bull* (1798), where the Court held that an act of the Connecticut legislature setting aside a probate court decree was not an ex post facto law and, therefore, not void under Article I, section 10, of the Constitution. Having delivered that judgment, Justice Samuel Chase, in what can only be described as *dicta*, went on to say that state authority is limited not only by express constitutional prohibitions but by the "first principles of the social compact."[2] While agreeing with the Court's judgment in the case, Justice James Iredell took strong exception to this statement of judicial power. "It is true," he said, "that some speculative jurists have held, that a legislative act against natural justice must, in itself, be void; but I cannot think that, under such a government, any court of Justice would possess a power to declare it so." Both the state and the federal constitutions, he pointed out, have defined with precision the objects of the legislative power and have restrained its exercise "within marked and settled boundaries."

> If [he continued] any act of Congress, or of a Legislature of a state, violates those constitutional provisions, it is unquestionably void; though, I admit, that as the authority to declare it void is of a delicate and awful nature, the Court will never resort to that authority, but in a clear and urgent case. If, on the other hand, the Legislature of the Union, or the Legislature of any member of the Union, shall pass a law, within the general scope of their constitutional power, the Court cannot pronounce it to be void, merely because it is, in their judgment, contrary to the principles of natural justice. The ideas of natural justice are regulated by no fixed standard: the ablest and the purest men have differed upon the subject.[3]

There is little question but that on this point Iredell was expressing the view of the framers and that they held this view largely for the reasons he gave, reasons as compelling—indeed, as I shall argue, more compelling—now as then.

True, on one occasion even John Marshall seemingly acknowledged the right of the Supreme Court to appeal to something akin to "natural justice" when declaring a statute unconstitutional. Announcing the judgment of the Court in the politically explosive case of *Fletcher v. Peck*, he said, "The state of Georgia was restrained [from passing the law in question] either by general principles, which are common to our free institutions, or by the particular provisions of the constitution of the United States"; this, he said, was "the unanimous opinion of the court."[4] But Marshall cannot fairly be cited by the proponents of what we have come to call an "activist" court. In his opinion, Marshall himself relied solely on an express provision of the Constitution; the Georgia law, he argued, was one "impairing the Obligations of Contracts" in violation of Article I, section 10. It was Justice William Johnson, alone among the seven justices who sat on the case, who had recourse to the idea of natural justice. "I do not hesitate to declare," he said in a concurring opinion, "that a state does not possess the power of revoking its own grants," but, he added, "I do it on a general principle, on the reason and nature of things: a principle which will impose laws even on the Deity."[5] It would appear that Marshall felt compelled by the political situation to announce an opinion that had the support of a "unanimous" Court and that it was this necessity that led him to refer to "general principles" in addition to an explicit provision of the Constitution.

Beyond *Calder v. Bull* and *Fletcher v. Peck*, there were even occasions—and long before the advent of contemporary "activism"—when the Court struck down state laws without any reference whatever to the Constitution. Prominent among these is a Kansas municipal bond case, *Savings and Loan Association v. Topeka*. Kansas law permitted municipalities to issue bonds and use the proceeds to attract industry to the cities. Speaking for the Court, Justice Samuel F. Miller held the law to be a form of "robbery," a taking of private money (in the form of taxes) and using it not for a public purpose but instead bestowing it on "favored [private] individuals." This, he said, "is not legislation [but rather] a decree under legislative forms."[6] This led Justice Nathan Clifford to protest that "Courts cannot nullify an Act of the State Legislature on the vague ground that they think it opposed to a general latent spirit supposed to pervade or underlie the Constitution, where neither the terms nor the implications of the instrument disclose any such restriction."[7]

"Natural Justice"

Put simply, the idea that judges are entitled to rest their decisions on the principles of "natural justice"—or any of its modern synonyms—is incompatible with the framers' idea of a written constitution. With a written text, they held, comes certainty, and with certainty comes legitimacy; and both certainty and legitimacy are put in jeopardy by rules of constitutional construction that, in effect, permit the judges to do as they will. James Madison even found reason to complain (albeit mildly) of Marshall's opinion in *McCulloch v. Maryland*:

> But it was anticipated I believe by few if any of the friends of the Constitution, that a rule of construction would be introduced as broad & as pliant as what has occurred. And those who recollect, and still more those who shared in what passed in the State Conventions, thro' which the people ratified the Constitution . . . cannot easily be persuaded that the

avowal of such a rule would not have prevented its ratification. . . .

There is certainly a reasonable medium between expounding the Constitution with the strictness of a penal law, or other ordinary statute, and expounding it with a laxity which may vary its essential character, and encroach on the local sovereignties with which it was meant to be reconcilable.[8]

If, as he said in a subsequent letter, the judges are not guided by the sense of the people who ratified the Constitution, "there can be no security for a consistent and stable, more than for a *faithful* exercise of its powers."[9] The legitimacy of government depends on adherence to the written text, the text that the people ratified or to which they gave their consent; so, too, does the possibility of limited or constitutional government.

The classic statement of these propositions can be found in Marshall's opinion for the Court in *Marbury v. Madison*: the "whole American fabric has been erected" on the principle that government derives from and is dependent on the will of the people. "This original and supreme will," Marshall said, "organizes the government, and assigns to different departments their respective powers." In the American case, it also assigns limits to those powers, and "that those limits may not be mistaken or forgotten, the constitution is written." It was for this reason that he (and, he suggested, all Americans) deemed a written constitution to be "the greatest improvement on political institutions."[10] Thomas Jefferson made the same point when he said that "the possession of a written Constitution [was America's] peculiar security."[11] As for the judiciary, its duty was to serve as its "faithful guardians."[12]

Statements of this sort abound in the literature of the time:

• "In a government which is emphatically stiled a government of laws, the least possible range ought to be left for the discretion of the judges."

• "If the constitution is to be expounded, not by its written text, but by the opinions of the rulers for the time being, whose opinions are to prevail, the first or the last? [And if the last] what certainty can there be in those powers [which it assigns and limits]?"

• "Would it not subvert the Constitution to subject the judges to popular opinion?"

• "Would it not make the constitution an instrument of flexible and changeable interpretation, and not a settled form of government with fixed limitations? Would it not become, instead of a supreme law for ourselves and our posterity, a mere oracle of the powers of the rulers of the day, to which implicit homage is to be paid, and speaking at different times the most opposite commands, and the most ambiguous voices?"[13] As Marshall put it in *Marbury*, the Constitution is to be fixed, made "unchangeable by ordinary means."

These various statements derive from a clear understanding of the principles informing the Constitution. No one governs by the grace of God; God (or "Nature's God") endowed men with the rights of life, liberty, and the pursuit of happiness, but He did not provide them with an effective means by which these rights might be secured. Their security required men to institute government, and, precisely because men are naturally all free and equal, the government derives its just powers from the consent of the governed. Or, to state it otherwise, because men are by nature free and equal, no one may govern another without his consent. In our case, that consent was rendered with and in the Constitution, which was ordained and established by us, "the people of the United States." By doing so, we agreed to exchange the natural right to govern ourselves for the civil right to be governed by laws to which we give our consent. As someone put it, consent is the needle's eye through which natural rights must pass in order to become the civil rights that government is empowered to secure; thus, what is secured by government is not so much the natural rights to life, liberty, and property, but the civil or constitutional right not to be deprived of them "without due process of law."

The Constitution then, is a fundamental law and was so described in *Federalist* 78, but it is not a "higher law" in the traditional sense of that term. As Robert Kraynak puts it, "Unlike divine or natural law [the Constitution] does not exist independently of the human will; it is created by the will of the people and may be altered or amended by the people according to preestablished rules."[14] Or, to return to *The Federalist*, "until the people have, by some solemn and authoritative act, annulled or changed the established form, it is binding on themselves collectively, as well as individually; and no presumption, or even knowledge of their sentiments, can warrant their representatives in a departure from it prior to such an act."

The Authority of Judges

But the authority denied to the legislature, and denied even to the people (except when they act in the prescribed "solemn and authoritative" manner), is now claimed by our judges. According to Justice William Brennan, popularly said to be the greatest of these, "The genius of the Constitution rests not in any static meaning it might have had in a world that is dead and gone, but in the adaptability of its great principles to cope with current problems and current needs."[15] And, as he demonstrated in case after case, it was he and his fellow judges who were charged with adapting it.

The temptation to adapt it, to keep it up to date, so to speak, seems to be irresistible, for "conservatives" like Rufus W. Peckham[16] as well as for liberals like Brennan and William O. Douglas.[17] Indeed, I suspect it would prove to be irresistible even for the most insistent critics of the practice, among whom I include myself. My first published article in the field had to do with *Buck v. Bell*, where the Court upheld a compulsory eugenical sterilization statute.[18] Surely, one would like to think, the Constitution does not permit surgical operations to be performed on unwilling patients. In support of its holding, the Court referred to an earlier case where it had upheld a statute requiring children to be vaccinated,[19] but is there not a difference between that and a statute requiring adult women to undergo salpingectomies? (As I put it thirty-odd years ago, no smallpox in the one case and no children in the other.) The state program was outrageous. A little investigation would have revealed that *Buck v. Bell* was a "friendly suit" and, therefore, not a case or controversy in the sense of Article III. The Court might have denied jurisdiction, but this would have had the effect of affirming the state court decision upholding the statute. On what ground might the Supreme Court have declared the statute unconstitutional? That it rested on "facts" that could not withstand scrutiny? They surely could not; the state's sterilization program rested on an already discredited Mendelian "recessive gene" theory. But such considerations are relevant in the legislative setting, not (we used to be told) in the judicial.

A little investigation would also have disclosed that some of the advocates of the program were admirers of Adolf Hitler, who, they said, deserved praise for adopting "many eugenic measures, including the sterilization law . . . and other measures to eliminate the non-Aryan element from Germany."[20] But of what constitutional relevance is that? Besides, not all the advocates of sterilization were admirers of Hitler. Then, what about the fact that the law applied only to the (alleged) mental defectives in state institutions and not to the "multitudes outside"? But by reaching all those "similarly situated," the law satisfied what were then understood to be the requirements of equal protection. In the event, the Court dismissed the complaint in a few paragraphs. "Three generations of imbeciles are enough," said Justice Oliver Wendell Holmes for the nearly unanimous Court, and that was that.

Justice Pierce Butler dissented, but without opinion. Rumor has it that, as the only Roman Catholic on the Court, he feared that anything he said would be misunderstood. On what could he have grounded his dissent? A few years later (in 1930), Pope Pius XI issued an encyclical (*Casti Conubii*) declaring sexual sterilization to be contrary to the natural law, and Butler might have been tempted to cite it if the encyclical had existed then. The Constitution, however, does not "enact" the natural law as expounded by the pope or, for that matter, by Thomas Aquinas, any more than the "Fourteenth Amendment [enacts] Mr. Herbert Spencer's Social Statics."[21] What, then, was left to Butler and those of us who opposed the statute other than some version of emanations radiating from those penumbras cast by the First, Fourth, Fifth, Ninth, and Fourteenth Amendments? As I said, the temptation to go beyond the text of the Constitution appears to be irresistible. It may even be inevitable.

Was it not the great chief justice himself who enjoined us never to forget that it was a constitution we were expounding, "a Constitution intended to endure for ages to come, and consequently, to be adapted to the various crises of human affairs"?[22] And what is this but to say that its vitality or viability depends on its adaptability?

The Failure of Congress

In fact, however, as I have pointed out before,[23] Marshall did not say that the Constitution may be adapted to the "various crises of human affairs"; he said that the legislative powers granted by the Constitution are adaptable to meet those crises. And much of what we regard as the inevitability of judicial activism is the result of Congress's failure to use its powers, specifically its powers under section five of the Fourteenth Amendment. Its failure to do so—for example, its failure in the course of time to declare that one of the privileges or immunities of American citizenship is to attend a nonsegregated public school—not only opened the door for the Court but made it *necessary* for the Court to assume a political role; and, as we say, the rest is history.

It is a history of employing constitutional clauses—equal protection and due process especially—in tasks for which they were not intended and are ill suited, tasks for which the legislative power *was* intended and *is* well suited. To invalidate poll taxes, for example, legislatures, unlike courts, have no need to invoke a principle that of necessity they must find either in the text or the interstices of the Constitution; nor do they have to say, as the Court did say, that "the Equal Protection Clause is not shackled to the political theory of a particular era [or] due process to a fixed catalogue of what was at a given time deemed to be the limits of fundamental rights."[24] They have only to decide that, under modern conditions, these taxes serve no useful and legitimate purpose. As Justice Hugo L. Black said in dissent, however, the Court had to invoke the familiar "natural-law-due-process formula," which, he suggested, is simply a cloak for what it thinks governmental policy should be.[25]

And so it is, and so it necessarily is, except that no one on the Court actually speaks of the natural law, natural justice, or "the first principles of the social compact": not in our day. Whatever might have been Justice Butler's inclinations when he dissented in *Buck v. Bell*, the traditional natural law rests on presuppositions that no contemporary judge or constitutional lawyer—or, at least, none known to me—would accept.[26] Their education forbids it. What about natural rights, or natural law as understood in the Declaration of Independence?

To justify our independence, we invoked "the Laws of Nature and of Nature's God," but our habit today is not to take that seriously. Even Carl Becker, the author of the one book devoted exclusively to explicating this first of our founding documents, does not take it seriously. As he would have it, Jefferson and his colleagues appealed to the laws of nature only because they had to appeal to something, and it is pointless to ask whether they were serious in their claims: "To ask whether the natural rights philosophy of the Declaration of Independence is true or false," he says, "is essentially a meaningless question."[27]

Others take it seriously but in the process demonstrate their unfamiliarity with the subject—the venerable Roscoe Pound for example. Hoping to breathe some life into the "forgotten" Ninth Amendment,[28] Pound seized upon the possibility that, with their reference to the "[rights] retained by the people," the framers had in mind natural rights or—he tends to confuse them—natural laws. But, an early opponent of the idea of original intent, he was not willing to accept the understanding of these rights or these laws current at the time of the founding. Instead, he came up with the idea of mutable rights and laws, mutable but—*mirabile dictu*—still natural. "From this standpoint," he said, "the Ninth Amendment is a solemn declaration that natural rights are not a fixed category of reasonable human expectations in civilized society laid down once for all in the several sections of the Constitution." And "unlike the law of nature of the eighteenth century," he said, "the revived natural law is not a fixed system of precisely formulated rules to stand fast forever."[29]

As I said, we began in 1776 with an appeal to the self-evident truth that all men are endowed by their creator with certain unalienable rights. It is altogether reasonable to assume that, in 1787–1788, when we gave our consent to the Constitution, we understood it to embody, or to be informed by, the principles of that Declaration and that we further assumed that occasions would arise when, to decide a case or controversy, it would be necessary *and* appropriate for the Court to invoke them. Which is to say, as it is in the *United States Code* (as well as other official compilations of our laws), we once understood the Declaration to be the first of our "organic laws."[30] Leo Strauss made this point in 1953 when he wrote that "about a generation ago, an American diplomat could still say that 'the natural and divine foundation of the rights of man . . . is self-evident to all Americans.'"[31] But Strauss went on to cast doubt whether that could still be said in his time. He referred to Germany, where the idea of natural right had been abandoned—where the term itself had become almost "incomprehensible"—and he suggested that this would happen in America. Indeed, if Sanford Levinson is right, that has now happened.

About a hundred years ago, Friedrich Nietzsche, the most influential of German thinkers, pronounced the death of God—"Nature's God," the god of the Declaration of Independence, as well as the God of the Bible—and we are indebted to Levinson, a leading American professor of constitutional law, for his candor when pointing to the consequences of this. "The death of constitutionalism," he declares, "may be the central event of our time, just as the death of God was that of the past century (and for much the same reason)."[32] Nature's God endowed us with rights and, through the agency of the founders, provided us with a Constitution that, to secure these rights, put constraints on the popular will. With his death, those constraints are deprived of all moral authority. In Levinson's words, "Law is stripped of any moral anchoring," with the consequence that there is nothing "to which the will [is] bound to submit"[33]—no moral order, no moral laws, and, as Nietzsche said, no reason to be burdened by guilt. Levinson claims—and who would contest him?—that his view of our situation is the one "emphasized today at most major law schools"—and not only in the law schools. Even as I was writing this chapter, I came across a letter, written by the chairman of the political theory program for the 1991 American Political Science Association annual meeting, saying that there was a flood of proposals for panels, most of them in the category of "postmodernism and critical theory." I have reason to believe the same situation prevails in the meetings of the Modern Language Association.

The Death of Constitutionalism

We now live in a postmodernist world, and it is important to understand what that implies: constitutionalism is dead. The thought that made it possible is no longer believed. Rationalism is dead. The idea of nature gave way to history and historicism, then radical historicism, and in our case to "postmodernist" legal thought. And this, as Levinson accurately portrays it and as Thomas L. Pangle pointed out in his review of Levinson's book, "is inspired by the brooding, anti-rationalist, quasi-religious and proto-fascist philosophies of Nietzsche and Heidegger, supplemented by their more recent French and American 'deconstructionist' epigones, Derrida, Foucault, Barthes, de Man and Richard Rorty."[34] There are, I would emphasize, no constitutionalists in this group, and, if Levinson is right, our law teachers, and ultimately our judges, will not be able to escape their influence.

But if constitutionalism is dead, so is the prospect for judicial review. If, as Levinson puts it with commendable candor, "there is nothing that is unsayable in the language of the Constitution,"[35] why should the people and their elected representatives defer to judgments rendered by an unelected judiciary? Levinson can think of no reason why they should, but Michael Perry (in some ways the most thoughtful of the "living" constitutionalists) says the judges speak for the people by appealing to their aspirations. The judges, he says, should be guided by the "beliefs or aspirations as to how the community's life, the life in common, should be lived." But he has to acknowledge that "different persons will have different views as to what an aspiration requires," and, this being so, he concludes that "the judge should rely on *her own beliefs* as to what the aspiration requires." How does "she" form those beliefs? By testing them "in the crucible of dialogic encounter with the wisdom of the past, of the tradition, including original beliefs, precedent, and anything else relevant and helpful."[36] The difference between this and a reliance on personal preferences is not readily discernible, and why the people and their elected representatives should defer to the judges' preferences is not at all evident. Why should they?

But Perry turns the question around. He asks, Why are today's public officials "morally obligated to defer to the beliefs either of the long-dead and mostly WASP men who ratified the original Constitution and the Bill of Rights or of the long-dead and mostly WASP men who ratified the second Constitution—the Civil War amendments"? He says that they are not so obliged, that it is "counterintuitive" to suppose that they are.[37]

Although Perry is a Roman Catholic and I am a latter-day WASP, it is not for that reason that I think this is a matter not to be decided by intuition. Would he think otherwise if the constitutional provision involved was of recent provenance, if, for example, it had been proposed last year by a convention called by the Congress on the application of two-thirds of the states and consisting of large numbers of non-

WASPs? Perhaps, but, assuming the later provision is not intended to repeal the earlier, what is it that gives the provision a greater claim to obedience? On what basis could Perry say that the later convention—acting, let it be noticed, under the authority of a provision adopted by the earlier—enjoys a status denied to the earlier?

Legitimacy and Authority

But let the matter be decided by intuition—the public's intuition—and ask which judge has a greater claim to obedience, the one who points to those five provisions indicating, in one way or another, that the Constitution permits the imposition of the death penalty[38] and, on the basis of this constitutional evidence and despite "her" own beliefs on the matter, concludes that death is not a cruel or unusual punishment, or the one (Justice Brennan) who, having discerned what he regards as our true "aspirations," decides that the death penalty is unconstitutional? Or, again, which judge has a greater claim to obedience, Justice Antonin Scalia, who concludes that Title VII of the 1964 Civil Rights Act means what it says when it forbids sexual preferences in hiring, or Justice Sandra Day O'Connor, who admits that Title VII has been interpreted, and is being interpreted, "to permit what its language read literally would prohibit," and who goes so far as to say that Justice Scalia had proved this "with excruciating clarity,"[39] but, nevertheless, after engaging in some of that Perry moral discourse, concludes that the statute must be read to permit what it literally forbids?

But this is a matter of legitimacy, which cannot be determined by intuition. Whether we can expect legislatures to defer to courts depends ultimately on the right of the people to adopt a constitution for themselves *and* for their posterity, a constitution binding upon themselves and, until "annulled or changed" in the prescribed manner, binding upon their posterity. That, in the words of *Federalist* 78, is the "fundamental principle of republican government." Judges may claim the obedience of other public officials because, and only because, they represent the people in their constituting capacity. Unlike elected officials, their constituents are those "long-dead and mostly WASP men" and, when acting in a "solemn and authoritative" manner, their living descendants. (Thanks to a series of constitutional amendments, these descendants are not necessarily either WASPs or men.)

The judges must acknowledge this. Even Justice Brennan claims to derive his authority from the Constitution, which, in this one respect at least, retains the meaning it had at the beginning. His decisions may derive from a *living* Constitution, but his authority to render them derives from that good old (in this one respect) "static" Constitution. The question is whether the people will continue to recognize that authority when the judges are no longer willing to limit themselves to enforcing the Constitution as written or, to quote Madison again, if the judges are not guided by the sense of the people who ratified it. I know of no one who has put this better than Fred Baumann of Kenyon College:

> The problem created by the doctrine of the living Constitution for the legitimacy of the Constitution is obvious. It is that the Constitution then preserves only a formal existence, that it becomes a kind of moral capital on which the Supreme Court ceaselessly draws but that it can never replenish. As that capital is drawn down, it becomes ever clearer that it is not the Constitution that lives but only its name; consequently neither the Constitution nor the Court deriving its justification from the Constitution can enjoy further legitimacy.[40]

We obviously have not reached that point yet. The idea of constitutionality—and its converse, unconstitutionality—is still accepted by the American people but only, I suspect, because, in their commendable innocence, they continue to believe that it is the Constitution whose provisions the Court is enforcing. One has to wonder what will happen when they come to understand, as Joseph Rauh, a prominent lay proponent of the "living Constitution," wants them to understand, that the "Supreme Court is part of our nation's political process." He says that "the sooner this is accepted as inevitable the better."[41] I doubt that. I think they think that political decisions should be made democratically, by their political representatives whom, under the Constitution, they elect to office and whom they can remove from office. If so, and if the Court were to proceed along the lines traced by Brennan and retraced by Perry, Rauh, and the others, the "living Constitution" is not calculated to enjoy a long life.

4

Guarding the Constitution from Legislative Tyranny

Joseph M. Bessette

> *In truth, the Legislative power is of such a nature that it scarcely can be restrained, either by the Constitution or by itself; and if the federal Government should lose its proper equilibrium within itself, I am persuaded that the effect will proceed from the encroachments of the Legislative department. . . . I am fully in the opinion that the numerous and immediate representatives of the people composing the . . . House [of Representatives] will decidedly predominate in the Government.*
>
> JAMES MADISON
> letter to Edmund Pendleton, June 21, 1789

Is the Supreme Court the guardian of the Constitution? This question may be divided into two parts: (1) Was the Supreme Court *designed* or *intended* to be the guardian of the Constitution? (2) Whatever the intention or original plan, has the Supreme Court actually functioned as the guardian of the Constitution throughout American history? I will treat mainly the first of these questions, with some reflections on the second later.

To begin, we must confront a preliminary question: what does it mean to be the guardian of the Constitution? Indeed, what do we mean by the Constitution of which the Court may be the guardian? In juxtaposing the Supreme Court with the issue of constitutional guardianship, it may appear that the *rights* secured by the Constitution—some in the original document of 1787, more in the Bill of Rights, and yet others in subsequent amendments—must be at issue. Yet this view is surely too narrow. For the Constitution that emerged from the Constitutional Convention says much less about rights than about the structure, powers, and duties of the institutions of government. The Constitution of 1787 is primarily a document constituting the organs of the new national government, not primarily a document articulating the rights of the people against unjust or arbitrary actions by that government.

This is not to belittle the extent and importance of the rights actually specified in the document of 1787. The list is impressive, including such protections as the right to the writ of habeas corpus (absent rebellion or invasion); the rights to be free from punishments through bills of attainder or ex post facto laws; the rights of creditors, merchants, and others to be free from state interference in the obligation of contracts and from the consequences of inflationary state laws on paper money; the right to trial by jury in criminal cases; the right of those accused of treason to a particularly high standard of proof; the right of citizens in each state to enjoy all the "Privileges and Immunities of Citizens in the several States"; the right of citizens in every state to a republican form of government; and the right of those otherwise qualified for federal office, elective or appointive, to be free from any religious test. While this list reminds us that rights were hardly ignored by the drafters of the original Constitution, the records of their debates and the text they produced fully reflect their view that constitution building meant primarily *institution* building, institutions that ideally would combine stability and energy with liberty and the republican form.[1] Lists of rights, after all, were but "parchment barriers" to the powers of government and had proved woefully inadequate at securing liberty in the states in the years leading up to the Constitutional Convention. If the "Blessings of Liberty" promised by the Preamble were to be secure, it would be mainly by designing a House of Representatives, Senate, presidency, and Court that together would govern with wisdom and effectiveness and fidelity to the enduring interests of the American people.

If the Constitution is understood as the framers themselves understood it—as the blueprint for a set of governing institutions— then what would it mean to be its guardian? To be the guardian of the Constitution must mean to guard it against some threat or danger. We are led to ask what danger threatened the institutional design incorporated in the Constitution of 1787 and what role the Supreme Court was to play in protecting the Constitution from such a danger. Insofar as *The Federalist Papers* of Alexander Hamilton, James Madison, and John Jay is an accurate indication of the founding fathers' concerns about preserving and perpetuating their constitutional design, the danger they most feared seems clear enough: legislative tyranny.

The Danger of Legislative Tyranny

"The accumulation of all powers, legislative, executive, and judiciary, in the same hands," wrote Publius (the pseudonym employed by Hamilton, Madison, and Jay), "whether of one, a few, or many, and whether hereditary, self-appointed, or elective, may justly be pronounced the very definition of tyranny."[2] No political truth was "of greater intrinsic value" than that "the preservation of liberty requires that the three great departments of power should be separate and distinct."[3] Preserving the institutional separation of the "three great departments" was an essential task of the American constitution makers, the failure at which would likely lead to some form of governmental tyranny even if under democratic forms. As Thomas Jefferson wrote in his *Notes on the State of Virginia:*

> An *elective despotism* was not the government we fought for; but one which should not only be founded on free principles, but in which the powers of government should be so divided and balanced among several bodies of magistracy, as that no one could transcend their legal limits, without being effectually checked and restrained by the others.[4]

From what quarter, then, was the drive toward consolidation likely to originate? Publius minced no words; his was not a subtle or esoteric argument: in a representative republic with a carefully limited executive,

> where the legislative power is exercised by an assembly . . . which is sufficiently numerous to feel all the passions which actuate a multitude, yet not so numerous as to be incapable of pursuing the objects of its passions by means which reason prescribes; it is against the enterprising ambition of this department that *the people ought to indulge all their jealousy and exhaust all their precautions.*[5]

The experiences under the new state constitutions had demonstrated nothing so clearly as the tendency of the popular assemblies to arrogate powers formally assigned to the executive or to the courts or to use their control over salaries, and in some cases over continuance in office, to undermine the genuine independence of the other branches. Publius cited the examples of Virginia, based on the authority of

Jefferson, who served as governor there from 1779 to 1781, and of Pennsylvania, where a council of censors had documented numerous examples of legislative usurpations of executive and judicial authority. Equally egregious examples from other states could well have been added to the list. As Publius so succinctly summarized the problem, "The legislative department is everywhere extending the sphere of its activity and drawing all power into its impetuous vortex."[6]

But how much should one make of this experience in the states during the eleven years after independence? Perhaps it reflects little more than a natural reaction to the decades of conflict during the colonial period between royally appointed governors and popularly elected assemblies. Were the despotic state legislatures of 1776–1787 merely a consequence of the historical context in which the new state governments were launched, or did the failure of the state constitutions to preserve balanced separation of powers systems reflect a deeper problem for democratic constitution building? Publius's view was clearly the latter: something about the legislative power in a representative democracy makes the legislature a real threat (and a much greater one than the other branches) to undermining the balance of the Constitution. Publius gave at least four distinct reasons for this view: (1) the constitutional powers of a legislature in a representative democracy are "more extensive, and less susceptible of precise limits" than those of the other branches; (2) the legislature alone "has access to the pockets of the people," thus giving it a direct control over resources not enjoyed by the executive and judiciary; (3) by determining the "pecuniary rewards" (that is, the salaries) of those who serve in the other branches, the legislature can bend these others to its will; and (4) the representative nature of legislative office in a democracy creates an alliance between the legislature and the people that fuels conflicts with the other branches and, as often as not, assures a legislative victory.[7]

The first three reasons derive from the nature of the legislative, or lawmaking, power: the difficulty in restricting its reach, its access to the resources of the community, and its ability to undermine the independent will of the other branches. The fourth reason, however, may be the deepest problem of all for it is tied to the fundamental nature of the regime itself. When separation of powers is joined to representative democracy, the democratic impulse will deform the carefully crafted institutional design through joint popular-legislative impatience and imperiousness. In institutional conflicts between the branches, the legislature will bring to bear the weight of public opinion, giving it "the irresistible force possessed by that branch of a free government, which has the people on its side."[8] Conversely, if the popular will feels thwarted by distant and unresponsive institutions, it will look to its representatives in the legislature, whom it regards as "the confidential guardians of the rights and liberties of the people," to press its claim.[9]

The following paragraph from Publius's defense of why the president in the new government should not be subservient to Congress captures the problems created by the conjunction of the democratic impulse and the legislative power:

> To what purpose separate the executive or the judiciary from the legislative, if both the executive and the judiciary are so constituted as to be at the absolute devotion of the legislative? Such a separation must be merely nominal, and incapable of producing the ends for which it was established. It is one thing to be subordinate to the laws, and another to be dependent on the legislative body. The first comports with, the last violates, the fundamental principles of good government; and, whatever may be the forms of the Constitution, unites all power in the same hands. The tendency of the legislative authority to absorb every other has been fully displayed and illustrated by examples in some preceding numbers. In governments purely republican, this tendency is almost irresistible. The representatives of the people, in a popular assembly, seem sometimes to fancy that they are the people themselves, and betray strong symptoms of impatience and disgust at the least sign of opposition from any other quarter; as if the exercise of its rights, by either the executive or judiciary, were a breach of their privilege and an outrage to their dignity. They often appear disposed to exert an imperious control over the other departments; and as they commonly have the people on their side, they always act with such momentum as to make it very difficult for the other members of the government to maintain the balance of the Constitution.[10]

There is a natural tendency in a representative democracy for those who serve in the popular assembly to identify their will with the will of the people. Often they are right: "The people [are] on their side." This is especially a problem for the executive or the courts when they oppose some deeply felt legislative desire; for if the people are the source of all authority and legitimacy, by what rights may their desires be thwarted? How will the "balance of the Constitution" be maintained in the face of a determined legislature allied with an equally determined populace? Legislative tyranny becomes the most likely mechanism through which the democratic impulse would undermine American constitutionalism.

Constitutional Balance

How, then, was this problem of legislative tyranny to be solved, this "almost irresistible" tendency in governments "purely republican" for the "legislative authority to absorb every other"? And what role was the Supreme Court to play, if any, in guarding the Constitution against legislative tyranny? The answer to the first question is the famous argument in *Federalist* 51. Although the basic argument is well known, it is worth reviewing here with a view to discerning the Court's role in preserving the "balance of the Constitution."

The overriding principle, with which Publius introduced the argument, is that the "interior structure of the government" must be so contrived that the several branches "may, by their mutual relations, be the means of keeping each other in their proper places."[11] Publius then laid out the Constitution's four-part plan for accomplishing this internal checking and balancing.

First, to ensure that each department has "a will of its own," each should have as little to do as possible with selecting the members of the other departments. Thus, the members of the House of Representatives were to be chosen by the people directly, senators by the state legislatures, and the president by specially appointed electors. Only the members of the federal judiciary were to be appointed through the agency of the other branches (the president nominating and the Senate confirming). This is defended on the basis of the special qualifications necessary for service in judicial office and the likelihood that the "permanent tenure" of federal judges would "soon destroy all sense of dependence on the authority" making the appointment.[12]

Second, the Constitution limits the legislature's control over the salaries, and thus over the will, of the president and judges. A sitting president's salary can be neither raised nor lowered during the term for which he was elected; the salary of judges cannot be lowered for the entire time they serve. (Judges' salaries, however, may be increased, thereby allowing the legislature to compensate for inflation during potentially lengthy terms of service.)

Third and best-known, those who run each department must be given "the necessary constitutional means and personal motives to resist encroachments of the others. . . . Ambition must be made to counteract ambition. The interest of the man must be connected with the constitutional rights of the place."[13] As elaborated elsewhere in the *Federalist*, the president must have not only a constitutional means of defending his office from legislative incursions—principally through the veto power—but also the powers, length of term, and possibility of reeligibility that will give him a real personal interest in protecting his office from legislative attack. The president's private interest must be made to coincide with the constitutional rights of the office. His personal ambition for power and honor must be made to counteract opposing ambitions centered in the legislature.

Merely separating the branches of government on paper does not guarantee that those who occupy the nonlegislative offices will have a personal ambition to oppose encroachments. Imagine, for example, a legislatively elected president with a one-year term of office, no reeligibility, and no veto power (much like many of the state governors under the original state constitutions). Would the occupant of such an office likely have the incentive, let alone the means, to fight to uphold the prerogatives of his office when threatened by the legislature? How would the president's self-interest or ambition be served by battling the legislature over a matter of constitutional power if his service in the executive office were limited to but one year of his professional life? He would obviously look elsewhere to fulfill his highest political ambitions. Make him eligible for reelection, and the problem is only exacerbated since he would now have powerful positive incentives to do the legislature's bidding. The point is that the president's ambition "must be made" through careful constitutional construction to promote the integrity and security of the executive office. In this way the private interests of officeholders will make up for their "defect of better motives"; for if better motives were in control, legislators would always respect the constitutional authorities of coordinate departments, and presidents would always resist encroachments on the executive office. This, then, is the "great security against a gradual concentration of the several powers in the same department."[14]

This famous principle of ambition counteracting ambition is not, it must be acknowledged, explicitly phrased in *Federalist* 51 in terms of presidents or the judiciary withstanding legislative encroachments. This explains why the two paragraphs elaborating this principle are not always read as directed to the specific problem of legislative tyranny. Indeed, the constitutional intention was that the members of each of the branches ought to resist intrusions upon their lawful authorities from whatever source. But the real world problem that the framers feared was not judicial tyranny or, perhaps more likely, executive tyranny but, as we have seen and about which Publius could hardly have been clearer, tyranny by the legislature.

In the final element of the four-part plan for preserving constitutional balance, Publius explicitly returned to the problem of legislative domination in representative democracies: "In republican government, the legislative authority necessarily predominates." This "inconveniency" is remedied by bicameralism: "Divide the legislature into different branches; and . . . render them, by different modes of election and different principles of action, as little connected with each other as the nature of their common functions and their common dependence on the society will admit."[15] To put it simply: weaken the legislature by creating two parallel institutions as unlike as possible (within the constraints of republicanism) and then require the approval of both before anything of consequence can be done (excepting the Senate's power over treaties and appointments). In the immediately following passages, Publius contrasted the need to weaken the naturally predominant legislature with the need to strengthen ("fortify" is his word) the naturally weaker executive.

The Court's Role

What, then, can we say about the contribution of the Supreme Court to this institutional solution to the problem of legislative tyranny? At one level, of course, the Court would enjoy the enhanced independence brought about by a life term (assuming no impeachments for inappropriate reasons) and salaries that could not be diminished during the term of a judge. And like presidents, federal judges would presumably have the personal motives to resist legislative encroachments, unless, that is, the promise of higher salaries alone was enough to undermine independence of will. Thus, insofar as legislative domination took the form of attempted incursions into the judicial domain—for example, calling judges before Congress to explain unpopular decisions (as the legislature of Rhode Island once did) or demanding to see drafts of opinions or the notes taken by judges in conference—we should expect steadfast resistance from the Court. Moreover, if Congress acts against the Court in a way that violates a specific constitutional provision—for example, passes an ex post facto law or bill of attainder to punish some individual exonerated through the legal process—the Court is obligated, according to Publius, to declare the offending statute void as violating the fundamental law of the Constitution. This obligation holds even if the legislature is supported in its actions by a majority of the people, although "it would require an uncommon portion of fortitude in the judges to do their duty as faithful guardians of the Constitution, where legislative invasions of it had been instigated by the major voice of the community."[16]

Thus, in deciding a specific legal controversy in which a party's injury is the result of an unconstitutional legislative action, federal judges are to function as "faithful guardians of the Constitution." But does the federal judiciary, and in particular the Supreme Court, properly embrace a kind of overarching guardianship for the constitutional order as a whole? Does it, more than the other branches, have a responsibility to guard the fundamental balance of the Constitution? The answer that I believe Publius would have given and that American history confirms is no.

Consider first the extreme case. Imagine that the political branches (the House of Representatives, Senate, and presidency), urged on by a determined majority of the people, are intent on visiting some injustice upon a substantial minority of the American people. Only the U.S. Constitution and the Supreme Court stand in their way. How likely is it that the Court could withstand such a combination of forces? Think of the weapons available to the political branches to enforce their will: they could deny the Court the appropriate appellate juris- diction under Article III, section 2 of the Constitution; they could stack the Court by adding a sufficient number of reliable votes (the Consti- tution places no restraints on Congress's authority to alter the size of the Court); they could impeach and remove from office the recalcitrant justices (as it was thought the Republican Congresses of Jefferson's administration might do to John Adams's Federalist appointees); or they (particularly the president) could simply refuse to enforce Supreme Court decisions. Upon what resources could the Court rely to withstand defeat in its lonely battle?

This thought experiment illustrates how utterly weak the Court is when standing alone against the political branches in alliance with a determined majority. Indeed, Publius acknowledged that "the judi- ciary is beyond comparison the weakest of the three departments of power."[17] Because of its "natural feebleness," it "is in continual jeopardy of being overpowered, awed, or influenced by its co-ordinate branches."[18] Such an institution could hardly serve as the principal preserver of the constitutional design, as the first line of defense against an aggrandizing legislature. Instead, it was to a wise and dispassionate Senate (bicameralism) and to a strong, vigorous, and independent presidency (a political, and not merely functional, separation of powers) that the framers looked for guarantors of the constitutional balance. These were to be the two great institutional barriers to democratic excesses pushed through the popular branch. If the Senate and pres- idency succumbed, no assemblage of justices, no matter how devoted to duty or how motivated by "stern virtue," could right the balance of the Constitution or in the end even protect their own lawful authority from debilitating encroachments.[19] Viewed in this light, the question then becomes: What role, if any, was the Supreme Court to play in assisting these other branches in resisting legislative tyranny and in thus protecting the constitutional equilibrium?

Consider bicameralism. As is well known, the Senate's six-year term, staggered elections, election by the state legislatures, and small size were all intended to create a representative institution that would be free from the kinds of democratic excesses expected to characterize the proceedings of the House of Representatives. The beauty of bicameralism as a device for thwarting legislative tyranny is that the popular branch is powerless to act without the formal consent of the less popular; two distinctly constituted independent institutions must concur for any measure to become the law of the land. The security that a well-designed and properly functioning Senate adds to the constitutional system is quite independent of anything the Supreme Court does. To the extent that bicameralism mitigates the dangers of legislative tyranny, the Court is irrelevant.

The matter is much, though not exactly, the same regarding the president's role in defending the Constitution against legislative usurpations. The framers expected and desired a dynamic tension between the legislative and executive branches. In giving the president the responsibility to recommend bills to Congress and the authority to veto all congressional measures ("Every Bill" as well as "Every Order, Resolution, or Vote"), the framers invested the president with a political responsibility unlike that found in mere administrators of the legislative will. The framers wanted a president who would "dare to act his own opinion with vigor and decision."[20] At times this would put him at odds with the legislature and even with the community itself. The hope was that the president would uphold the true interests of the people even if "at variance with their inclinations" and in so doing he would, over the course of a four-year term, "establish . . . himself in the esteem and good-will of his constituents." By giving "proofs . . . of his wisdom and integrity" he would acquire "the respect and attachment of his fellow citizens."[21] Insofar as the Congress believed that it, and not the president, had a better understanding of the true interests of the people, we would expect the two branches to compete for the approval of the citizenry in years of presidential elections (much the way that the election of 1832 became a referendum on the opposed positions of Congress and President Andrew Jackson on the fate of the national bank).

This is a political and institutional dynamic between the legislative and executive branches, not a legal one. Ambition counteracts ambition, power checks power, will opposes will. This is not counsel for the two branches battling it out in the courtroom; each branch is pushing its view, asserting its rights, and using all its institutional and political influence to carry the day. The process is contentious and it is untidy, but it is the essential dynamic for preserving the balance of the Constitution. And it is a dynamic in which the U.S.

Supreme Court plays no necessary role.

It may be asked, however, Why not have the Court serve as a neutral arbiter in disputes between the political branches? Surely this would be preferable to messy political disputes that hardly guarantee just results. To this, several things can be said. First, disputes between Congress and the president do not necessarily take a form that presents a properly justiciable issue for the Court. For this and other reasons, interbranch disputes may not reach the Court in a timely fashion. One has only to think of the history of the Tenure of Office Act of 1867, a duly enacted law that prevented the president from firing his highest-level subordinates without Senate approval—a law that remains arguably Congress's most serious assault on the powers of the presidency. Although this act overturned a settled precedent that went back to the First Congress, although its violation by President Andrew Johnson resulted in his impeachment and near conviction and removal from office, and although the act and an amended successor were a source of strife between the two branches until its repeal in 1887, the Court did not rule on the constitutionality of such congressional restraints on the president's removal power until the *Myers* case of 1926. Indeed, the law at issue in *Myers*, requiring Senate consent to presidential removal of postmasters, had itself been on the books since 1876, a half-century before.

Second, key to the framers' design is attaching personal interests to constitutional powers and rights. No constitutional officeholder other than the president can possibly feel the same personal interest in protecting the powers of his office as he does. It follows that one cannot rely on the Supreme Court to be sufficiently assertive in defending presidential prerogatives. The most emphatic recent illustration of this fact is the Court's seven-to-one decision in *Morrison v. Olson* (1988) upholding the independent counsel provisions of the Ethics in Government Act. All agree that by its express provisions the Ethics in Government Act was designed to, and does in fact, restrict the president's authority over a certain class of criminal prosecutions (in part by limiting his power to fire independent counsels). Yet it can hardly be disputed that criminal prosecutions are by their nature a part of the executive power. If we apply the same principle of constitutional construction of the executive power that, by Madison's testimony, was embraced by the First Congress during its debates on the president's removal power—"that the Executive power being in general terms vested in the President, *all power of an Executive nature* not particularly taken away must belong to that department"—it is hard to avoid the conclusion that in *Morrison v. Olson* the Court endorsed a congressional violation of the vesting clause of Article II of the

Constitution.[22] The irony, of course, is that in both 1983 and 1987 President Ronald Reagan signed legislation reauthorizing the act that he and his Department of Justice believed to be a direct infringement on the president's constitutional authority.

Two lessons would seem to follow from this incident: that a wise president ought not to rely on the wisdom of the Court to protect his lawful authority and that at least some recent presidents are less assertive in defending their constitutional powers and duties than the framers had intended. Think, for example, of how an Andrew Jackson might have responded to the independent counsel provisions of the Ethics in Government Act. Given Jackson's record in asserting the prerogatives of his office in conflicts with Congress (particularly over the national bank), is the following scenario unlikely? He would have vetoed the bill in the strongest possible language, language carefully crafted for public effect. If his veto were overridden by Congress, he would have publicly declared his view that all parts of the act that contravened his understanding of the president's authority were null and void. He would have instructed his subordinates, especially the attorney general, to ignore the offensive features of the act—features that specify, for example, when and how an attorney general must proceed with an investigation and when he must apply to the courts to appoint an independent counsel. Jackson would have gladly taken the issue to the people during the presidential campaign and would not have been hesitant to interpret reelection as public vindication of his position. Finally, to any who argued that the Supreme Court had settled all the key constitutional issues, he would have insisted that "the Congress, the Executive, and the Court must each for itself be guided by its own opinion of the Constitution. Each public officer who takes an oath to support the Constitution swears that he will support it as he understands it, and not as it is understood by others."[23] One can hardly imagine the firestorm of criticism that would descend upon a modern president who boldly adopted the Jacksonian approach on a matter upon which the Court had spoken so clearly (if not correctly).

Why, then, do our recent presidents fall so far short of the Jacksonian standard? The answer is complex, but two points may be elucidated. First, modern presidential ambition seems to have different effects from those desired by the framers. Instead of inclining presidents to assert their rightful powers against an encroaching legislature with the full awareness of the controversy to ensue, ambition now seems to divert both the first-term president with an eye on reelection and the second-termer with an eye on the history books from the kinds of controversial actions that might jeopardize approval ratings. The democratization of the presidency, begun by Jackson but not fully developed until the twentieth century, is a two-edged sword. When the president's position is also the popular one (like Jackson's opposition to the rechartering of the national bank), the executive's alliance with public opinion can be the source of great strength in a contest with Congress. As noted, Publius, thinking of the legislature, had written of "the irresistible force possessed by that branch of a free government, which has the people on its side."[24] On other occasions, however, the president's position cuts against the grain of public or elite opinion, as Reagan and his political advisers surely understood when the Ethics in Government Act arrived on his desk in 1983 and 1987. In such cases, self-interest (or at least perceived self-interest) may well dictate expedient measures at the expense of a defense of the full contours of the executive power vested by the Constitution. Thus it is that the democratization of the presidency that is so much a part of our contemporary political system, but not of the original design, fundamentally reshapes the calculus of presidential ambition in a way that may not contribute to the long-term well-being of the executive office.

The other principal reason why our recent presidents do not display the assertiveness that characterized Jackson is the now widespread acceptance of the view that the Court is indeed the principal guardian of the Constitution, the final arbiter of the true meaning of the fundamental law, and thus the impartial umpire of all disputes over separation of powers. We should not be surprised if presidents have been cowed by the authority of such a Court, however fallible its members and however imperfect its judgments. Yet a fair reading of the records of American history demonstrates both (1) that those who created the Court as one of three coequal branches never intended to raise the least representative institution to such an exalted position and (2) that in fact the Court has not been responsible during the past two centuries for preserving the integrity of the Constitution's institutional design. To raise the Court to the position of supreme guardian of the Constitution is to put excessive trust in fallible men and women, to enervate the American separation of powers dynamic, to jeopardize the constitutional rights of the political branches with serious consequences for governmental effectiveness, and ultimately to undermine the representative character of the American constitutional order.

5

Education, the Supreme Court, and the Constitution

Eva T. H. Brann

The subject of the relation of our Constitution to education can be taken in a narrow or in a broad sense. Narrow questions concern the way education is directly or indirectly included in the document and conversely the way the document appears in education. Broad questions concern the influence of the Constitution on the constitution of American life, on the shaping of a civic consensus, and on its current crisis.

Education and the Constitution in the Narrow Sense

The dramatic fact that must stand at the head of any discussion concerning the bearing of the Constitution on education is that it contains not a word about that topic.

A National University. That silence is not for want of speech on the part of James Madison. According to his *Notes of Debates in the Federal Convention,* he made two efforts. He reports that on August 18, 1787, he included in a list submitted for reference to the Committee of Detail the item "To establish a University" as a power proper to be added to those of the general legislature. Charles Pinckney of North Carolina similarly suggested: "To establish seminaries for the promotion of the arts and sciences." Again on September 14, both moved in the convention to insert in the list of powers vested in the Congress that of establishing "a

University, in which no preference or distinction should be allowed on account of Religion." James Wilson supported the motion, but Gouverneur Morris said that it was not necessary: "The exclusive power of the Seat of Government, will reach the object." The motion was defeated.[1]

As far as I can tell, no scheme for getting education into the Constitution was ever contemplated, other than the establishment of a national university or a college system. Why only a university was ever considered is as interesting as why the idea died so lingering a death.

Let us begin with the latter question. A national university was a matter of discussion not only at the Constitutional Convention but on college campuses, in commencement addresses, and in the numerous essays that were circulating on education for the new republic. Benjamin Rush, for example, in an article published under a pseudonym in the *Federal Gazette* of Philadelphia in 1788, proposed such a university as the agency for inspiring American citizens

> with federal principles, which can only be effected by our young men meeting and spending two or three years together in a national University and afterwards disseminating their knowledge and principles through every county, township and village of the United States.[2]

When in 1786 he had asked himself, in his *Thoughts upon the Mode of Education Proper to a Republic,* what was to be the aim of education in the public school system he was advocating, he put at the head the inculcation of religious principles:

> · The only foundation for useful education in a republic is to be laid in RELIGION . . . I had rather see the opinions of Confucius and Mohammed inculcated upon our youth than see them grow up wholly devoid of a system of religious principles. But the religion I mean to recommend in this place, is the religion of Jesus Christ.[3]

Therefore he advocates the use of the Bible as a schoolbook. Such use was opposed by a fellow essayist, Noah Webster. In his 1790 work *On the Education of Youth in America,* Webster gives the curious and cautious argument that familiarity breeds contempt, and thus the study of the Bible as a school text would weaken its power in promoting a system of religion and morality. I refer to the Bible question in this context because, although it arose with respect to the lower schools, it could not help but be a factor in the consideration of a national university. For the university was usually thought of as the culminating institution of a national system of education.

The most complete system was proposed by Samuel Harrison

Smith in his essay *Remarks on Education: Illustrating the Close Connection Between Virtue and Wisdom* of 1796, which won a prize given by the American Philosophical Society. It was favorably noticed by Jefferson. In his essay Smith set out a complete national system of education. It had the following features: (1) it was to be public in the old sense of that term in education—namely, of collecting the children in schools rather than having them instructed in the privacy of the house; (2) it was to be universal and compulsory in the sense that any parent unwilling to send his child to the public school was obligated to provide a similar education at home; (3) it was to be graded and selective, with a national university at the top, admitting one in ten of the students attending the lower-level colleges; and (4) it was to be supported by a tax on citizens in general.[4]

What is perhaps most remarkable about these essayistic plans, from a contemporary point of view, is that no author showed the slightest concern for any constitutional problem or the constitutional feasibility of such a system. Whether because constitutionality had not yet become an issue or because none of these early republican writers could imagine, any more than Gouverneur Morris, that the federal Constitution might not support so patent a national good as a national educational system culminating in a university, none referred to the new fundamental law, and none seemed very aware of the political difficulties that their stands on religion, selectivity, and federalism might cause.

The practical statesmen, however, were equally hopeful. Each of the first six presidents, from George Washington to John Quincy Adams, favored the national university. Washington, Thomas Jefferson, Madison, and John Quincy Adams urged Congress to establish the institution. Washington was most vigorous. On December 7, 1796, he addressed Congress for the second time concerning the project of establishing a military academy and a national university. He recommended it not only because "a flourishing state of the arts and sciences contributes to national prosperity and reputation," but also because

among the motives to such an institution, the assimilation of the principles, opinions, and manners of our countrymen, by the common education of a portion of our youth from every quarter, well deserves attention. The more homogeneous our citizens can be made in these particulars, the greater will be our prospect of permanent union; and a primary object of such a national institution should be the education of our youth in the science of government. In a republic, what species of knowledge can be equally important, and what duty more pressing on its legislature, than to patronize a plan for com-

municating it to those who are to be the future guardians of
the liberties of the country?[5]

This project was so important to Washington that he left in his testament
fifty shares in the Potomac Company toward the endowment of a
university to be established within the limits of the District of Columbia.
He explained:

> that as it has always been a source of serious regret with me
> to see the youth of these United States sent to foreign countries
> for the purpose of education, often before their minds were
> formed or they had imbibed any adequate ideas of the
> happiness of their own, contracting too frequently not only
> habits of dissipation and extravagance but principles un-
> friendly to republican government and to the true and genuine
> liberties of mankind, which thereafter are rarely overcome.
> For these reasons it has been my ardent wish to see a plan
> devised on a liberal scale which would have a tendency to
> spread systematic ideas through all parts of this rising empire,
> thereby to do away local attachments and state prejudices as
> far as the nature of things would, or, indeed, ought to admit
> from our national councils.[6]

But Washington did not succeed, even after his death. It would
appear that the homogenization of the young—their being turned into
"republican machines," as Rush so infelicitously termed the product
of a national education—offended the sectional sensibilities of the
people.

It was probably more than sectionalism that defeated the national
university. After all, it is hard to imagine that such an institution, had
it been established, would not have been heavily influenced by the
second most learned and the most intellectually enterprising of the
Founding Fathers—Jefferson. We know how the curriculum of his own
university was structured. It had a full complement of mathematics,
science, ancient and modern languages, and studies in government,
law, and Jefferson's favorite school of philosophy, "ideology;" but it
had no school of theology.

Samuel Knox, whose *Essay on the Best System of Liberal Education
Adapted to the Genius of the Government of the United States* had shared
the prize with Smith's in 1797, had excluded theology from the system
of national education he proposed. He recommended that the denomi-
nations carry on their own theological studies in a separate place. This
was exactly what Jefferson, who had evidently read the essays, wrote
into his 1822 annual report to the board of visitors of the university:

In conformity with the principles of constitution, which place all sects of religion on an equal footing, with the jealousies of the different sects in guarding that equality from encroachment or surprise, and with the sentiments of the legislature in freedom of religion, manifested on former occasions, they had not proposed that any professorship of divinity should be established in the University; that provision, however, was made for giving instruction in the Hebrew, Greek and Latin languages, the depositories of the originals, and of the earliest and most respected authorities of the faith of every sect, and for courses of ethical lectures, developing those moral obligations in which all sects agree. That, proceeding thus far, without offense to the constitution, they had left, at this point, to every sect to take into their own hands the office of further instruction in the peculiar tenet of each.[7]

A letter to Thomas Cooper lets the cat out of the bag—the truth behind the stately prose:

In our university you know there is no Professorship of Divinity. A handle has been made of this, to disseminate an idea that this is an institution, not merely of no religion, but against all religion. Occasion was taken at the last meeting of the Visitors, to bring forward an idea that might silence this calumny, which weighed on the minds of some honest friends to the institution. In our annual report to the legislature, after stating the constitutional reasons against a public establishment of any religious instruction, we suggest the expediency of encouraging the different religious sects to establish, each for itself, a professorship of their own tenets, on the confines of the university.[8]

My point here, as intimated above, is that the suspicion of antireligion would have been magnified for a nonsectarian national university—and nonsectarian it must surely have become, quite aside from the predilections of the founders, once the Bill of Rights was passed.

Moreover, Jefferson's plan for his university, like the various proposals for a national university, had a strong political intent. I am thinking here not of certain partisan—in fact, Anti-Federalist—elements but of the wider intention expressed by Jefferson in the minutes of the Board of Visitors meeting on March 4, 1825:

Whereas, it is the duty of this Board . . . to pay especial attention to the principles of government which shall be inculcated therein, and to provide that none shall be inculcated which are incompatible with those on which the Constitutions of this State, and of the United States were genuinely based, in the common opinion; and for this purpose it may be necessary to point out specially where these principles are to be found legitimately developed.[9]

Among the works fit to serve in this way, he then lists the Declaration of Independence, *The Federalist*, and Washington's Farewell Address of 1796, which contained the following reflections:

> Toward the preservation of your government and the permanency of your present happy state, it is requisite not only that you steadily discountenance irregular oppositions to its acknowledged authority but also that you resist with care the spirit of innovation upon its principles, however specious the pretexts. One method of assault may be to effect, in the forms of the Constitution, alterations which will impair the energy of the system and thus to undermine what cannot be directly overthrown.[10]

We may assume that the national university, intended to form a national American, that is, republican character, would have been shaped by the conservatism of successful revolutionaries; it would have inculcated the noblest of biases, but a bias nonetheless. What dogmatisms might such a premier school not have perpetrated in the years to come!

So the national university was rightly to be brought into being neither by an express power of Congress in the Constitution nor by a legislative proposal from the presidents. But if so delimited a thing, a national institution of higher education, was not viable, how would a more diffuse, extensive national plan of education have fared?

If one looks at samples of education articles in the state constitutions, one can see immediately why no other proposals on education were recorded as being offered at the Convention. Most of the state provisions are preoccupied with the funding of religious instruction. But the constitution of 1780 of Massachusetts had a provision for secular education:

> Wisdom and knowledge, as well as virtue, diffused generally among the people, being necessary for the preservation of their rights and liberties; and as these depend on spreading the opportunities and advantages of education . . . among the different orders of the people, it shall be the duty of legislatures and magistrates, in all future periods of this commonwealth, to cherish the interests of literature and the sciences, and all seminaries of them; especially the university at Cambridge, public schools, and grammar-schools in the towns; to encourage private societies and public institutions . . . for the promotion of agriculture, arts, sciences, com-

merce, trades, manufactures, and a natural history of the country; to countenance and inculcate the principles of humanity and general benevolence, public and private charity, industry and frugality, honesty and punctuality in their dealings; sincerity, and good humor, and all social affections and generous sentiments, among the people.[11]

The stated object of the preamble to the article—the wisdom, knowledge, and virtue of the people—is not among the objects mentioned in the Preamble to the Constitution. The latter does not aim to make the people wise, knowledgeable, or virtuous but to establish a government that is securely federal, just, tranquil, prosperous, and free. In other words, the legitimate business of making people better does not belong to the federal government, and therefore it belongs to the states. And that is a large part of the answer to the first question posed above: why no educational scheme of any sort appears in the Constitution.

The Supreme Court. Because education is not a federal power under the Constitution, the Supreme Court had relatively little to say about the subject until after World War II.

The case of greatest consequence came early. It was the *Dartmouth College* case, argued by Daniel Webster before Chief Justice John Marshall in 1818. The dispute was fairly dreary: a squabble between a proprietary president and a recalcitrant board of trustees. The question before the Court was whether Dartmouth College was subject to the legislature of New Hampshire, which had chartered it. Webster closed his argument with a tearful peroration:

> This sir, is my case. It is the case, not merely of that humble institution, it is the case of every college in the land. It is more. It is the case of every eleemosynary institution throughout our country . . . the case of every man who has property of which he may be stripped—for the question is simply this: Shall our state legislature be allowed to take that which is not their own, to turn it from its original use, and apply it to such ends or purposes as they, in their discretion, shall see fit? Sir, you may destroy this little institution . . . , but if you do . . . you must extinguish, one after another, all those great lights of science, which, for more than a century, have thrown their radiance over the land! It is, sir, as I have said, a small college, and yet there are those that love it.[12]

Chief Justice Marshall said that Dartmouth College was not a public but a private charitable institution. Its charter was a contract that had been violated by substituting the will of the state for that of the trustees: For the Constitution of the United States has imposed this additional limitation, that the legislature of a state shall pass no act "impairing the obligations of contract."

The founders of the college contracted, not merely for the perpetual application of the funds which they gave to the objects for which those funds were given; they contracted, also, to secure that application by the constitution of the corporation. They contracted for a system, which should, as far as human foresight can provide, retain forever the government of the literary institution they had formed in the hands of persons approved by themselves.

This system is totally changed. The charter of 1769 exists no longer. It is reorganized; and reorganized in such a manner as to convert a literary institution, molded according to the will of its founders and placed under the control of private literary men, into a machine entirely subservient to the will of government. This may be for the advantage of this college in particular, and may be for the advantage of literature in general, but it is not according to the will of the donors, and is subversive of that contract, on the faith of which their property was given.[13]

Thus the Constitution did soon play an unforeseeably momentous part in American education, through the contracts clause of Article I, section 10. For the *Dartmouth* decision made the world safe for small colleges; legislatures were not allowed to interfere with them—to attempt to convert them into state universities, for instance, or to control curricula. Thus they could compete freely in the educational marketplace. A great tide of denominational-college founding followed. The Constitution had indirectly lent itself to the establishment of scores of small colleges rather than directly to that of one great university.

The massive involvement of the Supreme Court in education in the post–World War II era is based far more on the amendments than on the body of the Constitution—particularly on the Bill of Rights and on the Fourteenth Amendment. The most active provisions, besides the obligation of contracts section mentioned above, are:

- Amendment 1: religion and free speech
- Amendment 5: due process
- Amendment 10: powers reserved to the states
- Amendment 14: no abridgment of rights by states, due process, equal protection of the laws

Accordingly, the cases before the Court fall mainly into the following categories: religion, race, academic freedom, student rights, and school financing. The Supreme Court, of course, intervenes only if there is a federal issue. Although education, since it is not a power mentioned in the Constitution, is by the Tenth Amendment reserved to the states, its operation must comport with the Constitution. As the list of interventions shows, most cases concern civil rights and liberties in educational settings. They have to do with the environment and conditions of education but rarely with its substance. In those rare cases where the Court has touched on curricular matters, the issue was never what must be taught but rather what may or may not be taught.

The important curricular case about what may be taught was *Epperson v. Arkansas* (1968). Arkansas had a law patterned after the Tennessee law upheld by the state supreme court in the Scopes "monkey trial" of 1927. Mrs. Susan Epperson, a biology teacher about to teach from a new book containing a chapter on the theory of evolution, sought an injunction against enforcement of the statute. The Supreme Court, while reiterating the state's right to control curricula, found that

> the first amendment does not permit the State to require that teaching and learning must be tailored to the principles or prohibitions of any religious sect or dogma. . . . In the present case there can be no doubt that Arkansas has sought to prevent its teachers from discussing the theory of evolution because it is contrary to the belief of some that the Book of Genesis must be the extensive source of doctrine as to the origin of man.[14]

Justice Abe Fortas led up to this judgment by citing a case of 1923, *Meyer v. State of Nebraska*, in which the Court had held unconstitutional a Nebraska law—pertinent to the English-as-second-language issues before the public at present—making it a crime to teach any subject in any language other than English to pupils who had not passed the eighth grade. Justice McReynolds's decision is interesting for present purposes because it discussed the ideas of Plato and the system of Sparta for the formation of ideal citizens, and it held that such a policy was not permissible under the Constitution:

> That the state may do much, go very far, indeed, in order to improve the quality of its citizens, physically, mentally and morally, is clear; but the individual has certain fundamental rights which must be respected.[15]

It is notable, however, that here only the teacher's right under the Fourteenth Amendment was amplified.

Hence not only the federal government's but also the state's right to seek to make its citizens good according to its lights is limited by the Constitution. A thorough civic education is precluded, certainly insofar as it involves political judgments leading to restrictions on educationally legitimate subject matter. The Nebraska law had been intended to discourage the rearing of children with a foreign language as their mother tongue because of the supposed deleterious effect on citizenship.

The chief subject on which the Court pronounced what may *not* be taught is Bible studies. The important case is *Abington School District v. Schempp* (1963). Justice Clark argued that the establishment clause and the free exercise clause of the First Amendment overlap, in that the first prohibits state support of any orthodoxy so that the second may have full scope. The net effect is that strict religious neutrality is required in the schools. Therefore the Bible may not be read religiously in the public schools. The approach that is consistent with the First Amendment is the study of the Bible for its literary or historic qualities, "presented objectively as part of a secular program of education." Justice Clark insisted that this decision did not impose a "religion of secularism"—that is, an affirmative opposition to religion.[16] Whether Justice Clark was right about the actual effect of a nonreligious reading of the Bible, the intention of the Court was certainly not that the Bible should disappear from public school curricula, although religion taught as dogma was so to disappear.

Thus the Supreme Court has pronounced on what may be taught and, in the single case of religion, what may not be taught in public schools. As far as I know, it has carefully refrained from saying what must be taught. So far, then, the content of education has been twice safeguarded under the Constitution. The curricula of public schools are subject only to the restrictions arising from fundamental, individual rights, and the private schools are free to teach what people will pay to learn. These constitutional protections may become extremely comforting to schools of all levels in the present climate, which has spread a—probably unwarranted—fear that accrediting agencies will dictate socially desirable alterations in curricula.

The Constitution in Education

I will begin by examining the writings of three men on the subject of education and the Constitution: Thomas Jefferson, Horace Mann, and John Dewey. In the *Rockfish Gap Report* of 1818, the founding prospectus for his university, Jefferson wrote that it must be among the objects of the higher branches of education

> to form the statesmen, legislators and judges, on whom public prosperity and individual happiness are so much to depend;

to expound the principles and structure of government.[17]

In 1825 he wrote to Joseph Cabell that

> in most public seminaries textbooks are prescribed to each of the several schools, as the *norma docendi* in that school; and this is generally done by authority of the trustees. I should not propose this generally in our University, because I believe none of us are so much at the heights of science in the several branches as to undertake this, and therefore that it will be better left to the Professors until occasion of interference shall be given. But there is one branch in which we are the best judges, in which heresies may be taught, of so interesting a character to our own State and to the United States, as to make it a duty in us to lay down the principles which are to be taught. It is that of government. Mr. Gilmer being withdrawn, we know not who his successor may be. He may be a Richmond lawyer, or one of that school of quondam federalism, now consolidation. It is our duty to guard against such principles being disseminated among our youth, and the diffusion of that poison, by a previous prescription of the texts to be followed in their discourses.[18]

He is referring to a resolution mentioned earlier, in which the board of the University of Virginia—in the person of Jefferson—resolved that in order "to provide that [no principles of government] shall be inculcated incompatible with the Constitution of the State and of the United States," certain texts were to be recommended, among them Locke's *Second Essay,* the Declaration, and "the book known by the title *The Federalist.*" We may infer that the Constitution was certainly to be read, but read under the aegis of *The Federalist,* which Jefferson evidently did not understand to be a document of "quondam federalism" or of the heresy of consolidation. It is interesting that a university that had no room for theology would nevertheless need to fear the peril of heresy—political heresy in the sectarian sense. The point here, however, is that the study of the Constitution had a mandated place in the first prestigious state university and the institution with the most modern curriculum.

Twenty-three years later, in 1848, Horace Mann published his *Twelfth Annual Report to the Massachusetts Board of Education.* It is one of the classics of American public school education. In it he explicitly recommends the study of the Constitution. His argument is that to omit it would be

> a proof of restored, or of never-removed barbarism, amongst us, to empower any individual to use the elective franchise,

without preparing him for so momentous a trust. Hence, the Constitution of the United States, and of our own State, should be made a study in our Public Schools. The partition of the powers of government into the three co-ordinate branches— legislative, judicial, and executive—with the duties appropri- ately devolving upon each; the mode of electing or of ap- pointing all officers, with the reason on which it was founded; and, especially, the duty of every citizen, in a government of laws, to appeal to the courts for redress, in all cases of alleged wrong, instead of undertaking to vindicate his own rights by his own arm; and, in a government where the people are the acknowledged sources of power, the duty of changing laws and rulers by an appeal to the ballot, and not by rebellion, should be taught to all the children until they are fully understood.[19]

There follow some remarkable pages. Mann first urges that the study of the Constitution will tend to substitute the well-considered use of the franchise for civic strife:

Had the obligations of the future citizen been sedulously incul- cated upon all the children of this Republic, would the patriot have had to mourn over so many instances, where the voter, not being able to accomplish his purpose by voting, has proceeded to accomplish it by violence; where, agreeing with his fellow- citizens, to use the machinery of the ballot, he makes a tacit reservation, that, if that machinery does not move according to his pleasure, he will wrest or break it? If the responsibleness and value of the elective franchise were duly appreciated, the day of our State and National elections would be among the most solemn and religious days in the calendar.

But then he considers the very quandary that tainted Jefferson's inclusion of the Constitution in his university studies:

But, perhaps, it will be objected, that the Constitution is subject to different readings, or that the policy of different administrations has become the subject of party strife; and, therefore, if any thing of constitutional or political law is introduced into our schools, there is danger that teachers will be chosen on account of their affinities to this or that political party; or that teachers will feign affinities which they do not feel, in order that they may be chosen; and so each schoolroom will at length become a miniature political club-room, ex- ploding with political resolves, or flaming out with political addresses, prepared, by beardless boys, in scarcely legible hand-writing, and in worse grammar.

The politicization of the classroom could scarcely be more vividly described. He goes on:

> With the most limited exercise of discretion, all apprehensions of this kind are wholly groundless. There are different readings of the Constitution, it is true; and there are partisan topics which agitate the country from side to side; but the controverted points, compared with those about which there is no dispute, do not bear the proportion of one to a hundred. And what is more, no man is qualified, or can be qualified, to discuss the disputable questions, unless previously and thoroughly versed in those questions, about which there is no dispute. In the terms and principles common to all, and recognized by all, is to be found the only common medium of language and of idea, by which the parties can become intelligible to each other; and there, too, is the only common ground, whence the arguments of the disputants can be drawn.

And he sets the problem aside as follows:

> With the most limited exercise of discretion, all apprehensions of this kind are wholly groundless.

There is sufficient ground in the middle between the parties, a large area of consensus, to avoid the catastrophe of turning the classroom into a political clubhouse—a calamity to the republic that he describes most pertinently:

> But to avoid such a catastrophe, shall all teaching, relative to the nature of our government, be banished from our schools; and shall our children be permitted to grow up in entire ignorance of the political history of their country? In the schools of a republic, shall the children be left without any distinct knowledge of the nature of a republican government; or only with such knowledge as they may pick up from angry political discussions, or from party newspapers; from caucus speeches, or Fourth of July orations,—the Apocrypha of Apocrypha?
>
> Surely, between these extremes, there must be a medium not difficult to be found. And is not this the middle course, which all sensible and judicious men, all patriots, and all genuine republicans, must approve?—namely, that those articles in the creed of republicanism, which are accepted by all, believed in by all, and which form the common basis of our political faith, shall be taught to all. But when the teacher, in the course of his lessons or lectures on the fundamental law, arrives at a controverted text, he is either to read it

without comment or remark; or, at most, he is only to say that the passage is the subject of disputation, and that the schoolroom is neither the tribunal to adjudicate, nor the forum to discuss it.[20]

Mann's solution seems to me to be the analog of the Supreme Court's 1963 proscription concerning Bible reading. Both rest on the judgment and faith that there is a common ground—a consensus of republican sentiment in the one case, a common notion concerning intellectual neutrality in the other—on which political and religious issues are defused.

I was taught under these consensual auspices. We had "civics," a bloodless and boring initiation into the machinery of democratic government. Like so many bloodless and boring subjects that are the bread and butter of any training of the young, this course entered our individual constitutions for good. Civics is gone now, replaced by a social science no longer bloodless or consensual.

Part of the explanation of the replacement is to be found in the influence of John Dewey on primary and secondary education. His preoccupations are signaled in his terms: the notion of educating republican citizens has given way to the project of forming a democratic society. Dewey entertains a suspicion of the individualistic ideal of the eighteenth century, which he interprets as an "unrestrained faith in Nature," the individual nature that was to come out once men were freed from the social limitations of thought and feeling. That individualism "lacked any agency for securing its ideal, as was evidenced in its falling back upon Nature." Dewey here speaks as if *Federalist* 10 and 51 had never been written, and as if the Constitution were not intended as the very agency for disciplining human nature for the sake of obtaining the maximum of freedom. In fact, the whole of *Democracy and Education* contains no injunction to study the political framework of this country. Indeed, Dewey sees a danger in an education for "civic efficiency or good citizenship" separated from "social efficiency," which is "industrial competency," in a wide and unconstraining sense:

> In the broadest sense, social efficiency is nothing less than that socialization of mind which is actively concerned in making experiences more communicable; in breaking down the barriers of social stratification which makes individuals impervious to the interests of others. When social efficiency is confined to the service rendered by overt acts, its chief constituent (because its only guarantee) is omitted—intelligent sympathy or good will. For sympathy as a desirable quality is something more than mere feeling; it is a cultivated im-

agination for what men have in common and a rebellion at whatever unnecessarily divides them. What is sometimes called a benevolent interest in others may be but an unwitting mask for an attempt to dictate to them what their good shall be, instead of an endeavor to free them so that they may seek and find the good of their own choice. Social efficiency, even social service, are hard and metallic things when severed from an active acknowledgment of the diversity of goods which life may afford to different persons, and from faith in the social utility of encouraging every individual to make his own choice intelligent.[21]

What seems to be characteristic here is the call to instill certain rather broadly conceived feelings and dispositions—the "socialization of mind"—rather than to inculcate knowledge of, and reflection on, the definite political frame of our social life. The aim of those who early on proposed a national university was to make Americans politically homogeneous. Dewey shifts to a vaguer socialization. Whatever its basis, it is not the study of a document, and its mode is not a knowledgeable reverence for a political framework—the conservatism of the republican revolution. It is rather a continuing critique of the social system, combined with the "cultivation or power to join freely and fully in shared or common activities"—social adjustment. The question is, of course, which of these will produce more salutary activity.

Portents of Restoration. It is generally agreed that in the era of the replacement of civics by social studies in the lower schools, common popular knowledge of the founding documents has all but lapsed. *The Federalist*, which Jefferson pointed out as the obvious text to support a study of the Constitution, is given only the sparest treatment in textbooks currently used. Fewer than half our seventeen-year-olds know that *The Federalist* was written in support of the Constitution, and the same sample achieved a "dismal average score of 54 percent on a nineteen-item test about the principles and issues of constitutional government in the United States."[22]

Efforts have been made, however, to remedy this ignorance—in particular, through a project developed for the National Trust for Historic Preservation, by the clearinghouse for social studies–social science education at Indiana University.[23] *James Madison and the Federalist Papers*, by John J. Patrick, is a resource book for high school teachers and students.[24] Besides its political balance, its virtues are that it supplies students with well-chosen and fairly extensive parts of *The Federalist*, with background documents, and that it uses *The Federalist*

73

Papers as expositions of the parts of the Constitution. The questions posed in each lesson are intended to induce a kind of reprise of the debates of the Constitutional Convention.

Patrick observes that *The Federalist* is ignored in established high-school curricula and that educators consider it above the abilities of students—a self-fulfilling prophesy. Furthermore, he discerns that "civic educators are committed to helping students know and deal with political reality. But suppose they believe that the central ideas of *The Federalist* are archaic and no longer applicable to the modern political world?" Educators consider the issues discussed during the writing of the Constitution and, implicitly, the document itself to be outdated. And this occurs in an epoch when the Supreme Court, by interpreting the Constitution, has been active in determining the composition of student bodies, the financing of school systems, and the restraints on curricular and extracurricular activities! Arguing to the contrary, Patrick gives as one reason for restoring the study of *The Federalist Papers* that "they reflect core values in the civic culture."[25] Such core values will be subject of the remainder of this chapter.

Education and the Constitution
in the Wider Sense

It would be an unprofitable expenditure of intellectual energy to balk at the conceptual framework within which the restoration of constitutional studies in secondary schools is bound to occur. Political thought is now taught under the aegis of social studies, as philosophy falls under the humanities and theology under religion. One might argue that this ranking frustrates at the very beginning the Constitution in the wider sense—namely the political philosophy underlying it—and so prevents its associated civic culture from shaping the citizens that live under it.

One might similarly argue that reference to core values undermines the shaping of a civic character, because a person of character does not live by values, ad libitum, but by goods, on principle. To disparage any effort, however, because it works within pervasive current conceptions is to take the futile tack of those social reformers who aver that nothing can be done until "the whole system is changed"—which means, in effect, that nothing will be done.

It is more worthwhile to gain a clear counterconception of what minimal elements would compose an American civic character shaped by the Constitution in the wider sense. What follows are my own reflections, fed by many similar inquiries and therefore largely presenting common ground. Indeed, it would be alarming if notions of

American citizenship diverged widely among those who were willing to admit a commonality to begin with.

Politics before Society. The notion of an American civic character would seem fundamental to life according to the Constitution. That document refers to the people, to the three branches of government, and to their members—the states and the citizens. It attributes no power or duties to society; responsibilities and rights belong entirely to political bodies or individuals. The system established in the Constitution is one of defined powers, duties, and rights. The Preamble asserts that their effect may be social—domestic tranquility and general welfare are certainly social goods. But their character is political—a matter of the law-guided choice of definite bodies composed of individuals, or of the individuals directly. Being a citizen under the Constitution requires the faith that, having made wide allowances for hard circumstances, personal choice rather than social conditions should be regarded as the ultimate determiner of conduct.

Liberty Always Actual, Equality Mostly Potential. The Preamble declares the securing of "the Blessings of Liberty" as a purpose. It does not mention the establishment of equality but of justice, whose condition is certainly "the equal protection of the laws" enjoined on the states in the Fourteenth Amendment. Life under the Constitution calls for an inclination to regard oneself as actually free under the law and to think that all should have an equal opportunity to work themselves into equality with those who are better off—and simultaneously into inequality with those they leave behind.

The People to Judge. Democratic sentiments are a part of citizenship under the Constitution in the sense that citizens need a certain broad faith in most of their fellow citizens—in their general good sense, in their stable, long-range judgment, and in the ultimate benevolence of their self-interest. This faith translates into the political willingness to accept majoritarian mandates while preserving a lively trust in the Constitution's arrangements for protecting minorities from excesses.

Fundamental Law as Embodiment of Ultimate Rights. It would be hard to live with proper reverence for the Constitution as our law of last appeal if it were not thought of as stating and protecting the most fundamental rights—whatever their source—we think we possess as political beings. An important service performed by the Bill of Rights for life under the rule of fundamental law is making explicit the assumptions of the Constitution, and so elevating the Constitution above merely positive law. We learn from the amendments who the Constitution implies that we are as political beings.

The Federal or Layered Disposition. The Constitution in the wider sense teaches the notion of split-level loyalties. First, there is a national American loyalty. We are "the people" of the Preamble, and we have the Constitution in the narrow sense—its machinery, duties, and rights—in common. This national civic culture is certainly independent of any unitary ethnic culture. It is even just barely conceivable without a common language—after all, biblical scripture has been potent in hundreds of versions. The national culture requires common information and understanding more than social similarity. As Tocqueville says,

> In examining the Constitution of the United States, which is the most perfect federal constitution that ever existed, one is startled at the variety of information and the amount of discernment that it presupposes in the people whom it is meant to govern. The government of the Union depends almost entirely upon legal fictions; the Union is an ideal nation, which exists, so to speak, only in the mind, and whose limits and extent can only be discerned by the understanding.[26]

Second are the states, once the most concretely important political entities for their citizens, and now returning to that status as federal financial support is increasingly withdrawn. Third are the lowest units, counties and cities, which also command political loyalty, particularly since they are where most public education takes place. But the Constitution—the *Dartmouth College* case is an example—also makes or at least leaves room for numerous pseudopolitical associations: private schools of all levels, lodges, organized interest groups. In these the political ethic here summarized is mirrored, and the largest part of the immediate life of citizens takes place. The habit of distributing loyalties and efforts in a balanced way among the levels of civic life, of not elevating one locus of loyalty to an exclusive status, is surely necessary to life in the light of the Constitution.

The Separation of Civic and Religious Life. Just as they must function on different political levels under the Constitution, Americans must live in separate worlds—the civic-secular and the religious-faithful. This constitutional solution to the church-state dilemma encoded in the First Amendment demands of citizen-believers a considerable act of suspension of their impulses. They have to accommodate themselves to the notion that the government must refrain from establishing religion precisely so that it may be freely exercised, and that the civic realm must be free of it so that it may flourish elsewhere. Thus an occasionally difficult double-consciousness is required of believers who are also active citizens: they must suspend in their civic life the expression of the dogmas that govern their moral life. This high tact and discretion is a peculiarly American mode; it is the antithesis of totalitarianism. When it collapses, sectarian aggression or moral indifferentism result.

Except for the first article in my list—the one requiring that citizens should consciously conceive their actions in political rather than social terms, and whose force has been waning throughout this century—the minimal list above might have been regarded as misguided, but scarcely as reprehensible, until the 1980s. In the 1990s its defense invites all sorts of reflections on the defender's decency: charges of social oppression, cultural imperialism, sexism, racism, philosophical absolutism, logocentrism. This attack on a national civic culture comes far more sharply and directly from the academy than did the slow erosion of citizen training in the public schools. Whether it takes the form of the deconstruction of the Constitution in the law schools or of the expulsion of the Euro-American canon from university curricula, the intellectual atmosphere is fiercely centrifugal. The name of the current movement against commonality is "diversity."

The Maximum of Diversity

It has been shown that the melting pot never prevailed in population centers where immigrants congregated.[27] Yet it was certainly still very much the ideal when I, a fairly new refugee, attended public school in Brooklyn during the 1940s. I can think of no better index of how seriously assimilation was taken than the ineffective but well-meant compulsory corrective speech classes that high-school students judged to have foreign or regional—Brooklyn—accents were required to take. Two decades later the melting pot as an ideal was superseded by a second stage: the notion of cultural and intellectual pluralism, which valued the regional, the ethnic, and all sorts of "alternative" communities, albeit in the name of a common American vision. Both of these ideals were practical responses to the actual social situation, ex post facto ideals, so to speak. Moreover, they were easily accommodated within the frame of political faith set out above.

The third stage, diversity, came into vogue in the late 1980s. It differs from the previous stages in two respects: it is prospective, in that it looks to a population situation forecast for the turn of the second millennium; and it is heavily ideological, in that it is consciously discontinuous with the American political tradition. It represents a marriage of sophisticated intellectual movements, such as Marxism and deconstructionism, with a hypertrophy of minority factionalism in Madison's sense in *Federalist* 10:

> a number of citizens, whether amounting to a majority or minority of the whole, who are united and actuated by some common impulse of passion, or of interest, adverse to the rights of other citizens, or to the permanent and aggregate interests of the community.[28]

But to Madison's chief impulse and interest, property—or rather, its contemporary counterpart, entitlement—there is added an urgent sense of group difference, a consciousness of defensive separation. In other words, the factions are encouraged by their leaders not to think of themselves as collections of similarly motivated individuals but as possessors of a common ethnic, linguistic, or racial identity.

If the melting pot was a social version of Washington's wish in his address to Congress of 1796 to see citizens become more "homogeneous by the assimilation of principles, opinions and manners of our countrymen"—a version that in public education tended to substitute consensual gentility for principled citizenship—then pluralism was the positive version of Madisonian factionalism. Instead of the dangers of interest, the profits of difference were emphasized. The search for roots was encouraged, and it was based on a respectable new scholarship recalling to the nation the contribution of minorities: "Differences among groups are a national resource rather than a problem to be solved."[29] What made the affirmation of cultural pluralism still continuous with the idea of the homogeneous national character so often called for in the early republic was the notion of a common, continuing civic ground. The formation of American citizens in the schools was not incompatible with the emphasis on difference.

The notion that has very recently succeeded that of pluralism abrogates the common ground quite consciously and decidedly. It goes by the term diversity, the call to substitute the separate cultures for the common base. Diane Ravitch has proposed that diversity is really particularism, or ethnocentrism.[30]

I shall conclude by characterizing briefly how educational diversity, in the sense of particularism, endangers our common constitutional ground as formulated in the six features outlined above.

First, the diversity movement is an element in an attempt to politicize the schools, particularly the university campuses. This new wave of politicization, known to students and to the media as "PC," or political correctness, is a disposition to observe oppression in every aspect of the American political and academic tradition and to fight it. This is done by identifying and suppressing biased speech while redistributing the resources and the course rosters of institutions to minorities, self-defined in an ad hoc fashion. A minority is a group not always numerically minor, nor including all historically unfortunate minority groups, that is currently felt to be in need of protection and compensation. Thus women, blacks, Hispanics, lesbians, male homosexuals, and the handicapped are each identified as minorities. The whole range of Asian-Americans, while included for some purposes among the protected minorities, have quotas directed against them by reason of their excellence in other respects, while Jewish- and Polish-Americans, again, are not minorities in the PC sense at all.

Such politicization of the schools and the social training or consciousness raising it involves run directly counter to the political life implied in the Constitution. That life demands that every citizen should first feel and judge as a member of the whole body politic and should in public matters put the realization of the law of the land before social particularism. The academy should surely be a place where liberty of thought is fostered and where the intellectual tradition that provides its theoretical ground and the political documents that make it practically possible are given a chance. "Particularism" and "university" are nearly a contradiction in terms.

Second, in the schools especially, liberty is of the essence. It is a more vital condition than equality, and certainly than equalization; the two latter are social aims without which schools may be less good but not impossible. One might argue that the constitutional mode, setting liberty somewhat above equality, is particularly in accord with the nature of learning. Learning is not, after all, a statistical but an individual effort; the demand for large-scale, socially significant outcomes must be mediated by the personal will to study. The egalitarianism of a good school is that of a community with a common task, not of a delivery system where services are equally apportioned and effects guaranteed. As freedom of the individual will and of public expression are the conditions of educational institutions, so conversely schools prepare students above all for a free life. This claim is currently much embattled, and I state it here without sufficient argument.

Third, in a democracy there ought to be a certain well-controlled deference to the majority and its sensibilities. The diversity movement takes its departure altogether from the needs of minorities, as formulated under certain sociological and psychological theories concerning the locus of self-esteem, the sources of political power, and the origin of standards of excellence. The diversity notion is not, of course, confined to the educational community, but it has its most powerful effect there. Granting that diversity is among other things a bona fide response to a problem both immediately and prospectively pressing, opposition to or contempt for the civic culture of the majority is a stance that is peculiarly endemic to academia and not always well-rooted in reality. For the academy lives almost by definition in critical tension with the people at large and with their unarticulated judgments.

Fourth, some feeling that the political order is just, and that the fundamental law is not merely positive but in some sense natural, is part of the constitutional disposition. The political justice of this polity is, of course, not so much questioned as denied by the criteria of social justice. Just as the decency of the liberal polity is attacked on social grounds, so the solidity of the traditional curriculum is opposed in the name of a social agenda. The denigration of the traditional curriculum begins with the claim that it embodies an oppressor's point of view. It is accused, for example, of representing the hegemony of gender-determined rationality (logocentrism), the intellectual imperialism of a white continent (Eurocentrism), and the class-induced elevation of a set of books (elitist canon). While on the critical side the common ground is undermined, on the positive side the demands concern access more than educational substance. The actual curricular proposals are not very coherent, nor are they offered with much argument for their intellectual solidity or permanent value. They are more like the numerous planks of a party platform.

Fifth, what goes by the board is the disposition, traditionally engendered by the federal Constitution, to live fairly comfortably on several levels and to value the willingness to acknowledge and to study in common, in the public schools and in the universities, the elements of what affects all citizens' lives. These elements are the theory of liberal, constitutional democracy, the roots of rational, mathematical science, and the common legacy of the English language.

Sixth, a special part of the split-level disposition fostered by the Constitution, best expressed in the separation of church and state, induces an aversion to ideology, the rationalistic analog to faith. The demand for political correctness to which the diversity movement has—paradox of paradoxes—acceded creates a general willingness to condone in the secular realm what one condemns in the life of the spirit; to allow in others what one condemns in oneself. To put it another way: the forced appreciation of and deference to particularity undermines the tolerant frame of mind that the Constitution engenders.

To conclude, diversity in the older sense of pluralism seems to be a public good. I say this not because difference is good in itself—there are diverse tastes about the relative values of difference and sameness in social life—but because under pluralism a large country can preserve and develop communities that have natures distinctive and exclusive enough to hold people's affection. Logic and life, however, unite in telling us that diversity needs a common ground, which for us happens to be our constitutional mode. And how is the message of logic and life to be propagated, if not by education?

6

One of the Guardians
Some of the Time

Louis Fisher

The last few generations of students have been taught that the ultimate safeguard of our constitutional liberties is the Supreme Court. This proposition suffers from two deficiencies. First, scarcely any evidence suggests that the framers ever advanced that notion. Second, the historical record provides ample documentation that the Court does a rather poor job in protecting individual rights. Over long periods of its history, the Court has been more likely to protect the exercise of governmental power (federal and state) or corporate interests. As a result, the task of guarding the Constitution has inevitably been shared with Congress, the president, the states, professional organizations, and ordinary citizens.

The Framers and Judicial Review

Although no explicit grant of judicial review appears in the Constitution, at least a plausible basis in the text suggests that federal courts must review the actions of state officials. The supremacy clause in Article VI provides that the Constitution, federal laws "made in Pursuance thereof," and all treaties shall be the supreme law of the land, "and the Judges in every State shall be bound thereby, any Thing in the Constitution or Law of any State to the Contrary notwithstanding." Because of the supremacy clause, federal judges are expected to review the actions of state governments to protect national powers.

Other language in the Constitution could be read to imply judicial review over Congress and the president, but the evidence is tenuous. When the supremacy clause speaks of federal laws "made in Pursuance thereof," presumably that might allow federal courts to strike down federal laws that are not made pursuant to the Constitution. That is a supposition, however, and has no explicit support in the constitutional debates. The more likely interpretation is that the jurisdiction of federal courts is limited to the specific conditions identified in the Constitution.

Under Article III, section 2, the judicial power extends to all cases "arising under this Constitution, the Laws of the United States, and Treaties made." Does the arising-under language give the Court carte blanche authority to review the acts of the coequal branches, Congress and the president? Probably not. The legislative history of the arising-under language points to judicial review of a specific type: over state actions.[1]

The framers made many direct statements on the need for judicial review against the states. Gouverneur Morris said that state actions inconsistent with the U.S. Constitution "would clearly not be valid," and judges "would consider them as null & void."[2] James Madison agreed: "A law violating a constitution established by the people themselves, would be considered by the Judges as null & void."[3] These statements, and others, were clearly limited to judicial control over state legislation.

A quite different claim, and one that is much more difficult to sustain, is judicial review directed against national institutions. Here the record is opaque, both in terms of the framers' intent and in the nature of our governmental structures. When Madison reviewed a draft constitution for Virginia in October 1788, he objected strongly to judicial supremacy. Courts had some power of review, but that function did not elevate the judiciary over other branches of government, for that would make "the Judiciary Dept paramount in fact to the Legislature, which was never intended and can never be proper."[4] Justice Oliver Wendell Holmes once remarked: "I do not think the United States could come to an end if [the Supreme Court] lost [its] power to declare an act of Congress void. I do think the Union would be imperiled if we would not make that declaration as to the laws of the several States."[5]

During the congressional debates in 1789, Madison offered what appears to be inconsistent positions on judicial review. As manager of the Bill of Rights, he predicted that once they were incorporated into the Constitution, "independent tribunals of justice will consider themselves in a peculiar manner the guardians of those rights; they will be an impenetrable bulwark against every assumption of power in the Legislative or Executive."[6] Yet nine days later, during debate on whether the president possessed the power to remove executive officials, Madison denied that Congress should defer to the courts on this constitutional issue. He begged to know on what principle it could be contended that "any one department draws from the Constitution greater power than another, in marking out the limits of the powers of the several departments." On questions regarding the boundaries between the branches, he did not see "that any one of these independent departments has more right than another to declare their sentiments on that point."[7]

During the first decade of the Supreme Court, the justices were uncertain about their power to strike down the acts of Congress and the president. In 1796 Justice Samuel Chase said it was unnecessary "*at this time*, for me to determine, whether this court, *constitutionally* possesses the power to declare an act of Congress *void* . . . but if the court have such power, I am free to declare, that I will never exercise it, *but in a very clear case*."[8] As late as 1800, just before John Marshall became chief justice, Chase said that even if it were agreed that a statute contrary to the constitution would be void, "it still remains a question, where the power resides to declare it void." The "general opinion," he said, is that the Supreme Court could declare an act of Congress unconstitutional, "but there is no adjudication of the Supreme Court itself upon the point."[9]

During this first decade, the federal courts failed to protect individual rights and liberties from the repressive Alien and Sedition Acts of 1798. Thomas Jefferson hoped that the courts would intercede and declare the act unconstitutional: "The laws of the land, administered by upright judges, would protect you from any exercise of power unauthorized by the Constitution of the United States."[10] Some members of Congress regarded the statute as a blatant violation of press freedoms protected by the First Amendment. Congressman Nathaniel Macon concluded that Congress lacked the constitutional authority to pass the statute and "could only hope that the Judges would exercise the power placed in them of determining the law an unconstitutional law, if, upon scrutiny, they find it to be so."[11]

Federalist judges, however, were unlikely to strike down a statute passed by a Federalist administration. The task of protecting individual rights fell to the president and Congress. After Jefferson took office as president in 1801, he "discharged every person under punishment or prosecution under the sedition law, because I considered, and now consider, that law to be a nullity, as absolute and as palpable as if congress had ordered us to fall down and worship a golden image."[12] He denied that the judiciary possessed a monopoly on deciding constitutional issues. To give judges the right to decide what laws are constitutional not only in their own "sphere of action" but in the legislative and executive spheres as well "would make the judiciary a despotic branch."[13]

Congress also entered the field left vacant by the judiciary. It passed private bills to reimburse individuals who had been fined under the sedition act. In 1840, for example, it appropriated $1,060.96, with interest from February 9, 1799, to the heirs of Matthew Lyon.[14] The House Committee on the Judiciary explained that these funds were being provided because the sedition act was "unconstitutional, null, and void, passed under a mistaken exercise of undelegated power, and the mistake ought to be corrected by returning the fine so obtained, with interest thereon, to the legal representatives of Matthew Lyon."[15] In 1964 the Supreme Court acknowledged that the sedition act was struck down not by a court of law but by the "court of history."[16]

Marbury v. Madison (1803) is supposedly the case in which Chief Justice Marshall declared that the Court is the ultimate authority on constitutional questions. In fact, the decision is much more modest in scope. Marshall stated that it is "emphatically the province and duty of the judicial department to say what the law is."[17] Obviously that rhetoric does not give the Court the final word on legal questions. His language can stand only for the simple proposition that the Court is responsible for stating what it thinks a statute means, after which Congress may enact another law to override the Court. It is just as accurate to say that it is emphatically the province and duty of the legislative department to say what the law is. The Court merely states what the law is on the day the decision comes down; the law may change after that.

Surely Marshall did not think he was powerful enough in 1803 to give orders to Congress and the president. He had few options. Marshall knew that he could not uphold the constitutionality of section 13 of the Judiciary Act of 1789 and direct Secretary of State Madison to deliver the commissions to the disappointed would-be judges. Jefferson and Madison would have ignored the order from Marshall. Everyone knew that, including Marshall. As Chief Justice Warren Burger has noted, "The Court could stand hard blows, but not ridicule, and the ale houses would rock with hilarious laughter" had Marshall issued a mandamus that the Jefferson administration ignored.[18]

There is further evidence from this period that Marshall did not believe the Court was supreme on legal questions. His behavior during the impeachment hearings of Judge John Pickering and Justice Chase suggest that he was quite willing to share that task with Congress

85

and the president. *Marbury* was decided on February 24, 1803. The House impeached Pickering on March 2, 1803, and the Senate convicted him on March 12, 1804. As soon as the House impeached Pickering, it turned to Chase. Had Chase been impeached and convicted, Marshall was likely to be next.

In this context Marshall wrote to Chase on January 23, 1804, suggesting that members of Congress did not have to take the drastic step of impeaching judges whenever Congress disagreed with their legal opinions. Instead, Congress could simply review those decisions and reverse them through the regular legislative process. The Court could say "what the law is," and so could Congress. Marshall's letter is somewhat ambiguous. He could have been referring to congressional reversals of statutory interpretation by the courts, not constitutional interpretation, but Marshall did not make this distinction. Given the temper of the times, Marshall most likely meant constitutional as well as statutory interpretations. Here is his language:

> I think the modern doctrine of impeachment should yield to an appellate jurisdiction in the legislature. A reversal of those legal opinions deemed unsound by the legislature would certainly better comport with the mildness of our character than [would] a removal of the Judge who has rendered them unknowing of his fault.[19]

Alexander Hamilton's *Federalist* 78 is the clearest statement from the framers in favor of judicial review, but even Hamilton recognized that judicial review did not mean judicial supremacy. If judges rendered unsound decisions, they would be subject to impeachment. As Hamilton noted in *Federalist* 81, Congress had adequate checks to rein in an overactive Court:

> The inference is greatly fortified by the consideration of the important constitutional check which the power of instituting impeachments in one part of the legislative body, and of determining upon them in the other, would give to that body upon the members of the judicial department. This is alone a complete security. There never can be danger that the judges, by a series of deliberate usurpations on the authority of the legislature, would hazard the united resentment of the body entrusted with it, while this body was possessed of the means of punishing their presumption, by degrading them from their stations.[20]

We often ignore the fact that Marshall never struck down another act of Congress. After *Marbury* he consistently upheld the power of Congress to exercise its commerce power, to create a U.S. bank, and to discharge other constitutional responsibilities, whether express or implied. With regard to congressional power, the Marshall Court functioned as a yea-saying, not a negative, branch. *Marbury* does not deserve the inflated significance given it by future generations. As Professor Walter Murphy has written, "For his part, Marshall in *Marbury* never claimed a judicial monopoly on constitutional interpretation, nor did he allege judicial supremacy, only authority to interpret the Constitution in cases before the Court."[21]

The Court and Individual Liberties

The court-packing plan offered by President Franklin D. Roosevelt in 1937 unleashed a storm of protest. Roosevelt was accused of using deception to jeopardize the coequal status of the judiciary. Several opponents of the plan objected in particular to any tampering with the Court's historic role as guardian of the Constitution. When the Senate Judiciary Committee reported the reorganization bill adversely, it said that the bill "applies force to the judiciary . . . its initial and ultimate effect would undermine the independence of the courts . . . it undermines the protection our constitutional system gives to minorities and is subversive of the rights of individuals."[22] The committee report in other places emphasized the importance of maintaining an independent judiciary:

> It is essential to the continuance of our constitutional democracy that the judiciary be completely independent of both the executive and legislative branches of the Government, and we assert that independent courts are the last safeguard of the citizen, where his rights, reserved to him by the express and implied provisions of the Constitution, come in conflict with the power of governmental agencies.[23]

The committee further claimed that the framers "never wavered in their belief that an independent judiciary and a Constitution defining with clarity the rights of the people, were the only safeguards of the citizen."[24] Omitted from this assessment was the responsibility of Congress and the president to safeguard constitutional rights. The committee also lapsed into hyperbole by stating, "Minority political groups, no less than religious and racial groups, have never failed, when forced to appeal to the Supreme Court of the United States, to find in its opinions the reassurance and protection of their constitutional rights."[25] The committee report included several examples to show how the Court protected human rights in cases involving Chinese, blacks, the press, and labor unions.[26] The committee concluded that the independence of the judiciary was "the only certain shield of individual rights."[27]

At the time of the Senate's consideration of the court-packing bill, Henry W. Edgerton, who would later become a federal judge, had completed an analysis of Charles Warren's assertion in his legal history that judicial review had protected individual liberties against congressional intrusions. Edgerton began his article in 1922 and completed most of it by the summer of 1936, months before Roosevelt made his proposal. Edgerton's study was published in the April 1937 issue of the *Cornell Law Quarterly*.[28]

Edgerton focused on the cases in which the Supreme Court held an act of Congress, or part of the act, unconstitutional. He began by pointing out that the Court is not needed to prevent contravention of "the black-and-white clauses of the Constitution, like that which allots two Senators to each State."[29] Instead, the conflicts between Congress and the Court related to the "indefinite" clauses, including those that deal with interstate commerce and due process. In reviewing these cases, Edgerton did not judge whether the Court's opinions were reasonable or technically sound. His objective was more specific: "Has judicial supremacy been, on the whole, neutral in its incidence; or has it tended to protect the interests of a relatively poor and unprivileged majority on the one hand, or of a relatively well-to-do minority on the other?"[30]

In his defense of judicial supremacy, Warren argued that the Court had prevented Congress from invading the functions of the states and from infringing personal liberty.[31] Edgerton reviewed the cases cited by Warren and concluded that they "give small support to the theory that Congress had attacked, and judicial supremacy defended, 'the citizen's liberty.'"[32] Edgerton also examined the many cases where the Court, instead of protecting a citizen against governmental action, protected the government against a citizen's complaint. *Marbury v. Madison* was a case of that sort. Marbury sought to gain his commission, but the Court, through elaborate reasoning, denied the relief. As Edgerton notes, "The doctrine of judicial review served precisely as a justification for refusing to give to the individual the protection which Congress sought to provide."[33]

Edgerton explored other categories of cases decided by the Supreme Court. Judicial review was used to deprive blacks of protection granted by Congress. Of the prominent *Dred Scott v. Sandford* (1857), Charles Warren could say only: "It was cured by the result of the Civil War. It is now of only historical interest."[34] In fact, *Dred Scott* is an excellent example to illustrate how constitutional rights are created and settled outside the judiciary.

James Buchanan, after his election in 1856, sought guidance from the Supreme Court on a portion of his inaugural address dealing with the slavery issue. On the question whether the Court was about to decide *Dred Scott*, Justice John Catron wrote to Buchanan on February 19, 1857, suggesting that Buchanan could "safely" say at the inaugural

> That the question involving the constitutionality of the Missouri Compromise line is presented to the appropriate tribunal to decide; to wit, to the Supreme Court of the United States. It is due to its high and independent character to suppose that it will decide & settle a controversy which has so long and seriously agitated the country, and which *must* ultimately be decided by the Supreme Court.[35]

With this guidance, Buchanan proceeded to draft his inaugural address, placing within it the naive expectation that the smoldering issue of slavery could be decided solely by the Supreme Court. The dispute over slavery in the territories, he told the nation, "is a judicial question, which legitimately belongs to the Supreme Court of the United States, before whom it is now pending, and will, it is understood, be speedily and finally settled."[36] *Dred Scott,* handed down two days later, did not "finally settle" this issue.

Abraham Lincoln did not accept the Court as the ultimate guardian of individual rights. While he accepted the decision as it affected the particular litigants, he did not accept the larger policy questions decided by the Court, which denied blacks the right to be citizens and prohibited Congress from excluding slavery in the territories. Lincoln considered those parts of the decision to be a nullity, requiring resolution outside the courts.[37] He believed that Congress had the constitutional authority to exclude slavery from the territories and insisted that the Declaration of Independence, in saying that all men were created equal, meant blacks as well as whites.

Lincoln refused to accept the moral and political teaching of *Dred Scott*. He regarded the Court as a coequal, not a superior, branch of government. In his inaugural address in 1861, Lincoln denied that constitutional questions could be settled solely by the Court. If government policy on "vital questions affecting the whole people is to be irrevocably fixed" by the Supreme Court, "the people will have ceased to be their own rulers, having to that extent practically resigned their Government into the hands of that eminent tribunal."[38]

Although *Dred Scott* was eventually overturned by the Civil War amendments, it had already been repudiated by congressional and executive action. Congress passed legislation in 1862 to prohibit slavery in the territories.[39] I read through the congressional debates on that statute and thought that someone in the House or Senate would challenge the authority of Congress to overturn by mere statute a constitutional decision of the Supreme Court. *Dred Scott* was never mentioned. Members of Congress never doubted their constitutional authority to prohibit slavery in the territories and announce that as national policy, with or without the Court.

Also in 1862, Attorney General Edward Bates released a long opinion in which he held that neither color nor race could deny American blacks the right of citizenship. He pointed out that "freedmen of all colors" had voted in some of the states.[40] The idea of denying citizenship on the ground of color was received by other nations "with incredulity, if not disgust."[41] The Constitution was "silent about *race* as it is about *color*."[42] Bates did not ignore *Dred Scott* but held that the case, "as it stands of record, does not determine, nor purport to determine," the question of blacks to be citizens.[43] What Chief Justice Roger Taney said about citizenship was pure dictum and "of no authority as a judicial decision."[44] Bates concluded, "The free man of color, . . . if born in the United States, is a citizen of the United States."[45]

The Court's record in guarding constitutional rights after the Civil War was not much better than before the conflict. One of the great losses in individual liberties came with the *Civil Rights Cases* of 1883, which struck down legislation passed by Congress in 1875 giving blacks equal access to public accommodations. Congress did not attempt to make blacks and whites equal on a social plane. That development was left to private choices. What it did intend, and had the right to require, was granting blacks equal access to inns, theaters, public transportation, and other accommodations available to the general public. In the *Civil Rights Cases*, the Court declared that Congress had exceeded its authority under the Thirteenth and Fourteenth Amendments.[46]

Charles Warren regarded the *Civil Rights Cases* of 1883 as of little significance. He included the decision in his list of statutes struck down by the Court, but of the fifty-three statutes invalidated at the time of the 1925 edition, "only eleven have ever received any serious criticism; and the others have been recognized not only as correct, but as vitally important in preserving the rights of individuals and of the States as against encroachments by the Federal Government."[47] Surely the *Civil Rights Cases* did not preserve the rights of black citizens. As Edgerton correctly noted, the "interest which the decision protected was that of a dominant race in excluding a depressed race from opportunity and comfort."[48] Not until the Civil Rights Act of 1964 were blacks given equal access to public accommodations.

At the same time that the Court was denying blacks their rights, it was according women a similar treatment. In 1873 the Court held that denying women the right to practice law was not a violation of the Fourteenth Amendment guarantee of privileges and immunities.[49] It was left to Congress to remove the legal disabilities that prevented women from practicing law. The House of Representatives, voting 169 to 87, passed legislation in 1878 providing that any woman who was a member of the bar of the highest court of any state or territory or of the Supreme Court of the District of Columbia for at least three years, maintained a good standing before such court, and was a person of good moral character, should be admitted to practice before the U.S. Supreme Court.

The Senate Judiciary Committee reported the bill adversely, arguing that the Supreme Court should be left to itself to decide whether it wanted to change its rules to permit women to practice before it.[50] The Senate delayed action until the next year, when it passed the bill thirty-nine to twenty. Senator Aaron Sargent argued forcefully and eloquently for the legislation, showing a sensitivity to women's rights that could not have come from the courts:

> It is generally recognized that women are taking to themselves a wider sphere of action and filling it well. . . . The medical universities of the world are receiving women and instructing them in medicine and surgery. . . . There are in the various States of the Union women lawyers; and women in literature have won a very high place. No man has a right to put a limit to the exertions or the sphere of woman. That is a right which only can be possessed by that sex itself.
>
> I say again, men have not the right, in contradiction to the intentions, the wishes, the ambition, of women, to say that their sphere shall be circumscribed, that bounds shall be set which they cannot pass. The enjoyment of liberty, the pursuit of happiness in her own way, is as much the birthright of woman as of man. In this land man has ceased to dominate over his fellow—let him cease to dominate over his sister; for he has no higher right to do the latter than the former. It is mere oppression to say to the bread-seeking woman, you shall labor only in certain narrow ways for your living, we will hedge you out by law from profitable employments, and monopolize them for ourselves.[51]

Within a few weeks after enactment of this law, Belva Lockwood (who had lobbied for the bill) became the first woman admitted to practice before the U.S. Supreme Court. When she was denied the right to practice in Virginia and took an appeal to the U.S. Supreme Court, the Court accepted the restriction by deferring to the state court's ruling that state law limited the practice of law to men.[52] The Court maintained this sorry record until 1971, when it finally struck down sex discrimination on constitutional grounds.[53] A review of judicial decisions on women's rights convinced two male researchers "that by and large the performance of American judges in the area of sex discrimination can be succinctly described as ranging from poor to abominable."[54]

Edgerton reviewed other decisions by the Supreme Court, including a series of cases between 1908 and 1923 in which the Court "nullified a variety of efforts on the part of Congress to benefit the working class."[55] These cases did not protect the rights of individuals. They supported the interests of the business class, as did other cases that shielded businesses from taxation[56] or that protected private incomes from taxation[57] or property rights in general.[58] Edgerton summarized his research:

> Of the pre-New Deal cases in which the Supreme Court annulled acts of Congress, one group protected mistreatment of colored people; another group protected businesses or business methods hurtful to the majority; another, compromising employers' liability, workmen's compensation, minimum wage, child labor, and union membership cases, protected owners of business at the direct expense of labor; another protected owners of business against taxation; another protected the recipients of substantial incomes, gifts, and inheritances against taxation; and other cases protected the interests of property owners in other ways.[59]

Edgerton's critique goes even further than questions of the employee against employer or the disadvantaged against the propertied. In the whole series of cases he could not find one that protected the civil liberties of speech, press, and assembly. The espionage act was not merely upheld by the Court but extended by it.[60] Not one case protected the right to vote. On the contrary, "congressional attempts to protect the voting rights of Negroes were defeated by the Court."[61] At no point did the Court protect the interests of the "working majority of the population in organizing or in wages; on the contrary, congressional efforts to protect those interests were frustrated by the Court."[62]

Joint Guardianship of Constitutional Rights

The Court is given great credit for its decision in 1943 striking down a compulsory flag salute. Unquestionably, Justice Robert Jackson's opinion for the majority represents an eloquent defense by the judiciary in safeguarding the interests of a minority.[63] The context of that opinion, however, casts a shadow over the Court's role. Three years earlier, Justice Felix Frankfurter upheld a compulsory flag-salute law in Pennsylvania.[64] Seven other justices joined Frankfurter in running roughshod over the minority interests of the Jehovah's Witnesses, who regarded a salute to a secular symbol a violation of their religious faith. Justice Harlan Stone was the only dissenter.

The reaction to the decision was almost unanimously hostile. Law journals, newspaper editorials, and religious organizations found Frankfurter's opinion intolerable. Newspapers accused the Court of violating constitutional rights and buckling to popular hysteria.[65] From all sectors of society, the Court received the same message: "You do not understand the Constitution, minority rights, or religious liberty. Your opinion is offensive. Change it." Following Frankfurter's opinion, the persecution of Jehovah's Witnesses increased.

By 1942, three members of Frankfurter's majority publicly apologized for their vote. In an extraordinary move, Justices Hugo Black, William Douglas, and Frank Murphy announced that the Court's opinion in 1940 was "wrongly decided."[66] That is as close as justices ever come to saying that they bungled a case. With the loss of those three, Frankfurter now had, at best, a five-four majority. His opinion was even more vulnerable because two members of the 1940 majority had left the Court. Stone's original dissent, plus the three justices who changed their minds, plus Jackson and Wiley Rutledge (the new justices), produced a six-three majority in defense of a religious minority.

Jackson's opinion in this case is magnificent to read, but the real credit for safeguarding constitutional rights belongs to all the individuals and associations in the country who objected vehemently to Frankfurter's opinion. Although we tend to forget it, public opinion can be more discerning than judicial rulings mired in technical doctrine. William Howard Taft, during his service as a federal judge, wrote, "If the law is but the essence of common sense, the protest of many average men may evidence a defect in a judicial conclusion though based on the nicest legal reasoning and profoundest learning.[67]

The Japanese-American cases of 1943 and 1944 illustrate the danger of depending too much on the judiciary to safeguard the Constitution. In the first case, a unanimous Court upheld a curfew order directed against more than 100,000 Japanese-Americans, about two-thirds of them native-born U.S. citizens.[68] A year later, split this time six-three, the Court upheld the placement of Japanese-Americans in detention camps.[69] In one of the dissents, Justice Murphy objected that the Court had supported the "legalization of racism."[70] In another dissent, Justice Jackson warned of the dangers when the Court gives its endorsement to military orders:

Once a judicial opinion rationalizes such an order to show that it conforms to the Constitution, or rather rationalizes the Constitution to show that the Constitution sanctions such an order, the Court for all time has validated the principle of racial discrimination in criminal procedure and of transplanting American citizens.[71]

Earl Warren was attorney general of California during this period and favored the actions taken against the Japanese-Americans. Later, as chief justice, he regretted those policies and particularly the approval granted by the judiciary. Writing in 1962, he penned this extraordinary sentence: "The fact that the Court rules in a case like *Hirabayashi* that a given program is constitutional, does not necessarily answer the question whether, in a broader sense, it actually is."[72] His message is clear. The Court is not always a dependable guardian of the Constitution. It makes errors, sometimes of monumental proportions.

If the Court at times defers to unconstitutional practices, where must we look for guidance? Warren advised that in a democratic society "it is still the Legislature and the elected Executive who have the primary responsibility for fashioning and executing policy consistent with the Constitution."[73] Only an "occasional aberration from norms of operation" is likely to be brought to the Court by litigants.[74] The primary task of defending the Constitution therefore falls on nonjudicial officers in the executive and legislative branches. Warren even cautioned against relying solely on governmental officers for the protection of constitutional values: "The day-to-day job of upholding the Constitution really lies elsewhere. It rests, realistically, on the shoulders of every citizen."[75]

In 1980 Congress established a commission to study the actions against the Japanese-Americans to determine whether any wrong was committed. The commission reported two years later that the actions were not justified "by military necessity. . . . The broad historical causes which shaped these decisions were race prejudice, war hysteria and a failure of political leadership."[76] Although the decisions of 1943 and 1944 had never been overruled and thus remained "good law," the commission concluded that the decision in *Korematsu* "lies overruled in the court of history."[77]

Congress passed legislation in 1988 to implement the commission's recommendations, acknowledging "the fundamental injustice of the evacuation, relocation, and internment of United States citizens and permanent resident aliens of Japanese ancestry during World War II."[78] Congress apologized for "these fundamental violations of the basic civil liberties and constitutional rights of these individuals of Japanese ancestry."[79] As part of the reparations authorized by this legislation, the United States paid $20,000 in compensation to each of the surviving Japanese-Americans interned in prison camps during World War II. Attorney General Dick Thornburgh, while handing out the checks, made this point: "By finally admitting a wrong, a nation does not destroy its integrity, but rather reinforces the sincerity of its commitment to the Constitution, and hence to the people. In forcing us to reexamine our history, you have made us only stronger and more proud."[80]

The responsibility of guarding the civil rights of Americans has been carried out by all three branches. In *Brown v. Board of Education* (1954), the Court did much to arouse the public conscience and to articulate constitutional values. That decision by itself, however, did little to integrate public schools. As late as 1964, the Court conceded that there "has been entirely too much deliberation and not enough speed" in implementing *Brown*.[81] The pivotal events were a series of landmark statutes passed by Congress: the Civil Rights Act of 1964, the Voting Rights Act of 1965, and the Fair Housing Act of 1968. The struggle against racial discrimination required the conscientious effort of all three branches, backed by a genuine bipartisan spirit.

The recent Civil Rights Act of 1991 reversed or modified nine Supreme Court decisions to grant additional rights to blacks and women. This statute, in the making for two years, provides further evidence that individual rights are often better protected through the legislative rather than the judicial process. Organizations that once relied heavily on litigation to achieve their goals, such as the American Civil Liberties Union and the National Abortion Rights Action League, now look to Congress as the court of last resort.

Two other examples illustrate the range of constitutional values that are protected by legislative action. In 1978 the Supreme Court held that law enforcement officials could obtain a warrant and come onto the premises of a newspaper to conduct a search for evidence regarding an offense by another party.[82] By approving third-party searches and intrusions into the newsroom, the decision set off an alarm bell in the First Amendment community.

Congress responded by holding hearings and listening to witnesses decry the coming of a police state. Congress had to go through the same process as the Court: balance the conflicting interests of law enforcement and a free press. Congress chose to give the press much greater protection than was available under the Court ruling. Legislation enacted in 1980 limited newsroom searches by requiring, with certain exceptions, a subpoena instead of a warrant.[83] If a newspaper or anyone with a First Amendment interest is required by subpoena to respond, they surrender only the requested document. Law enforcement officials do not enter their space to begin a general search through files, wastepaper baskets, and other sources.

To take another example involving First Amendment interests, this time involving religious freedom, Captain Simcha Goldman was told by the air force that he could not wear his yarmulke indoors while on duty. He and his attorney attempted to convince the air force to change the departmental regulation, but to no avail. The next stop was the judiciary, with the case finally reaching the Supreme Court in 1986. To the attorney's disappointment, the Court upheld the air force regulation as a legitimate method of furthering the department's interest in military discipline, unity, and order. Goldman's need to exercise his religion freely was subordinated to governmental power.[84]

Goldman and his attorney worked with Congress to overturn the decision. Every year Congress passes a military authorization bill. In 1987 Congress adopted an amendment to this bill, directing the air force to change its regulation to permit military personnel to wear religious apparel while on duty, provided there is no interference with military duties.[85] The debate in the House and the Senate provides impressive evidence that members of Congress are fully capable of considering constitutional rights and giving greater protection than is available in the federal courts.[86]

The examples given thus far reveal how often the political branches must intercede to guard constitutional rights. Similar illustrations can be drawn from the efforts of state courts when they define state constitutions broadly to protect individual rights and liberties. State judges frequently reject U.S. Supreme Court doctrines as overly restrictive. The areas affected by the rulings include free speech, obscenity, religious liberty, jury procedures, search and seizure, the exclusionary rule, school financing, and abortion.[87]

A few cases can demonstrate the activity of state courts in defending constitutional rights. In the state of Washington, a university student carrying a bottle of gin was stopped by a campus policeman because the student seemed under age. The policeman followed the student back to his dorm to see his identification card. From the hallway the officer noticed what appeared to be drug paraphernalia and entered the student's room to seize the material. The Supreme Court of Washington held that the evidence was obtained illegally and could not be introduced at trial, but the U.S. Supreme Court reversed by reasoning that the evidence was admissible because it was in "plain view."[88] When the case came back to the Supreme Court of Washington, the state court refused to accept the High Court's verdict. The state court ruled that the evidence—under the state constitution and state law—could not be admitted in court.[89]

Another example involves the issue of abortion. After the Supreme

Court held in *Roe v. Wade* (1973) that women have a constitutional right to abortion during the first and second trimesters, Congress passed the Hyde amendment to prohibit the use of federal funds to finance abortions for indigent women, with certain exceptions. The Supreme Court upheld the Hyde amendment in *Harris v. McRae* (1980).[90] State legislatures passed similar types of amendments to restrict public funding of abortion. Despite the Supreme Court's ruling, several state courts found the funding restrictions to be in violation of the state constitution.[91]

The Supreme Court's ruling in *Webster v. Reproductive Health Services* in 1989 pushed the volatile issue of abortion back to the states for resolution. There is some doubt whether *Roe* can survive the current composition of the William Rehnquist Court. If *Roe* is overturned, the responsibility for protecting women's rights will fall increasingly on state governments. As the Florida Supreme Court noted some months after *Webster*, "While the federal Constitution traditionally shields enumerated and implied individual liberties from encroachment by state or federal government, the federal Court has long held that state constitutions may provide even greater protection."[92] As one of the justices in that case remarked, if the U.S. Supreme Court "were to subsequently recede from *Roe v. Wade,* this would not diminish the abortion rights now provided by the privacy amendment of the Florida Constitution."[93]

The record of the past two centuries provides ample testimony that judicial review is not used uniformly to safeguard constitutional rights. Again and again the Court has nullified the efforts of political branches to expand individual rights and freedoms. Repeatedly the political branches have been forced to reverse Court decisions, sometimes by constitutional amendment but more frequently through the regular legislative process. The Court is only one participant in the complex process of guarding constitutional rights. It necessarily shares that profound responsibility with Congress, the president, the states, and the general public. We are all guardians all of the time.

7

The Supreme Court as Republican Schoolmaster

Ralph Lerner

For thinking revolutionaries it was axiomatic that securing the republic depended on first forming a certain kind of citizenry. This was not a task to which responsible governors might affect indifference or remain aloof. Accordingly, every organ of the new republican government could be expected to do its part, each in the mode most becoming to it.

In the case of the judiciary, this obligation entailed, among other things, a test of the narrow limits within which the judge and his public customarily met and took one another's measure. Judges, after all, were empowered primarily to deal with the particular case or controversy at hand. Their license to adjudicate hardly predisposed prudent judges or their wary publics to expect a relaxation of those restraints. The picture of a sitting judge as propagandist, haranguer, or part-time philosopher would warm few hearts, then or now.

And yet a thoughtful judge, reflecting on the close connection between judicial power and public opinion, might have reason to wonder whether the judge's task narrowly conceived is adequately conceived. All the more would this doubt arise in the context of democratic politics. It is enough to recognize that no regime can safely or for long avoid hard, politically unpopular decisions—and, with that, to ponder the means by which such necessary measures may be rendered palatable to a modern democratic people. These difficulties are more readily stirred than resolved.[1]

It comes as no surprise to learn that Alexis de Tocqueville was acutely alert to this problem. In conceiving of a democratic people as benevolently inclined but little given to self-denial, he was expressing some of his profoundest preoccupations and misgivings. Here, it seemed to him, lawyers generally and judges in particular have much to contribute. Their quasi-aristocratic habits of mind fit them to serve as needed and politically acceptable counterweights to popular impatience and injustice.

The consequence of so regarding the judge is to thrust him (and the whole machinery of justice) into the role of an educator, molder, or guardian of those manners, morals, and beliefs that sustain republican government. And yet the political effectiveness of a judge in gently shaping and even checking democratic opinion is itself dependent on that very opinion. Thus, for Tocqueville, while their ordinary jurisdiction offers justices of the Supreme Court vast opportunities for the exercise of power,

> it is power springing from opinion. They are all-powerful so long as the people consent to obey the law; they can do nothing when they scorn it. Now, of all powers, that of opinion is the hardest to use, for it is impossible to say exactly where its limits come. Often it is as dangerous to lag behind as to outstrip it.
>
> The federal judges therefore must not only be good citizens and men of education and integrity, qualities necessary for all magistrates, but must also be statesmen; they must know how to understand the spirit of the age, to confront those obstacles that can be overcome, and to steer out of the current when the tide threatens to carry them away, and with them the sovereignty of the Union and obedience to its laws.[2]

A democratic regime, then, requires a judiciary that is both upright and subtle, equally attentive to its opportunities and dangers, and averse to seeming either diffident or overbearing. So Tocqueville maintained, and so too did some of the shapers and leaders of the early national judiciary. Less obvious is whether the earliest generation of national judges consciously acted as statesmen-teachers or, indeed, whether they were supposed to assume any such role. In seeking to recover and to assess that historical evidence, one looks, not for a ready-made model for the modern judge, but for a deeper understanding of the founders' political science.

Itinerant Sermonizing: Use and Abuse

The legislative history of Senate Bill 1 of the first session of the First Congress must, in many interesting particulars of motive and intention, remain hidden from us. The genesis of what was to be called the Judiciary Act of 1789 has been examined and reexamined, sometimes with great care,[3] but always with a number of questions unanswered and perhaps unanswerable. The secrecy in which the Senate then conducted its business and the heedless indifference with which Americans long treated their public records obscure the purposes Congress intended to serve in enacting the Judiciary Act. What broad political functions were the justices of the highest court of the land expected to perform? We can give at best a probable answer. To what extent were the political and psychological premises underlying the national judicial establishment of a piece with those on which the other parts of the new government were founded? On such a fundamental question we are obliged to speak with no less caution. We are dealing with matters that not only admit of speculation but fairly require it.

Not only such large questions are difficult to answer with confidence. Many narrower problems are equally beset with ambiguities and uncertainties. Consider the simple question, What led Congress to send members of the Supreme Court riding circuit over the length and breadth of the land? There may be parallels between the organization of the circuit courts and the English assize system or the colonial or state courts.[4] But earlier practice contained no precise analogy to the way members of the nation's highest court were brought directly into the milieu of local laws and usages, local lawyers and jurors. Members of the Supreme Court, sitting as circuit court judges, instructed grand juries and presided over trials while disposing of the considerable original jurisdiction vested in the circuit courts. It bespeaks some legislative purpose, not to say single-mindedness, to compel the disgruntled members of the highest national tribunal to perform tiring and hazardous circuit duties. It is plausible, even likely, that nothing more lies behind this feature of the judicial system than a close-fisted Connecticut concern to get value for money. The early expectations for the Supreme Court's business, both original and appellate, suggested that ennui rather than exhaustion would be the justices' probable occupational hazard. Jealous guardians of the public purse may well have seen circuit riding as a cure to boredom and a way of serving both justice and economy, to neither's disadvantage.[5]

However onerous members of the Supreme Court felt their circuit duties to be, it cannot be said that they failed to take advantage of the opportunities thus presented. The justices of the Federalist period sensed and were reminded of the novelty of giving substance to the Constitutional Convention's founding act. It is not farfetched to suspect that the justices saw themselves as having a unique responsibility, beyond those shared by other courts in the system. They were all Federalists. They were not narrow professional lawyers but revolutionary patriots and statesmen whose involvement in the founding and ratification controversies made it natural for them to think politically and to feel some proprietary relationship to the new order. The justices were quick to see and to seize the chance to proselytize for the new government and to inculcate habits and teachings most necessary in their view for the maintenance of self-government. (In so doing, they left later interpreters with the problem of distinguishing a defense of the regime and of the Constitution from a defense of an administration and of a party.) The main vehicle for this instruction was the charge to the grand jury, with which the presiding judge formally opened the proceedings of a circuit court session.

The Political-Judicial Charge. The prevailing practice was for a judge to summarize for a newly empaneled grand jury the statutes and in the state courts the common law, relevant to the performance of their duty. It was the grand jury's duty to return such indictments and presentments alleging violations of the laws as in its judgment were warranted by the evidence already known to it or presented to it. In the state courts the grand jury commonly presented grievances about poor administration of the laws and the need for new laws, reaching down to matters of narrow local concern and great specificity.[6] None of this was new or extraordinary. But out of the years of stress that preceded and led to the break with Britain, another kind of dialogue between judge and jurors matured. In a growing number of instances, the judge came to regard himself as an exhorter and teacher, obliged at all times (but above all at moments of crisis) "boldly [to] declare the law to the people, and instruct them in their civil rights." By 1785 John Dickinson could write to members of the Pennsylvania Supreme Court, about to go on circuit,

> that besides the Terror of legal Penalties, all the Influence to be derived from your Characters, and the Dignity of your Stations, might be applied in disseminating the best Principles & setting forward the most effectual Regulations for the prevention of offences. You Gentlemen, well know how vain are Laws without Manners.[7]

That the judges would respond to such instructions with differing degrees of avidity may safely be presumed. But for two reasons we can be quite certain that when they did undertake political education, they did so with self-awareness. The political charge was a deviation from the ordinary and recognized as such by the judges who used it. James Iredell, at the time a North Carolina judge, could cut short, after five pages, a sermon on natural rights and patriotism—itself a sort of prelude to a brief grand jury charge—by recalling that "the time, and even the occasion, [would] not properly permit" his elaborating on these themes. Another North Carolina judge, Samuel Ashe, could surround a long and impassioned plea that "the love of our country rise superior to the turpid and base passion for gain" with unmistakable signs that he knew his political charge was not of a piece with his just-concluded statement of the law: "Gentlemen, give me leave now, before you retire to business, to address a few words to you in another character. . . . Gentlemen, you will, I hope, excuse my traveling out of the line of Business for which you have been summoned here at this time."[8] This self-consciousness when delivering political charges persisted. Indeed, this open self-consciousness was in later days often a sign of sensible use of the political charge. American oratory at large may have made this kind of speech familiar but not to the extent that the members of the new national judiciary could forget the customary bounds of judicial propriety, even while exceeding them.

Chief Justice John Jay defended himself by saying in the charge delivered on his first circuit, "These remarks may not appear very pertinent to the present occasion, and yet it will be readily admitted that occasions of promoting good-will, and good-temper, and the progress of useful truths among our fellow-citizens should not be omitted." Similarly, a district judge, John Sitgreaves, could declare to a grand jury that "to forbear to speak of this government on this occasion, (altho it may not be necessary to the business for which you are now assembled) might argue an insensibility towards it, which no citizen should ever feel." Having said this much, he was free to extol the new Constitution through contrast with the old and through hopeful anticipation of public prosperity.[9]

Not only the novelty of the political charge led the judges to signal their auditors (and themselves) of a departure from customary decorum. At least as powerful an inducement to judicial self-awareness and self-control were the uneven and fluctuating reactions to the practice by grand juries. If there were times when judge and jurors sang in beautiful harmony—now in outrage against the British, then in stirring defense of the revolutionary cause—there were other times when cacophony prevailed. The political charge could and did exacerbate political differences—most evidently before the Revolution when Loyalist judges chastised grand juries for failing to make presentments and indictments against libelers and tea burners and other local revolutionaries, less dramatically after the Revolution when state judges' urgings of moderation in the treatment of Loyalists were received with little enthusiasm by grand jurors.[10] During the first decade of the national judiciary, the political charge was subjected yet again to the full cycle of popular applause and disdain. Toward the end of the period, one state judge, Richard Parker of Virginia, could exhort a grand jury to steer clear of political presentments, "not [to] think of introducing politics into a court of justice which *cannot* or *ought not* to have anything to do with it," and to keep to the business of grand juries as defined by the state legislature. By the end of the period, the publication of collected grand jury charges of another state judge, Alexander Addison, required this kind of prefatory defense:

> A stronger evidence of a disposition in some men, to monopolize the direction of public opinion, can hardly be given, than the harsh censures which have been propagated on what are called *Political Charges;* nor of the depravity of public opinion, than the approbation with which those censures have been received. While so many set themselves up as political instructors, and, in this capacity, with all the confidence, industry, and zeal of inspired missionaries, preach error and sedition; it would seem hard, if men whose education, habits, and experience, may have qualified them to think justly on public affairs, should be condemned to silence; or, while interposing their sentiments against the torrent of delusion, deny them the solemnity of a public station. I flatter myself, that such censures come not from the wisest and best part of the community.[11]

But by then the days of the political charge (and of Judge Addison's tenure) were numbered.

The reports of the manner in which these charges were delivered and received suggest a cross between a political sermon and a speech from the throne.[12] It would be a mistake, as the substance of the statements shows, to dismiss these charges as the merest Federalist propaganda, although one of their intended effects was to bolster Federalist theories and practices. Lumping all these charges and reducing them to simple apologetic would make it hard to discriminate between Chief Justice Jay's use and Justice Samuel Chase's abuse of the judicial charge. Some of these political sermons ought to be considered rather as carefully composed, self-conscious appeals to that portion of the population which was then politically influential—appeals to be good republicans coupled with some rules for being good republicans. Depending on the judge and the occasion, the political charges presented the full range from judicial elevation to intemperate special pleading. These appeals were often printed in the newspapers at the request of the grand jurors and then reprinted farther afield.

The justices knew that their audience extended beyond the confines of the courtroom. An occasion for a ceremonial pronouncement was seized, the pronouncement itself given a character both judicial and political—like, yet unlike, what a president might say—and a certain conception of the public good promoted through a calculated exhortation. Before one can judge the adequacy and fairness of the conception of the public good implicit in the exhortation, one has to see precisely what the judicial teaching was.

Themes of the Justices. Chief Justice Jay, in his charge to grand juries repeated throughout the eastern circuit on the occasion of his first convening these courts in the spring of 1790, opened appropriately enough with the question to which the history of the United States was to provide the answer. In accents reminiscent of the initial paragraph of *Federalist* 1, the chief justice began:

> Whether any people can long govern themselves in an equal, uniform, and orderly manner, is a question which the advocates for free government justly consider as being exceedingly important to the cause of liberty. This question, like others whose solution depends on facts, can only be determined by experience. It is a question on which many think some room for doubt still remains.

It had fallen—providentially fallen—to the Americans to have "more perfect opportunities of choosing, and more effectual means of establishing their own government, than any other nation has hitherto enjoyed." The force and fraud that seem to have shaped constitutions and governments in most other times and places appear to have been frustrated, at least for the while. The sometimes painful experiences of establishing and correcting state governments "have operated as useful experiments, and conspired to promote our advancement in this interesting science." Similarly, the future lessons of time and experience will be applied to improve this new national government as long as the people rely—and have reason to rely—on their own good sense.[13]

Other Supreme Court justices, such as Iredell and Oliver Ellsworth, elaborated upon this theme. "The noble experiment" that the Americans had undertaken would test the limits of human nature as well as the cause of "a government of reason." "A higher degree of freedom [than that provided by the Constitution], consistent with any government at all, is not exercisable by human nature." At the same time, "no people . . . can rationally desire more than that they should themselves choose the government under which they are to live." Jay cautioned his audience to temper their theory with some sober practice, just as Thomas Jefferson was to appeal to his fellow citizens not to abandon the experiment represented by "this Government, the world's best hope," on the basis of some "theoretic and visionary fear." "If, then," Jay continued,

> so much depends on our rightly improving the before-mentioned opportunities, if the most discerning and enlightened minds may be mistaken relative to theories unconfirmed by practice, if on such difficult questions men may differ in opinion and yet be patriots, and if the merits of our opinions can only be ascertained by experience, let us patiently abide the trial, and unite our endeavors to render it a fair and an impartial one.

It was in this mixed spirit of high hope and sober sense, equally removed from the doctrinaire and from cold legalism, that some justices instructed the people in republicanism.[14]

The foremost of the themes repeated and elaborated upon by the justices was the close connection between self-restraint and true liberty. The justices showed an awareness that the civil liberty of a people free to choose its governors cannot for long be restrained in a manner that is not generally accepted. No matter how well born or high toned they are, governors dependent on the popular franchise cannot expect simply to prescribe opinions and codes that will be authoritative. The more intelligent justices recognized this from the outset and took such steps as they could to persuade others to adopt their opinions. While the courtroom circumstances in which the charges were delivered could have brought to mind ex cathedra pronouncement, the rhetoric actually employed shows that the justices chose not to rest with appeals to their authority. They began, rather, by appealing to fairly narrow calculations of self-interest, broadening the range of considerations as the argument moved from self to nation to type of regime: "It cannot be too strongly impressed on the minds of us all how greatly our individual prosperity depends on our national prosperity, and how greatly our national prosperity depends on a well organized, vigorous government." Jay was quick to reassure his listeners that such a government is not "unfriendly to liberty—to that liberty which is really inestimable." And having gone so far, he proceeded to define civil liberty as "an equal right to all the citizens to have, enjoy, and to do . . . whatever the equal and constitutional laws of the country admit to be consistent with the public good."[15]

It is true that Jay, like Iredell and Ellsworth, was prone to see a divine plan (or the tracks of one) in political affairs, but that was not

105

the sole or main thrust of his argument. If an appeal was to be made to his contemporaries it had to be to both "the duty and the interest . . . of all good citizens."[16] Once led to see the connection between their material well-being and law-abidingness, they would be less apt to be startled by false alarms. They would be better able to distinguish "true liberty" from the "unbounded liberty of the strongest man" or the "unlimited sway of a majority" or "unlicensed indulgence to all the passions of men." "Let each man consider, that his liberty and his property cannot be secured without forming a common interest with all the other members of the society to which he belongs." The cultivation of this common interest, the adjustment as far as possible of "the common welfare of the whole jointly" to the welfare of the individuals and states forming the whole, are tasks to which "moderation and good sense" are indispensable.[17]

The recent history of American public affairs might well have contained important and even salutary lessons, but as can be seen here, those lessons were subject to interpretations. That the cause of individual liberty requires a price to be paid to a larger whole and that genuine liberty is fundamentally dependent on law-abidingness are propositions to which no thinking person could take exception. But thoughtful people could and did disagree about the environment most favorable to liberty.

A frequent Anti-Federalist argument—and one with respectable theoretical credentials—was that liberty was neither safe nor securable under a single government extending over so large and varied a country. More than one response was possible, and more than one was made. A comparison of Ellsworth's language (voiced while on circuit at Savannah) with Jay's in *Federalist* 2 reveals, not that one response was more mythopoeic than the other, but that the voice of the judge speaking as judge had a rhetoric of its own. To the contention that America was too extensive and heterogeneous to have one will (unless it were coerced by Janizaries), Jay, writing as Publius, replied by denying the significance and even the existence of barriers to union. In contrast, Ellsworth, speaking as chief justice, turned the argument around. Far from being too vast to be bound together by good laws, this country would be held together precisely and above all by good laws. Not the ties of kinship, not the memories of common disasters and victories—important as these were—but the ligatures of national laws were most to be relied on. It was for a judge, a teaching judge, to make this point and to create the occasions for reiterating it. Beneath the laws lay political preconditions; beyond the laws stretched political consequences. For a moment there merged the inclination and the opportunity to expound these matters to the citizenry.[18]

Advocating Civic Conduct. Implicit and often explicit in the political charges of the Supreme Court justices was the advocacy of a certain kind of conduct, corresponding to a certain type of citizen: plainspoken, self-possessed, manly in a quiet rather than gallus-tugging fashion; jealous of his rights but aware of his duties and the self-esteem of others. Arguably the justices were at least as concerned with sustaining an already existing type as with creating a model republican. The republic itself showed such moderation and presupposed it in its citizens.[19]

This confidence, however, was not to be taken for granted. Popular government, more than other forms, tries citizens' capacities for enduring disappointment gracefully. After being invited—indeed obliged—to declare their views on the public business, the citizens of a republic are further obliged "cheerfully [to] submit" to constitutional majority determinations. This "deference of private sentiment to that of the public" is "the very basis of all republican governments." The greater diffusion of political rights carries with it a need for a more broadly distributed sense of political responsibility, the quality of which is seen most clearly perhaps in the way public discussion is conducted. The freer the government, the greater is its dependence on popular confidence; that confidence, to be worth anything, requires each citizen to exercise the right of public comment so "that he may neither be unwarily misled himself, nor unwarily mislead others." Such considerations—to say nothing for the moment of the special problem of those who deliberately deceive the public—point to "that salutary caution with which all public measures ought to be discussed." Nowhere is this more needed than in discussions of policy "because nothing is more fallible than human judgment when it extends its views into a futurity." Diffidence, moderation, and a cautious weighing of inconveniences and advantages are in order: "Any other mode of considering great questions of public policy is idle and insignificant." Above all, the enlightened citizen will remember that "things and not names ought to decide our judgments."[20]

There are lessons to be drawn from the past, lessons to be passed on to present and future generations. In this continuous process of extraction and transmission, many of the justices saw their relations to the grand jury as central. Every nation, but especially "an extensive country," has to learn to cope with those who, "impelled by avarice or ambition, or by both," are prepared to gratify their longings at the expense of the public good. Add to this peril the natural effects of partisanship on even "the best men": "Our wishes and partialities becoming inflamed by opposition, often cause indiscretions, and lead us to say and to do things that had better have been omitted." Between these arts of the deceitful and the weaknesses of the honest, republics

107

have come to ruin. For these old dangers, remedies—both old and new—are needed: government by representatives, a divided and balancing legislature, a vigorous executive. As fundamental as any of these are the qualities called for by Ellsworth: "vigilance, constant diligence, and fidelity for the execution of laws"—traits needed in any good republican but especially in a republican grand juror.[21] And from the grand juror would go forth the law, both the knowledge of it and the spirit of it. "I offer no apology, gentlemen, for the nature or the length of this address," Justice James Wilson said in concluding a charge whose printed version could not easily have taken less than an hour to deliver. "In the situation, in which I have the honour to be placed, I deem it my duty to embrace every proper opportunity of disseminating the knowledge of [the criminal code] far and speedily. Can this be done with more propriety than in an address to a grand jury?" And later: "Inform and practically convince every one within your respective spheres of action and intercourse, that, as excellent laws improve the virtue of the citizens, so the virtue of the citizens has a reciprocal and benign energy in heightening the excellence of the law."[22]

These admonitions and appeals ought not to be mistaken for simple declarations of the need for vigorous administration and good government. Some measure of popular self-restraint is indispensable for good government, while one of the surest effects of good administration is the way it secures the voluntary attachment of the people. If there can be no good government without some citizen virtue, there can be no highly developed sense of citizenship without good government. The itinerant justice, in this early stage of national life, improved the judicial occasion by drawing out the deeper implications of national law enforcement for both liberty and union. When he did his work with finesse, the teaching judge was more than a scrupulous craftsman, if less than a philosopher-king, and quite other than the partisan. It is not hard to see that the task of political education would be complicated and even defeated once it fell to the hands of coarse judges and once harsher party conflicts emerged. For however salutary the lessons to be conveyed, a sensible teacher first heeds the context of the instruction. In the measure of care that the justices took in considering those limits, we find a way of discriminating the use from the abuse of the judicial charge. By examining two of the instances where judicial pronouncements ran counter to strong popular and partisan opinion, we can get a sense of the strengths and weaknesses of this variety of judicial politics.

The conduct of foreign policy became a theme of judicial teaching in two ways. To the extent that the grand jury's duty to investigate suspected breaches of the laws of the United States touched upon treaties, the law of nations, and the like, it was beyond debate that the justices, out of their superior judicial understanding of international law, should instruct the grand jury. This the justices did, but not only this. Prompted by the occasion, and by the passions quickened by George Washington's Proclamation of Neutrality of April 22, 1793, the justices went on to pronounce some lessons in foreign policy. In their remarks they tried to steer a narrow course between an examination of the particulars that vexed domestic politics throughout most of the first decade of the new government and an overly vague statement of what constituted good manners in international conduct. Chief Justice Jay's grand jury charge at Richmond, delivered a month after Washington's proclamation, is a fair sample of the concerns for policy and professional duty that merged in the political charge.[23]

The grand theme running through Jay's charge is that the demands of duty and interest coincide, that neither individuals nor nation will find their genuine interests slighted when they act in an honorable fashion. The aptness of this theme is illustrated in various ways. Thus the old maxim that one should use one's own property so as not to harm others is generalized beyond the realm of property to comprehend liberty, power, "and other blessings of every kind." The very purpose of free government is to restrain people to act in accord with this maxim. Precisely in a regime where all powers are derived from the popular will, the need for strong government is most acute, for it is there that the number of rights to be protected and the difficulty in restraining the citizenry are greatest. Above all in a free government, "the duty and interest of us all, that the laws be observed, and irresistibly executed," are clearest, for above all in such a government, the laws express the will, and secure the benefit, of the citizens as a whole.[24]

In reviewing the laws of which the grand jurors ought to take cognizance, Jay was careful to instruct the jurors in the "general principles" that guided relations among the nations and, going beyond this, to argue that utility and justice coincided in recommending a policy of neutrality for the United States. The bulk of the charge is taken up with a discussion of the relevant laws, under the headings of treaties, law of nations, and the Constitution and statutes. Treaties ought not to be mistaken for statutes; the unilateral discretion available for changing and repealing the latter does not apply to the former. The special standing that treaties enjoy as part of the supreme law of the land is a token of the practical restrictions on each contracting power. Maxims and principles of the law of nations prescribe and define fidelity to treaties. Not who the parties are, but the fact of their mutual pledge, makes the obligation binding. Similarly, the law of nations imposes duties as well as rights on the United States. In urging "a conduct friendly and impartial towards the belligerent powers," Washington's proclamation "is exactly consistent with and declaratory of the conduct enjoined by the law of nations." Its domestic consequences, restricting citizens and aliens alike from behaving in a manner that jeopardizes that neutrality, are well supported by the law of nations. "The respect which every nation owes to itself imposes a duty on its government to cause all its laws to be respected and obeyed." Considerations of duty, interest, and disposition all support a policy of neutrality and bind the grand jurors to ferret out those seeking to frustrate that policy. As though this would not suffice, Jay proceeded to defend the wisdom of the proclamation of neutrality in terms going beyond the judge's or jurors' province strictly defined. It is not enough to "be faithful to all—kind to all—but let us also be just to ourselves." America now enjoyed peace, liberty, safety, and unparalleled prosperity. A policy of neutrality left her free to pursue her offices of humanity and benevolence—as well as her commerce—toward all belligerents.[25]

An enlightened self-interest also dictated that Americans act with an awareness of the domestic causes that might lead the country into war. War might arise from the narrowly self-regarding actions of those who would "not hesitate to gratify [their] passions [of avarice or ambition or both] at the expense of the blood and tears even of those who are free from blame." Or war might equally arise from the partisan indiscretions from which even the best citizens are not exempt. "Prudence directs us to look forward to such an event, and to endeavour not only to avert, but also to be prepared for it." The principal precaution is "union in sentiments and measures relative to national objects," the avoidance of parties that are partisans of one foreign power or another. In short, a particular conduct befits a free people in peace and war:

> But, if neither integrity nor prudence on our part should prove sufficient to shield us from war, we may then meet it with fortitude, and a firm dependence on the Divine protection; whenever it shall become impossible to preserve peace by avoiding offences, it will be our duty to refuse to purchase it by sacrifices and humiliations, unworthy of a free and magnanimous people, either to demand or submit to.[26]

However one regards the law of nations—as rules for relations between states or (with Justice Wilson) as "the duties which a nation owes to itself"—it is to be understood in the light of a few well-known facts. In Chief Justice Jay's words, "Nations are, in respect to each other, in the same situation as independent individuals in a state of nature." Having no common judge on earth, these nations "have a perfect right to establish such governments and build such houses as they prefer, and their neighbors have no right to pull down either because not fashioned according to their ideas of perfection." The indisputably superior merit and justice of the American form of government (and none of the justices was shy about so judging it) ought to commend it to the world, but they do not entail a general commission to remake the world after the American likeness. Nonintervention and self-determination seem, rather, to be the standing order. But if "strict impartiality" is the rule—"it is no less our interest than our duty to act accordingly"—it is a rule open to qualifications and, in any event, is not to be mistaken for indifference. There are standards of conduct, standards of civility, to which nations, no less than individuals, ought to be held. Unless prior treaty commitments require it, Americans ought not to be partisans of one belligerent or the other. If the war is about objects in which America is not interested, Americans ought not to interfere except as mediators and friends to peace.[27]

In Wilson's formulation there are certain self-regarding duties that neither states nor individuals can properly shirk. Predictably, "self-preservation is a primary duty." Beyond that is the duty to "love and to deserve an honest fame." In the midst of the controversy over the proclamation of neutrality, Jay could declare in a grand jury charge: "A just war is an evil, but it is not the greatest; oppression and disgrace are greater. War is not to be sought, but it is not to be fled from. Let us do exactly what is just and right, and then remain without fear, but not without care about the consequences." Honest fame, a due regard for national dignity and character, required a state of mind that would neither give nor brook insult and disgrace.[28]

The justices' international and domestic teachings were as one. They saw a need in each case to elevate self-interest into republican virtue, manly independence, self-respect, and patriotism. In the course of reciting the reasoning that in his judgment gave issue to the Washingtonian policy, the chief justice could not but be aware of the fact that the merits of that policy were a subject of bitter partisan dispute. Yet even here there was a lesson to be learned, a moral to be drawn. However heated the controversy and debatable the policy, as law of the land the proclamation bound judge and juror alike. The duty to enforce the law overbore individual scruples and misgivings. Outside the courtroom, in the political forum, "as free citizens we have a right to think and speak our sentiments on this subject, in terms becoming freemen—that is, in terms explicit, plain, and decorous." Within the courtroom, in the act of performing an unpleasant duty, grand jurors would have occasion to learn the truth of "the excellent principle" that "the interests and the duties of men are inseparable."[29]

There seems to be general agreement that the use of the charge as a means of political education was the introduction of a new purpose to what originally had been a mere abstract of crimes and punishments. But not every such introduction is impudent meddling. What saves Jay's charges (and those like his) from the scorn justly directed toward hot-headed political preachments from the bench is precisely the consciousness that he "was treading on delicate ground." Jay enacted in the courtroom the very spirit and teaching that he would inculcate in others. He knew, and acted and spoke as though he knew, that "on such difficult questions men may differ in opinion and yet be patriots." It is one thing to declaim (like Ellsworth) against the evil effects of disorganization and impiety, showing that, "unhinged and imperious, the mind revolts at every institution which can preserve order, or protect right, while the heart, demoralized, becomes insensible to social and civil obligations." But it is another, and more difficult, thing to avoid both the erroneous doctrine and the erroneous manner of "heated divines" and of "some enthusiastic politicians."[30]

Justice Chase's Impeachment. The troubles of Justice Chase flowed from various causes, some of them peculiar to that able but intemperate man. The larger political controversies behind the impeachment are not my concern now. Nor do I mean to assert—what cannot be proved one way or the other—that more cautious charges could long have preserved the Federalist judiciary from the watchful hostility of the Jeffersonian administration and Congress. Nonetheless, it is possible and even useful to try to detect that respect in which Chase's style in his political charges differed from Jay's.[31]

Justice Chase's scandalizing charge may be considered in its three parts: an exordium stating the problem and the speaker's credentials to speak to it, a critique of three accomplished or proposed changes in the laws, and finally an analysis and rejection of the theoretical foundations of those changes in the laws. The political charge itself is seen as extra matter, the delivery of which was prompted by a concern for the welfare of the country. Chase saw his task as countering pleasant-sounding nonsense, even at the risk of saying things "repugnant to popular prejudice." Yet there is more than a consciousness of good intentions; he identified himself as a man of 1776, an authentic long-time republican. The problem as it emerges in the charge is that a change is occurring in the ordinary understanding of representation and liberty; the change is such, according to Chase, that the "fast approaching" result will be that "the people are *not free*, wh[a]tever may be their form of government."

Indicative of this evil end are the institutional changes condemned and deplored by Chase in the central part of his charge:

> You know, gentlemen, that our state and national institutions were framed to secure to every member of the society, equal liberty and equal rights; but the late alteration of the federal judiciary by the abolition of the offices of the sixteen circuit judges, and the recent change in our state [Maryland] constitution, by the establishing of universal suffrage, and the further alteration that is contemplated in our state judiciary (if adopted) will, in my judgment, take away all security for property and personal liberty. The independence of the national judiciary, is already shaken to its foundation, and the virtue of the people alone can restore it. The independence of the judges of this state will be entirely destroyed, if the bill for the abolition of the two supreme courts should be ratified by the next general assembly. The change of the state constitution, by allowing universal suffrage, will, in my opinion, certainly and rapidly destroy all protection to property, and all security to personal liberty; and our republican constitution will sink into a mobocracy, the worst of all possible governments.
>
> I can only lament, that the main pillar of our state constitution, has already been thrown down by the establishment of universal suffrage. By this shock alone, the whole building totters to its base, and will crumble into ruins, before many years elapse, unless it be restored to its original state. If the independency of your state judges, which your bill of rights wisely declares "to be essential to the impartial administration of justice, and the great security to the rights and liberties of the people," shall be taken away by the ratification of the bill passed for that purpose, it will precipitate the destruction of your whole state constitution; and there will be nothing left in it, worthy the care or support of freemen.

What is one to make of this prose? Let us grant that the Judiciary Act of 1802 threatened the independence of the national judiciary, although this proposition is not easily supported by Chase's behavior here or by that of a unanimous Supreme Court less than ten weeks before in *Marbury v. Madison* or by the Court's acquiescence in *Stuart v. Laird* in the reestablishment of the circuit-riding system prescribed by the Judiciary Act of 1789.[32] Even granting this, though, what can be intended by the appeal to the virtue of the people? Could Chase

have expected that those who had entrusted and reentrusted their
affairs to the Jeffersonians would throw the rascals out the next time
around for their repeal of the Judiciary Act of 1801?[33] The attack on
the extension of the Maryland suffrage to a population beyond those
"who have property in, a common interest with, and an attachment
to, the community" seems, if anything, even more futile than the attack
on the Judiciary Act of 1802. By what stretch of a political imagination
can the narrowing of a once-extended suffrage be envisioned through
reinstituted property qualifications? To what majority is such an appeal
addressed?

The practices Chase censured stem from bad opinions, and it was
to those opinions, or rather to the theoretical underpinnings of those
opinions, that he turned in the final part of his charge:

> The declarations, respecting the natural rights of man, which
> originated from the claim of the British parliament to make
> laws to bind America in all cases whatsoever; the publications,
> since that period, of visionary and theoretical writers, asserting
> that men, in a state of society, are entitled to exercise rights
> which they possessed in a state of nature; and the modern
> doctrines by our late reformers, that all men, in a state of
> society, are entitled to enjoy equal liberty and equal rights,
> have brought this mighty mischief upon us; and I fear that
> it will rapidly progress, until peace and order, freedom and
> property, shall be destroyed. Our people are taught as a
> political creed, that men, living under an established govern-
> ment, are nevertheless entitled to exercise certain rights which
> they possessed in a state of nature; and also, that every
> member of this government is entitled to enjoy an equality
> of liberty and rights.

The justice's critique of these opinions would not seem strange
to anyone who knew *Reflections on the Revolution in France*, yet Chase's
attack, if similar to Edmund Burke's, is also more extreme than Burke's.
Chase mounted an attack against a fallacious doctrine—but he did so
in the name of a doctrine or from a doctrinal position. His critique
displays an insufficient regard to what Burke held to be of central
importance: circumstances. To the assertion of the natural rights of
man, Chase brought the counterassertion that there are no natural
rights; nor, in his view, is there any state of nature. "I really consider
a state of nature as a creature of the imagination only, although great
names give a sanction to a contrary opinion." In this categorical denial,
Chase went beyond Burke, and—what is more revealing—Chase was
recklessly separating himself from such "founding Federalists" as Jay
and Wilson by rejecting one of the fundamentals of the Revolution.

To the views of those "visionary and theoretical writers" who argued that men could enjoy their natural rights in society, Chase replied with a denial that there could be any personal liberty and rights before, or outside of, society. All rights are social, conventional. And to the egalitarian doctrines of latter-day reformers, Chase replied in a fashion that can best be summarized by Burke's dictum: "In this partnership all men have equal rights; but not to equal things."[34]

Most striking about Chase's grand jury charge, if compared with that of Jay, is not that his teaching was bizarre but that it was propounded immoderately. Jay was upholding the law and calling for obedience; Chase was attacking the laws and calling for resistance, repeal, and restoration. Although Chase's teaching perhaps resembled Jonathan Boucher's too much to suit contemporary tastes, his general political position was sound Federalism. Chase was not playing Sir Robert Filmer to nineteenth-century Americans, but his words give little sign that he appreciated how irrelevant his mode of teaching had been rendered by the change in opinions that he was deploring. In the eyes of Jefferson and his followers, the results of the election of 1800 were as momentous as the events of 1776 (more than a few Federalists agreed). The principles of 1776 were now triumphant, the last vestiges of monocratic power would be erased, and the promise of the great documents and pamphlets of the revolutionary struggle would be fulfilled. Yet if the election of 1800 was a political revolution, it was one secured by a margin of eight electoral votes. It was an election in which Maryland had split evenly and following which the state Federalist party retained significant strength.

Chase, however, showed no sign of acting on the premise that a more moderate political charge would be likely to receive a respectful hearing or have the desired effect. Instead, he mounted a frontal attack against Jeffersonian doctrine. That exhilarating teaching (however remote from Jeffersonian practice) had kindled the imaginations and aspirations of New England and Appalachia alike. In the face of widespread expectations that political life was to be restored, purified, raised to new heights, how could Chase have expected to move men with a categorical rejection of Jeffersonian doctrine and with an appeal of this sort?

> I cannot but remember the great and patriotic characters, by whom your state constitution was framed. I cannot but recollect that attempts were then made in favor of universal suffrage; and to render the judges dependent upon the legislature. You may believe, that the gentlemen who framed your constitution, possessed the full confidence of the people of Maryland, and that they were esteemed for their talents and

patriotism, and for their public and private virtues. You must have heard that many of them held the highest civil and military stations, and that they, at every risk and danger, assisted to obtain and establish your independence. Their names are enrolled on the journals of the first Congress, and may be seen in the proceedings of the convention that framed our form of government. With great concern I observe, that the sons of some of these characters have united to pull down the beautiful fabric of wisdom and republicanism, that their fathers erected!

Chase, a leading framer of the Maryland constitution of 1776, found all the more rankling the participation of the sons (many of them young Federalists) in the undoing of their fathers' handiwork. But his appeal from the new to the old Federalists fell on deaf ears. Starting not from where his audience was, but from where (in his judgment) they ought to be, Chase made his argument out of exhortation, remonstrance, and appeal to venerable authority. His impatience with the errors of his audience deprived him of the ingratiating arts and courteous consideration that might have moved his audience to recognize some reasonableness in his position. Even more did his impatience deprive him of a recognition of the deeper calculations that would lead one of the most aristocratic of states to introduce the most democratic forms.[35] Taking arms, as he did, against a sea of troubles, Justice Chase would have drowned—had not his firm but prudent counsel adopted another style in addressing the Senate when it sat as a court of impeachment.

It is easy to see that Chase's excesses and subsequent impeachment would have effects beyond merely cooling intemperate judges. Both sides at his trial held to the tacit premise that the day of the political charge had passed. Even Chase's counsel felt obliged to say that using the grand jury charge as a vehicle for arguing against a public measure "may, perhaps, be ill-judged indiscreet or ill-timed. I am ready to admit that it is so: for I am one of those who have always thought, that political subjects ought never to be mentioned in courts of justice." The real issue, however, was criminality, and here the defense was that the political charge had become customary and that its use had been explicitly and implicitly approved. "From the time of Judge Drayton to the time of Judge Chase, it has been considered as innocent." In Chase's own words:

> It has been the practice in this country, ever since the beginning of the revolution, which separated us from Great Britain, for the judges to express from the bench, by way of charge to the grand jury, and to enforce to the utmost of their ability,

such political opinions as they thought correct and useful. There have been instances in which the legislative bodies of this country, have recommended this practice of the judges; and it was adopted by the judges of the supreme court of the United States, as soon as the present judicial system was established.

If this was prescription, it was not old prescription. Nor was the appeal to practice a sufficient response to the allegation of impropriety. This was not a strong defense against an attack that could point to "a judge of the United States, passing judgment of condemnation on the laws which he was bound to conform to, and execute, and with the policy of which, in his judicial character, he had nothing to do."[36]

A comparison of Jay and Chase in their capacity as teaching judges supports the truth and aptness of Tocqueville's standard for measuring judicial behavior. In the passage quoted at the beginning of this essay, Tocqueville stressed the need for judges who combined legal learning, civic rectitude, and political adroitness. The manner in which the judge performed his duties was of decisive importance. Jay tied his political teaching, however broadly stated, to the proper business of a grand jury—in this instance, enforcing the Neutrality Proclamation as declared national policy. He combined his character as judge with his larger function. Chase, in contrast, appeared more nakedly as a partisan political advocate, and at that as an opponent of the laws of the land. His sense of the rightness of his intentions could not make up for the lack of prudence displayed in his exhortation.

Using the grand jury charge as a means of political education took high political finesse. Abuse led to disuse, and disuse led to a kind of forgetfulness. Barely four decades after one chief justice, Jay, could speak of not omitting occasions for promoting goodwill, good temper, and the progress of useful truths among the citizenry, another chief justice, Roger Taney, could opine confidently to a grand jury that "it would be a waste of time in the court to engage itself in discussing principles, and enlarging upon topics which are not to lead us to some practical result. . . . Not a moment should be wasted in unnecessary forms."[37]

Judges and the Perpetuation of Political Institutions

Members of the pre-Marshall Supreme Court could, while on circuit, fairly be called teachers to the citizenry. In this phase of its role as republican schoolmaster, the Supreme Court seized upon the expedient of the grand jury charge but with uneven success. A series of bitter partisan conflicts—centering on the Neutrality Proclamation, the Alien and Sedition Acts, and the overthrow of Federalist hegemony—contributed to the disappearance of the political charge. The unfashionable became repulsive, finally foolhardy. Chase's impeachment only ratified that result. Nonetheless, the first justices of the Supreme Court—among them men such as Jay, Wilson, and Ellsworth, who had been singularly important in the drafting or defense of the Constitution and of the Judiciary Act of 1789—adopted this mode of political education as fitting, even necessary. I now look beyond the sermon charge (a passing phase), beyond the circuit riding (only one aspect of the judicial role), to the larger problem subsuming all these, and more. The temporary and particular manifestations draw our attention to the fundamental reasoning for an institution designed to play a broad and permanent part in the life of the nation. That fundamental reasoning touches circuit duties only incidentally and outright political preaching to the people only by remote construction. Political preaching presumes a kind of superiority in the judge. Was that superiority (as distinguished from the explicit preaching) taken to be an essential feature of the national judiciary?

Transcending Enlightened Self-Interest. The question is not so much whether the courts, and more particularly the Supreme Court, were expected to be "a bevy of Platonic Guardians"[38] as whether the authors and defenders of the Constitution conceived of the courts, and of the Supreme Court more than any, as acting and speaking on principles of public-spiritedness and civic devotion beyond the probable range of other governmental officials, to say nothing of the ordinary citizens. To what extent did the new plan of government require a body of judges disposed and able to transcend considerations of enlightened self-interest? That question, in turn, raises the larger issue: How did the framers of the Constitution expect to sustain and perpetuate a republican regime? The manner in which the Federalists addressed themselves to this question leaves much to be desired. The Anti-Federalist complaint of a profound disharmony in the new system was neither forced nor fatuous. The preconditions of republican virtue, as then understood, were not fulfilled in the extended republic envisaged by the apologists for the Constitution. When Federalist debaters chose to speak on this theme, they did not meet the issue in a uniformly candid or persuasive manner. In the preceding pages I have examined the connection between extraordinary qualities of leadership and the need for widespread citizen virtue by considering how judicial statesmen, through their teaching, tried to promote and sustain republican virtue. Here I am concerned with identifying the kind of citizen virtue and the kind of statesmanship the

Federalists believed necessary for the perpetuation of their political institutions.

Although all—Federalists and Anti-Federalists—agreed that the new government, whatever form it might take, had to accord with the temper and genius of the American people, there were great differences on what that temper and genius were. Benjamin Franklin could argue against paying the executive, adducing foreign examples and that of General Washington "to shew that the pleasure of doing good & serving their Country and the respect such conduct entitles them to, are sufficient motives with some minds to give up a great portion of their time to the Public without the mean inducement of pecuniary satisfaction." Conversely, Noah Webster could propose improving the "system of the great Montesquieu" by striking out the word "virtue" wherever it appeared in the *Spirit of Laws* and substituting "property or lands in fee simple." "*Virtue*, patriotism, or love of country, never was and never will be, till men's natures are changed, a fixed, permanent principle and support of government."[39]

In the midst of a heated debate, Patrick Henry could lament the Constitution's dangerously delusive reliance on the governors' "fair, disinterested patriotism" and on good, but naturally weak, "luminous characters." "The real rock of political salvation is self-love, perpetuated from age to age in every human breast, and manifested in every action." To rely on men's higher motives (and to the extent Henry saw the Constitution as doing that) was in effect to turn the government over to the watchful wicked, notwithstanding the republican virtue of the people at large. This argument—a strange marriage of ward-politics reasoning and deserted-house imaginings—was answered by two of the least starry-eyed defenders of the Constitution. According to John Marshall, Henry could search in vain for some American analogue to the British "exclusive personal stock of interest." The American way was so to blend public and private interests that all men (or most) would have a sense of their stake in society. When the American "promotes his own [interest], he promotes that of the community. When we consult the common good, we consult our own." With such a population—alert, wary, and interested—one might establish a government of sufficient energy to rule an extensive republic, relatively safe in the confidence that its abuses would be checked. James Madison went even further in challenging Henry's pitting of the cunningly corrupt against the drowsily virtuous; it was neither a fair match nor a credible one.

I go on this great republican principle, that the people will

119

have virtue and intelligence to select men of virtue and wisdom. Is there no virtue among us? If there be not, we are in a wretched situation. No theoretical checks, no form of government, can render us secure. To suppose that any form of government will secure liberty or happiness without any virtue in the people, is a chimerical idea. If there be sufficient virtue and intelligence in the community, it will be exercised in the selection of these men; so that we do not depend on their virtue, or put confidence in our rulers, but in the people who are to choose them.[40]

Words like these suggest that Madison was carried very far indeed by the mood and movement of the Virginia debate. It would be hard to find in this language a concession that a political task was involved in sustaining the virtue of the people. Is then the people's republican virtue a given—enduring, available, sufficient? Not quite. Although in speaking at all to the issue Madison differed from many Federalists, his discussion remains incomplete and hence problematic. The Federalists surely were aware of the insufficiency of their response to nagging Anti-Federalist questions about republican virtue. They may well have avoided a detailed discussion of that theme out of fear that the answer they would be obliged to give could only harm the more urgent cause of ratification. Moreover, since the main attack on the Constitution was mounted in the name of popular liberty, the Federalists were supplied with a double opportunity to thrash the Anti-Federalists on that issue while eluding a confrontation on the problem of sustaining popular virtue.

What I have identified as the larger issue—how best to sustain and to perpetuate the regime—is connected with the need for republican virtue, but the Federalists did not always choose to dwell on that connection. Alexander Hamilton, for example, could address himself to the need for statesmen and uncommon leaders (and did so repeatedly) without appearing to have to discuss popular virtue as a problem. Even when the attachment and confidence of the people were taken up as an explicit theme by him in the New York debates, the problem seemed to turn less on the need for a certain kind of citizen than on the need for a certain kind of ruler:

All governments, even the most despotic, depend, in a great degree, on opinion. In free republics, it is most peculiarly the case. In these, the will of the people makes the essential principle of the government; and the laws which control the community receive their tone and spirit from the public wishes. It is the fortunate situation of our country, that the minds of the people are exceedingly enlightened and refined.

Here, then, we may expect the laws to be proportionably agreeable to the standard of perfect policy, and the wisdom of public measures to consist with the most intimate conformity between the views of the representative and his constituent. . . .

It was remarked yesterday, that a numerous representation was necessary to obtain the confidence of the people. This is not generally true. The confidence of the people will easily be gained by a good administration. This is the true touchstone. . . . The popular confidence depends on circumstances very distinct from considerations of number. Probably the public attachment is more strongly secured by a train of prosperous events, which are the result of wise deliberation and vigorous execution, and to which large bodies are much less competent than small ones.[41]

The intelligence needed to produce "a chain of prosperous events" is to be found in the men whom the people have chosen. This was a subject to which Hamilton warmed and spoke at length. At a considerably lower level is the popular intelligence that sees or feels the advantages of a "chain of prosperous events" and knows enough to connect the presence or absence of such advantages with what the government does. This was not a subject requiring much elaboration.

Sustaining a System of Government. We are left to wonder at the Federalists' discussion. When sustaining republican virtue is the theme, the treatment is muted and surprisingly incomplete. When the question is how to sustain the necessary conditions for popular government, the Federalists usually move the emphasis away from the need for statesmanship and uncommon leadership without quite ruling out the possibility that such leadership may be indispensable. Why they should have followed this tack is another of those problems admitting of more speculation than certainty. It might be said that, by arguing in a manner that neither foreclosed nor required statesmanship for the conduct of the new republic, the Federalists' thinking showed its origins and its limits. The leading founders were not philosophers but gentlemen. Their thinking, while precise and often acute, was not thorough; their goal was a sufficient understanding, not an elaborated theory. In this sense, what they thought and argued and built was very good indeed. They envisioned a government whose business would be conducted by men such as themselves; in such hands the public business would be well placed and diligently executed. "A Federalist gentleman differed only in his political views from a Republican gentleman."[42]

Credible as such an interpretation is, it is not altogether convincing. An analysis of the argument of *The Federalist* shows that its authors

121

relied on quasi-aristocratic leaders and teachers, like the national judiciary, to sustain and to guide the kind of public their regime presupposed. Why the defenders of the Constitution, in the stress of hard fights for state ratification, would prefer to emphasize those features that made it appear to be a self-sustaining system is immediately intelligible. The Constitution was, they argued, peculiarly fit for this particular people. And, in truth, the framers, in their clear-eyed, unsentimental way, had cut the Constitution to the pattern of ordinary American citizens (as they were or were likely to become). But aware of the extraordinary efforts they themselves had had to make to have a Constitution to recommend, did they believe that their Constitution would obviate such efforts by future generations? More narrowly, would the system "wholly popular" survive, even thrive, on talents wholly popular? A review of Publius's calculations and anticipations in *The Federalist*—and though polemical, they were no less careful— suggests that the answer is no. The founding of the American regime was an act of men whose talents were both great and not wholly popular. Those men thought the preservation of that regime under their Constitution, if it did not require equally great men, at least stood in need of some men who were not wholly popular.

Publius was calm by nature, not given to exaggerated enthusiasms or fears, though not above playing on such feelings. In judging human nature, he was inclined to be less, rather than more, sanguine about its capacities and about its inclination with respect to good and bad; but in this judgment, as in so many other matters, he aimed at some kind of balance: "As there is a degree of depravity in mankind which requires a certain degree of circumspection and distrust: So there are other qualities in human nature, which justify a certain portion of esteem and confidence." That portion might not be great; neither did Publius trouble himself to name or describe those "other qualities." But certainly republican government, more than any other form, depended on their existence. In all such political calculations, excess was to be avoided: "The supposition of universal venality in human nature is little less an error in political reasoning than the supposition of universal rectitude." The famous and distinctive solution of *Federalist* 51, based on the "policy of supplying by opposite and rival interests, the defect of better motives," does not deny the existence of those motives, still less declare them superfluous. If the insufficiency of virtue and honor is repeatedly shown, if a reliance on "superior virtue" is misplaced in republics, that does not settle the question.[43] True, the Constitution presupposes that its powers will be administered with only "a common share of prudence." The virtue of the citizens may be little more than this: that they "understand their rights and are disposed to defend them." And yet Publius showed, again and again, that he was indifferent to neither the utility, beauty, nor necessity of higher and finer motives. He knew and admired "men, who under any circumstances will have the courage to do their duty at every hazard." But he also knew that "this stern virtue is the growth of few soils." Its presence, therefore, was not to be depended on, if that could be avoided. Still, Publius had no a priori way of knowing that all problems likely to arise under the new Constitution could be accommodated satisfactorily by merely self-interested groups. He surely must have considered whether a nation could do without some leaders (like those in the Constitutional Convention itself) who had "a deep conviction of the necessity of sacrificing private opinions and partial interests to the public good."[44]

In fact, the promotion of the public happiness, indeed the republican cause, requires men who have "courage and magnanimity enough" to serve the people while risking popular displeasure. Why, we may ask, do these men act as they do—saving the people's interests from the consequences of their foolish inclinations—under a cloud of popular scorn and blame? Are the "lasting monuments of their gratitude" with which the people may ultimately reward their guardians likely to be a sufficient inducement? And wherein lies the magnanimity of these guardians? Might they as easily, perhaps more easily, have set snares for the unwary, flattering their prejudices to betray their interests?[45] These lines, I suggest, presuppose a sense of duty—rare, needful of institutional support, but in the last (and desperate) instant, indispensable. Hypocritical self-serving governors and a mean-spirited populace were Publius's Scylla and Charybdis. He dared not separate the case for good government from the case for popular government. He knew that severally and together those cases needed something more in both the leaders and the people than an overpowering absorption in self-interest. Uniting those cases was at once a political necessity and an act of high statesmanship.

No branch of government was more likely to shelter and to provide a political platform for that presupposed sense of duty as a regular matter of course than the judiciary. There especially might this rare, nonpopular, and often unpopular virtue be fostered and used to best effect. Little, it had to be confessed, was to be expected of the House of Representatives in this respect. Although not utterly devoid of elevation, its virtue would be its commonness, its similitude to the interests and sentiments of the great body of the people. "Similitude" does not mean perfect congruence. If it is true "that the people commonly *intend* the PUBLIC GOOD," the House may be said to borrow that intent, refining it a bit, but also possibly deflecting it by its own special humors. Its commonness, moreover, would best be secured by *avoiding* commonness as the proper basis of representation. Publius could defend the House against attack by showing that the interests and feelings of all classes of the people would best be expressed in that body by representatives drawn from certain particular classes. "Bound to fidelity and sympathy" with the people by cords of "duty, gratitude, interest, [and] ambition itself," it was to be presumed that "in general" these men, "distinguished by the preference" of their fellows, would be "somewhat distinguished also, by those qualities which entitle them to it."[46]

Somewhat more might be hoped for in the Senate: "there is reason to presume" that the state legislatures will choose "those men only who have become the most distinguished by their abilities and virtue." In such a small body, where each member can receive "a sensible degree" of praise and blame, there is the motive to devote oneself to studying and attending to the public business. It is not altogether clear whether the Senate would have a "permanent motive" to do so, and if so, what that motive would be. A properly constituted Senate should supply "the want of a due sense of national character," thus providing a remedy for the unenlightened, variable, and blundering policies of the Confederation. The special responsibility in foreign affairs with which the Senate (in association with the president) is charged gives added weight to the peculiar virtues that are needed and expected in that body. But the very motives of patriotism and national dignity that might encourage a Senate to take a strong stand for the national honor would also lead it to eschew "absolute inflexibility." In resisting the will of the more popular branch, it would be "particularly sensible to every prospect of public danger, or of a dishonorable stagnation in public affairs." The Senate will moderate its intransigence so as to avoid deadlock because of "the interest which [the senators] will individually feel in whatever concerns the government."[47]

In comparison with either branch of the legislature, the president appears likely to be much better situated to give public expression to his "livelier sense of duty" and his "more exact regard to reputation." Publius foresaw "a constant probability" that the presidency would be occupied by "characters pre-eminent for ability and virtue." One of the marks of the national government's superiority over the states is the need for "other talents and a different kind of merit" to raise a man to "first honors" in the nation as a whole. Yet in contemplating a president's temptations "to sacrifice his duty to his interest, which it would require superlative virtue to withstand," Publius, sensibly enough, did not make gratuitous assumptions: "The history of human conduct does not warrant that exalted opinion of human virtue." His discussion of the executive veto gives a fair measure of his expectations:

> In the case for which it is chiefly designed, that of an immediate attack upon the constitutional rights of the executive, or in a case in which the public good was evidently and palpably sacrificed, a man of tolerable firmness would avail himself of his constitutional means of defence, and would listen to the admonitions of duty and responsibility. In the former supposition, his fortitude would be stimulated by his immediate interest in the power of his office; in the latter by the probability of the sanction of his constituents; who though they would naturally incline to the legislative body in a doubtful case, would hardly suffer their partiality to delude them in a very plain case. I speak now with an eye to a magistrate possessing only a common share of firmness. There are men, who under any circumstances will have the courage to do their duty at every hazard.[48]

What sustains a president of tolerable, common firmness in his inclination to protect the common good? Not the certainty of popular approbation; not any immediate self-interest. Standing alone, a president can count on only the probability of public approval; yet that approval, if it comes, is his alone. We ought not to be surprised to find the president considering himself both "under stronger obligations, and more interested" to fulfill his responsibilities.[49] But striking as the effects of executive leadership can be, especially in critical cases, the motivations to such public-spirited acts are unreliable and insufficient. We have not yet before us the full union of private motives, institutional supports, and special training.

The Locus of High Statesmanship. Of the judges, and only of the judges, did Publius declare that they would be "too far removed from the people to share much in their prepossessions." Precisely this dissimilarity, this nonpopular character, would especially qualify the judiciary to be "an intermediate body between the people and the legislature." The judiciary is the only branch of the government whose members require special training and competence, and one of the effects of that training is to set those individuals apart from the populace. The judicial function itself occupies some sort of middle ground between a technician's deductions from general rules and a legislator's pure reason prescribing such general rules. In construing the Constitution, the judge performs a political duty through the exercise of a technical duty. When Publius rejected the theory in which each branch of government would make an authoritative construction of its powers binding upon the other branches, he at the same time candidly avowed that the courts would stand in a closer relation to the deliberate will of the people as expressed in the Constitution than would the representatives of the people. The courts would be peculiarly fit to discover in the Constitution what the will of the people was. Even bolder was his conjuring of a situation in which the judges would stand in need of "an uncommon portion of fortitude":

> Until the people have by some solemn and authoritative act annulled or changed the established form, it is binding upon themselves collectively, as well as individually; and no presumption, or *even knowledge of their sentiments*, can warrant their representatives in a departure from it, prior to such an act. But it is easy to see that it would require an uncommon portion of fortitude in the judges to do their duty as faithful guardians of the constitution, where legislative invasions of it had been instigated by the major voice of the community.

One may still speak of the sense of the people ruling but in a manner that vividly brings to mind the "courage and magnanimity" needed to serve the people "at the peril of their displeasure."[50]

If Publius wished to suggest that a locus of high statesmanship—cautious, politic, yet able and willing to cope with popular excesses—would be found in the national courts, he did not leave it at these indirections. His general, thematic discussion of the judiciary anticipates, and surely does not preclude, judges who would view themselves as teachers of republicanism using the text of the Constitution and the national laws interpreted in a judicial spirit of moderation and fairness. The preliminary impression conveyed by Publius's account is that somewhat incompatible elements are being stirred together. If the judiciary was the least dangerous branch, it might well also be considered the least to be trusted.[51] To complicate matters, no prima facie evidence showed that it would be the least influential branch. The subject had to be treated judiciously. Perhaps nothing illustrates this quite as well as these famous lines:

> Whoever attentively considers the different departments of power must perceive, that in a government in which they are separated from each other, the judiciary, from the nature of its functions, will always be the least dangerous to the political rights of the constitution; because it will be least in a capacity to annoy or injure them. . . . The judiciary . . . has no influence over either the sword or the purse, no direction either of the strength or of the wealth of the society, and can take no active resolution whatever. It may truly be said to have neither Force nor Will, but merely judgment; and must ultimately depend upon the aid of the executive arm even for the efficacy of its judgments.[52]

One doubts whether we smile much more at this comparison than Publius did. His next sentence begins with the words "this simple view of the matter." Although the argument is offered in a spirit that does not disgrace the cause of truth, this view is indeed simple even considered on the premises of Publius's psychology; the view is kept simple because of the demands of Publius's rhetoric. The too sharp distinction between will and judgment defied, then as now, the good sense of any discerning mind. Madison could speak in the Constitutional Convention of the analogy between the executive and judiciary, while stressing that one of the differences was that "in the administration of the [executive] much greater latitude is left to opinion and discretion than in the administration of the [judiciary]." Nothing suggests here that the judicial function is free of every influence of opinion and discretion. Nor is Publius one to mistake names for things; he knows better.

> The faculties of the mind itself have never yet been distinguished and defined, with satisfactory precision, by all the efforts of the most acute and metaphysical Philosophers. Sense, perception, *judgment*, desire, *volition*, memory, imagination, are found to be separated by such delicate shades, and minute gradations, that their boundaries have eluded the most subtle investigations, and remain a pregnant source of ingenious disquisition and controversy.[53]

It is unreasonable, then, to assume that Publius thought of judicial decision making as a thin-blooded exercise in deduction in which discretion and will had no place or effect. He chose to speak in this manner, rather, to strengthen the impression that the judiciary could safely be accorded special, extraordinary supports and defenses. And he could speak in this manner because what he said was essentially, though not simply, true. That very statement characterizing the judiciary as "least dangerous" does not assert that it is weak. The Supreme Court will be innocuous: "the political rights of the constitution," "the general liberty of the people," will not be threatened by an independent and separate judiciary. But the Supreme Court will not be weak or ineffectual, save in the most extreme political controversies in which its will (for we must call it that) is pitted against the constitutional will of the representatives of the people. The provisions of the Constitution and the prudence of the judges will warn off the courts from most such confrontations. But within the large domain remaining, the judiciary will hardly be unnoticed. The problem of judicial review of national legislation aside, the judiciary will serve as an instrument of national supremacy. Publius never suggested any weakness in the

Supreme Court's carrying the authority of the Constitution and the laws to the people and in its facing local injustice and plain localism backed by popular feelings. In its capacity for harming individuals, even large numbers of individuals, the judiciary is terrible, as Montesquieu had said. But the judiciary cannot (or is not likely to) take over the government the way the other branches of government can, and in that specifically political sense it is "next to nothing." The full force of the words is to be accorded Publius's statement of why the Supreme Court was not united with the Senate to form a court of impeachments: "I forbear to remark upon the additional pretext for clamour, against the Judiciary, which so considerable an augmentation of its authority would have afforded." There were already pretexts enough.[54]

Separate and Independent. Publius's case for an independent judiciary is inseparable from, even as it goes beyond, his case for the separation of powers. By "contriving the interior structure of the government" in the proper way, it is possible to achieve that measure of a separation of powers that is "admitted on all hands to be essential to the preservation of liberty." The basis of that separation is, more fundamentally, the desired independence of each of the branches of government. By being in a position and of a mind to resist the encroachments of the others, each branch is able to perform its distinctive function and also to serve as an effective element in the system of checks and balances. A prerequisite, then, to the separation of powers is that each branch "should have a will of its own"; this in turn requires, strictly speaking, that all appointments to the three branches "be drawn from the same fountain of authority, the people, through channels, having no communication whatever with one another." The separation of powers presupposes separate derivations from the people, if only to prevent any one branch from preempting the right to speak in the name of the people. In a government wholly popular, the independence of the branches of government vis-à-vis one another rests on the separate dependence of each on the sovereign people.[55] This dependence is, however, separate but unequal.

Although each branch of government has its connection with the people, each also has a certain distance or separation from them. *"The total exclusion of the people in their collective capacity* from any share" in the American republics forms the "true distinction" between them and the ancient republics. Decisive as this difference may be, further distinctions are to be drawn, no less interesting, within the structure of the American republic. Nowhere is the separation from the people more complete and more necessary than in the judicial branch. If there is to be a judiciary equal to its tasks and adequate for the preservation of liberty, there must be some relaxation of the principle of unmediated derivations from the people. That this relaxation is politically safe is suggested by two considerations. The peculiar qualifications and qualities of the judges remind us that we are discussing the "least dangerous" branch and hence the one in least need of direct popular control. Then, too, the permanent tenure with which judges hold office entails the least risk that their will may be hostage to the appointing power. There must, moreover, be a departure from "the characteristic policy of republican government" (popular election of rulers) and from the "most effectual" means of maintaining "a proper responsibility to the people" (limited terms of appointment).[56] The cause of free government requires a qualification of popular government.

Adherence to the republican principle, to the spirit of a government wholly popular, in no way entails "an unqualified complaisance to every sudden breeze of passion, or to every transient impulse which the people may receive from the arts of men, who flatter their prejudices to betray their interests." Publius, like Rousseau, knew that while "the people commonly *intend* the PUBLIC GOOD," they do not always "*reason right* about the *means* of promoting it." Indeed, the deepest justification of a separate and independent judiciary may be the expectation that, more often than is politically safe, "the interests of the people are at variance with their inclinations." If the "republican principle demands, that the deliberate sense of the community should govern the conduct of those to whom they entrust the management of their affairs," it also imposes a "duty" on "the guardians of those interests" to call the people to their senses or at least to give the people the chance to come to their senses. A government ought to have an unlimited range of powers, adequate to its objects and "free from every other control, but a regard to the public good and to the sense of the people."[57] A free government is one in which the sense of the people or the sense of the majority is controlling.

But to secure the public good in a manner compatible with the republican principle requires that the deliberate sense of the community prevail. And that sense is not taken simply or unqualifiedly from what the people or a majority say to their legislative representatives at any given moment. The "deliberate sense" is found in a blend of voices, from the people and their representatives, direct and remote, present and past.[58] In the extreme, critical, and interesting case, that sense may be taken from what "men, who [have] courage and magnanimity enough to serve them at the peril of their displeasure" declare to be in the people's interest. Insofar as these forms of resistance to temporary passions refer to the protection of minorities, securing the rights of all may be said to have a democratic source. Thus the popular credentials of the American regime are in no way impugned by asserting "that the whole power of the proposed government is to be in the hands of the representatives of the people" rather than in the hands of the people themselves. More than this was neither necessary nor safe, in Publius's eyes. Ultimately, the people's "cool and deliberate sense" prevails over the views of their rulers; but at any given moment, their freely chosen rulers act "to suspend the blow meditated by the people against themselves."[59]

In such a context Publius could look forward to the judiciary's "faithful performance of so arduous a duty" as guarding the Constitution against legislative encroachments and to the thwarting of certain popular "ill humours" by the judges. When the separate judicial establishment performs its distinct function and when it serves as a complicating element in the system of checks and balances, the judiciary is but one of the three branches of the government and as such is unexceptionable. But at still another level—transcending its other functions and implied in the technical knowledge needed by this branch of government alone—the judiciary acts as a special guardian of the principles of the Constitution. In this role it is no longer merely one of three and no longer weak. To the extent that it can remove itself from its popular source of power, the judiciary is able to display and to act in its unique character. Ultimately, the judges ought to hold their office with permanent tenure to sustain their "necessary independence" of the executive and the legislature and the people. If such tenure did not in fact "soon destroy all sense of dependence," if fear and a concern for popularity were to affect the quality of justice, the complications and safeguards of the Constitution would be a hollow joke.[60] Uniquely situated and uniquely protected, the judges were not expected to behave like ordinary men.

For Publius it was sufficient to remind "considerate men of every description" of the larger political benefits to be derived from a judiciary whose temper was marked by "integrity and moderation." The tone and quality of the highest national court would prove decisive for the entire administration of justice since

> the national and state systems are to be regarded as ONE WHOLE. The courts of the latter will of course be natural auxiliaries to the execution of the laws of the union, and an appeal from them will as naturally lie to that tribunal, which is destined to unite and assimilate the principles of national justice and the rules of national decisions.

Such a tribunal, so placed, could display political wisdom as well as legal craftsmanship. It opportunities and risks would be correlative.

Publius could safely have adopted as his own Aratus's understanding of the political position of the North Carolina courts:

> The *Judicial* of our democracy runs an equal pace with a monarchical judiciary, but steps forward to an almost undetermined distance—not only acting in all law occurrences . . . as the monarchical judiciary; but from the nature of our government, as may be easily deduced from the constitution itself, *pro salutate reipublicae*, it advances higher, and becomes the *equilibrium* or *pendulum* thereof.[61]

The national judiciary—independent, public-spirited, and impelled by a pride in its special competence—was expected to serve as an instrument and symbol of the power of "a more perfect Union." Such an understanding was clear and widespread.[62] But it was debatable whether more should be expected of the justices, that is, whether their political counsel should be sought and indeed required for making public policy. The Constitutional Convention repeatedly discussed a "council of revision" (first proposed by Governor Edmund Randolph in his presentation of the Virginia Plan and presumably modeled after the New York arrangement); these discussions revealed quite differing views about the province and function of judicial power. According to the Virginia Plan, a council of revision, composed of the national executive and "a convenient number" of the national judiciary, would possess a qualified veto over every act of the national legislature, including the latter's act of negativing any state law "contravening in the opinion of the National Legislature the articles of Union."[63]

The involvement of the judiciary in this automatic review of all national legislative authority was the occasion of much debate. Madison saw in this involvement an apt way of bolstering a chief executive who was all too likely to be in need of whatever support he could get and perhaps also in need of being reminded of his duty. According to this argument, the American chief executive, representing the monarchic principle (and the responsibilities and temptations of solitary rule), needed to be supported and restrained in a manner that took due account of the entire republican setting in which he would act. "Mr. Elseworth," who was to be the principal draftsman of the Judiciary Act and its jealous manager through committee and floor debates, "approved heartily of the motion" for a council of revision: "The aid of the judges will give more wisdom & firmness to the Executive." Madison, early in the debates, drew attention to a power of review that was not exhausted by considerations of constitutionality:

> In short, whether the object of the revisionary power was to restrain the Legislature from encroaching on the other co-or-

dinate Departments, or on the rights of the people at large; or from passing laws unwise in their principle, or incorrect in their form, the utility of annexing the wisdom and weight of the Judiciary to the Executive seemed incontestable.

This expectation that the judges would not limit themselves to judgments of constitutionality—and ought not to so limit themselves—was made even more forcefully by Wilson:

> Laws may be unjust, may be unwise, may be dangerous, may be destructive; and yet not be so unconstitutional as to justify the Judges in refusing to give them effect. Let them have a share in the Revisionary power, and they will have an opportunity of taking notice of these characters of a law, and of counteracting, by the weight of their opinions the improper views of the Legislature.[64]

These arguments, however, were unavailing. The notion that judges ought to be charged explicitly with the delicate task of assessing the wisdom of proposed legislation was successfully attacked on grounds of competence and propriety. Nathaniel Gorham doubted whether as judges they were "to be presumed to possess any peculiar knowledge of the mere policy of public measures." Elbridge Gerry saw in the proposal "an improper coalition": "It was making Statesmen of the Judges; and setting them up as the guardians of the Rights of the people." So far was this trust mistaken, that he feared that the executive could rather "be covered by the sanction & seduced by the sophistry of the Judges." Although the council of revision lacked nothing in the way of able and persistent advocates, it was decisively rejected. In a final effort to extend the formal influence of the judiciary in the new government, Gouverneur Morris proposed a "council of state" to assist and advise the president. Heading the list of cabinet officers was to be the

> Chief Justice of the Supreme Court, who shall from time to time recommend such alterations of and additions to the laws of the U.S. as may in his opinion be necessary to the due administration of Justice, and such as may promote useful learning and inculcate sound morality throughout the Union.

Having once been referred to the Committee of Detail, this proposal never emerged again. Faced with clearly stated alternatives, the majority of the Convention appear to have been of the mind that "it is impossible to keep the Judges too distinct from every other avocation than that of expounding the laws."[65]

We are left with an equivocal conclusion: while some of the leading framers of the Constitution proposed making use of the judges' political wisdom—and indeed in so recommending implied that the judges would not otherwise have these broader duties or opportunities—the majority of the Constitutional Convention (and even the leading defenders of its work) emphatically rejected such a plan on the grounds that judges ought to be kept "judicial." The attack on the revisionary power, then, was mounted mainly for the sake of securing the proper separation of powers, that is, for the sake of an effective check on the other branches of government. But the ground of that attack was the notion that it is best that judges do what they are trained for.[66] Yet that technical competence points to another, higher judicial function—safeguarding the legal and political principles of the regime. Indeed, those very characteristics of the judiciary so well set forth in *Federalist* 78 make it more likely that the purposes envisioned for the council of revision are better served under the present arrangement. The judiciary can better perform its higher function indirectly, through its more "technical" acts, than directly. The judges—and the judges alone of all government officials—needed to have special training and character in order to do their job at all. Set apart from most citizens by temperament, education, acquired tastes, and responsibilities, the judges (at their best) could make the most of such opportunities as came their way to act as faithful sustainers and guardians of the regime. The political grand jury charge was one response to that challenge but not the last.

Political Limits and Judicial Discretion

An examination of the Supreme Court's work during its first decade of circuit riding discloses that the judges were concerned about educating their audience politically. Further, evidence of the early intentions and expectations for the national judiciary points to a political role for the courts. This conception starts from the premise that "government must be framed for man as he is, and not for man as he would be if he were free from vice." It is not embarrassed when discussing the likelihood that "the faithful discharge" of the judicial power will not win the general acclaim and support of a people no longer virtuous; rather, this conception of judicial power flatly accepts the great probability of some significant political tension when the court acts as an equilibrium *pro salute reipublicae*: "We are well aware this doctrine will sound ruffly in the ears of many of our demagogues of power."[67]

Recognizing the near certainty of heated confrontations, the early justices took it upon themselves to mold public sentiment to the degree that it lay in their power to do so. Teaching a people how to be good republicans meant more than making judicial power secure. It would have the far greater effect of making the republicans safe for the republic. The justices (in this respect anticipating Abraham Lincoln) acted on the understanding that "in this and like communities, public sentiment is everything." On this premise they sought to mold and educate that public. Doing so presupposed an educable people as well as a population who are emphatically citizens. For yet another member of the second generation, John Quincy Adams, this was the lesson to be drawn from the revolutionary generation's deeds.

> This was the platform upon which the Constitution of the United States had been erected. Its VIRTUES, its republican character, consisted in its conformity to the principles proclaimed in the Declaration of Independence, and as its administration must necessarily be always pliable to the fluctuating varieties of public opinion; its stability and duration by a like overruling and irresistible necessity, was to depend upon the stability and duration in the hearts and minds of the people of that *virtue*, or in other words, of those principles proclaimed in the Declaration of Independence, and embodied in the Constitution of the United States.

The first justices of the Supreme Court acted in such a way as to counter the habit of mind that insisted that "there is no right principle of action but *self-interest*" and to inculcate civic virtue. More, perhaps, than any other branch of the government, they were in a position and of a character to do so.[68]

Subsequent changes in the organization of the courts and in the style of political discourse led the Supreme Court to give up the political charge. Yet in so doing, the justices merely replaced one mode of shaping public beliefs and opinions with another—one that could be equally, probably more, effective. Much of Chief Justice John Marshall's greatness lay in his success in, so to speak, putting the Supreme Court as a whole on circuit. By explicitly taking the higher role of guardian of the principles of the regime and by speaking with one voice through opinions of the court, the Supreme Court, under Marshall's politic and artful guidance, was able to survive and even to prevail in ways not easily foreseeable in 1801. Today the Supreme Court is, in some respects, more evidently and continuously on circuit and its work more often before the public eye than the warmest supporters of circuit riding could have hoped.

One of the reasons Congress persisted in requiring members of the Supreme Court to ride circuit in the nineteenth century was a fear of the political consequences of isolating the judiciary from its public. The argument that was made pointed perhaps as much to judges learning as to judges teaching. Precisely because judges have "political functions to discharge," they should be attentive to their political support; "they should be conversant with public opinion, and imbibe the spirit of the times." Although not important alone, the judges should have a clear and vivid sense of being tethered but not shackled to public opinion. Perhaps even more important, in the long run, the people at large should have a clear and vivid sense that "a harmony of opinion and of action" exists between the Supreme Court and the inferior courts and between the judiciary and the people for whom it is meant to establish justice. "In a Government founded on opinion, it is necessary that the People should be satisfied with judicial decisions."[69]

In requiring circuit duty, Congress acted as though it believed that this harmony could be fostered by the confrontation of judges with a larger public of lawyers, court officials, litigants, and bystanders. In that encounter the political charge after the Chase impeachment was neither appropriate nor significant, but the judges could resort to another way of teaching, more politic and effective because more obviously "judicial," and hence less visible. Then, as now, the judges had the option of teaching by cases. By their decisions, and especially through a coherent explanation of the grounds of their decisions, the judges could partially introduce the language of the law into the vulgar tongue. And more important, they could transfer to the minds of the citizens the modes of thought lying behind legal language and the notions of right fundamental to the regime. The political sophistication needed, then and now, for conveying these lessons is surpassed only by the sense of political responsibility that continues to set judges the task of being republican schoolmasters.

8

The Supreme Court and Public Policy

Herman Schwartz

The issue of the Supreme Court and public policy raises the fundamental question about the role of the judiciary in American democracy: How much power should this unaccountable, countermajoritarian institution exercise? I will focus on two current issues arising from that basic question: (1) Whether the Court should provide more protection for property rights and (2) what the Court's proper role in statutory construction is.

Public Policy or Law?

To the ordinary person, the title of this essay is itself a piece of the puzzle I will discuss: Doesn't the Court always deal with public policy, no matter what it does? Does the phrase have a special lawyer's meaning, and if so, isn't that an artificial meaning?

The answer to both these questions is yes. In American and British law, the phrase "public policy" has come to have a rather special meaning, one easier to adumbrate in functional terms than to define or even to identify. Unlike Justice Potter Stewart's claim about obscenity—despite his doubts about whether he could define it, he said, "I know it when I see it"[1]—public policy can be neither defined satisfactorily nor readily known when seen. Its functional "definition" is essentially a negative question-begging conclusion: "public policy" refers to matters that are not law, and therefore not the business of the judiciary but of the other governmental branches. But as to what these nonlaw matters are, or even whether these distinctions are feasible, the definition offers not a clue.

The distinction between public policy, by whatever name, and law is an old one. As far back as 1803, in *Marbury v. Madison*, Chief Justice John Marshall wrote that "questions, in their nature political, or which are, by the constitution and laws submitted to the executive, can never be made in this court."[2] Indeed, historians as far apart in their attitudes as Jennifer Nedelsky and George Haskins are agreed that Marshall's great contribution was to develop the distinction between law and politics, reserving the former for the courts and the latter for the other branches. A few decades later an English judge of no particular note uttered a line that gave him a shred of immortality: "Public policy is an unruly and dangerous horse to ride."[3] In somewhat more detail, a statement by a British judge in 1853 reflects the conventional view on both sides of the Atlantic:

> Public policy is a vague and unsatisfactory term [that] . . . in its ordinary sense mean[s] "political expedience" or that which is best for the common good of the community. . . . It is the province of the statesman, and not the lawyer, to discuss, and of the Legislature to determine what is best for the public good and to provide for it by proper enactment. It is the province of the Judge to expound the law only . . . not to speculate upon what is the best in his opinion for the advantage of the community.[4]

More recently, American judges like Potter Stewart, Warren Burger, and Oliver Wendell Holmes have complained that the Court was getting into policy and going beyond the law. Although they sometimes shared the Court's policy judgments, they did not think the Court should adopt these positions as a matter of constitutional law.[5]

Their notion seems to be that law involves some kind of arcane science that is above politics and partisanship, calling only for exposition of what is revealed after long study by a disinterested value-neutral mind, whereas public policy involves judgments of "what is best for the public good."[6] Obviously, legal realism and the even sharper criticism of the critical legal studies movement have destroyed the plausibility of this distinction. In deciding many of the most important cases, and particularly—though not exclusively—constitutional issues, courts must consider whatever is involved in the common-sense notion of public policy as "the public good." In these cases the real distinction is not between public policy and law but between different kinds of public policy, some of which are indeed only for the legislative branches and some of which are appropriate for judicial determination. The hard question is which kinds are for which branch.

Nevertheless, the claim for some platonically distinguishable difference between law and policy continues to be made. It underlies, for example, the argument always made on behalf of judicial nominees that the nomination process should be lifted out of politics and that only neutral value-free factors—intelligence, integrity, experience—should be considered and not the nominee's views on abortion or civil rights. Why this kind of argument is given even a polite reception remains a mystery except perhaps for the continuing power of the law-policy distinction. For if one thing is clear to everyone, Supreme Court (and often lower court) nominations are almost always intended to implement the president's vision of what is an appropriate public policy for the nation, what is best for the public good.[7] Given the power of the Supreme Court in American life, a president would be untrue to his oath if he acted any other way. And nobody is really fooled, for whether a Republican president nominates Robert Bork or a Democrat nominates Abe Fortas as chief justice, the opposition goes after him for his views on what is best for the public good, and the supporters protest that only the nominee's brains and character should be considered.[8]

The continuing mythological strength of the law–public policy distinction thus would seem to have little or no impact on the nomination process since it is not taken too seriously, at least in this context. But a real impact appears not in the occasional controversial Supreme Court nominee like Bork or even David Souter but in the less contentious Supreme Court nominations and in lower court appointments. The distinction makes it easier for the Senate to ignore the impact on public policy of these "noncontroversial" selections and to let them slide through with only perfunctory scrutiny. Senators do not like these fights anyway, for they are messy and have no political payoff unless the nomination affects the home state directly, which nominations to the Supreme Court and court of appeals rarely do.

Europeans are much more honest about this. They have recognized that their constitutional courts are in the business of making public policy. Indeed, the German court has the authority to ban political parties for being Nazi or Communist; the Czechoslovak Constitutional Court, created in February 1991, has a similar authority, as well as jurisdiction over electoral issues. Each has also been given jurisdiction over delicate questions of federalism and over basic human rights questions; the German and French courts, for example, have each taken on the abortion issue.[9]

In recognition of the obvious policy-oriented jurisdiction of these courts, all these countries have provided for an explicit political selection process. As the leading student of the German court put it, "The rules themselves could hardly be more calculated to politicize the selection process," for the members of the court are chosen by the political parties and other political forces, such as the state ministers and state government representatives.[10] In Belgium and Czechoslovakia the national divisions between Czechs and Slovaks, Flemings and Walloons must be reflected in the composition of the constitutional court. Yet Mauro Cappelletti, the foremost student of constitutional courts and comparative judicial review, and others have concluded that these politically chosen judges act objectively and impartially, though not without reflecting and expressing their values.[11]

Before turning to the actual operation of public policy considerations in the two areas I wish to discuss—constitutional protection for property rights and statutory construction—a brief discussion of two lesser-known contexts in which the distinction between law and public policy operates will illustrate both where it belongs and where it is only a smoke screen for a decision based on public policy considerations.

Political Questions. The first, not surprisingly, is the area of political questions. Going back to Marshall in *Marbury,* our courts have always set apart one set of issues that they will not even hear because they raise "political questions." Many of these issues arise in a foreign policy context, and for once the Court has been fairly straight about its reasons for not considering these issues. In Justice William J. Brennan's landmark opinion on political questions, in *Baker v. Carr,* he set out six factors that would induce the federal courts not to hear a case on this ground:

> a textually demonstrable constitutional commitment of the issue to a coordinate political department; or a lack of both liability and remedy judicially discoverable and manageable standards for resolving it; or the impossibility of deciding without an initial policy determination of a kind clearly for nonjudicial discretion; or the impossibility of a court's undertaking independent resolution without expressing lack of the respect due coordinate branches of government; or an unusual need for unquestioning adherence to a political decision already made; or the potentiality of embarrassment from multifarious pronouncements by various departments on one question.[12]

Most of these, particularly something like the lack of judicially manageable standards, are clearly functional: they focus on what the courts can do and the consequences of their action.

139

Standing Law. The other area with something like the law–public policy distinction is the mess known as standing law, where the Supreme Court has erected a barrier to litigants' entry into the federal courts for cases involving social and related issues. The decisions are ostensibly based on the technical legal notion that the Constitution requires someone filing a lawsuit to have a real interest in the outcome to ensure that he prosecutes the case wholeheartedly and the Court can thereby get a good picture of the controversy. In fact, the Court has developed the doctrine into a basis for requiring a complicated, expensive preliminary minitrial of such crucial issues as causation and harm. The explicit purpose and effect are to block access to the federal courts for challenges to official actions that at this stage of the suit are considered unconstitutional or illegal. Standing rules have been used to exclude cases involving civil rights, civil liberties, and other social causes,[13] although they have sometimes been manipulated to allow the Court to consider a challenge to something the validity of which the majority wants to uphold.[14] The justification for the strict standing rules, now explicit in a recent case like *Allen v. Wright* but adverted to in the earliest of the restrictive standing cases in 1971 and 1974, is that some areas are not proper for the courts to get into but are solely the jurisdiction of the popular branches: standing requirements are necessary to prevent the federal courts from becoming "virtual . . . continuing monitors of the wisdom and soundness of executive action."[15]

This justification, of course, makes the standing doctrine equivalent to the "political question" doctrine, though turning not on the functional matters set out in *Baker v. Carr* but on some notion of what is appropriate solely for the elected branches of government. As Justice John Paul Stevens pointed out in a recent dissent, "The strength of the plaintiff's interest [which is what standing law is concerned about] has nothing to do with whether the relief it seeks would intrude upon the prerogatives of other branches of government." Here as elsewhere the dissenters accused the majority of deciding these cases on the merits—and always against the challengers to the official action—in the guise of applying neutral legal principles about what is appropriate for the courts and what should be left to the democratic process.[16]

Where, then, is the line to be drawn between something called law and something called public policy, the former considered proper for the courts, that is, ultimately the Supreme Court, and the latter not? More concretely and functionally, in what areas should this essentially unaccountable countermajoritarian institution, the Supreme Court, invoke its awesome power of annulling the judgments and enactments of the democratically elected branches either to protect or expand established rights or to create new ones?

Property Rights

Let us return to the matter of constitutional protection for property rights, one context in which the question has recently arisen: Should the Court go back to the attitude that has dominated most of its history and abandon its recent indifference to property values in order to create what the *Wall Street Journal* calls economic civil rights?

Historical View. Whatever the meaning of "property" either in our formative years or today,[17] until recently protecting those who have tangible property, or to put it more plainly, material wealth, from efforts at public control, redistribution, or the development of countervailing powers such as unions or consumers, had clearly been a primary concern of the Supreme Court from the beginning. Regardless of whether Madison would have approved of *Lochner v. New York*,[18] and whether his conception of "property" encompassed spiritual values of conscience and belief, *Federalist* 10 makes it clear that he was unhappy about the "rage for paper money, the abolition of debts, for an equal division of property," which he characterized as "improper or wicked project[s]."[19] And although property rights have always been limited for the public good,[20] the Federalists' concern for its protection has persisted and generally dominated American constitutional law until comparatively recently. Whether the reliance was on the contract clause, as in the *Dartmouth College* case and *Fletcher v. Peck*,[21] or natural law, as in Justice William Johnson's concurrence in *Fletcher*,[22] or the due process clause, as in *Dred Scott* and *Lochner*, or a narrow reading of the federal commerce clause and the federal taxing and spending powers, as in *E. C. Knight*, *Hammer v. Dagenhart* (child labor),[23] and the New Deal cases, the goal has generally been to protect vested property, or to put it plainly, those who have money against those who do not.

For our purposes, the most significant efforts involved the contract clause and the due process clause, for these purported to lift the issue out of "politics," into the realm of higher law, which is beyond policy. The contract clause had its heyday during the first third of the nineteenth century and then declined in importance, except for municipal bond cases, until about 1977, when it enjoyed a momentary revival.[24] As we know, the due process and to some extent the equal protection clause governed these cases from 1897 through the 1930s. By 1963, however, the Court had almost abdicated any scrutiny whatsoever of economic regulation, invoking the usual talk about policy and law.[25]

Though probably a gross oversimplification, the Court's initial protection for property has not seemed much out of line with what most Americans have wanted. C. Peter Magrath has pointed out that whereas many of Marshall's decisions involving the contract clause "may have been 'conservative' . . . they did not do violence to the national political consensus. . . . [T]he nineteenth century American . . . if he was not already, hoped soon to be his own little capitalist."[26] That consensus may have continued into the first third of the twentieth century as well, at least until the depression, when both the Court and the country changed radically in their attitude toward property, redistribution, and government regulation.

Economic Civil Rights. Today voices are again being raised publicly, both in scholarly settings and in media like the *Wall Street Journal*, for restoring property rights to the pantheon of highly protected constitutional rights. The most extreme form of this argument has been presented by Professors Richard Epstein of the University of Chicago Law School and Bernard Siegan of the San Diego Law School, who is also a product of the Chicago Law School. Their argument is that the Constitution was built around a concern for property rights and that this is crucial for both individual liberty and economic prosperity. Their target is any form of redistribution that does not benefit both distributee and distributor equally. Their argument comes down to an attack on virtually every kind of governmental check on property rights, including almost every kind of regulation: estate and gift taxes, urban renewal, zoning, rent control, land reform, licensing, most welfare laws, almost all labor legislation, minimum wage and maximum hours legislation, and more. As Epstein proclaims, "My position invalidates much of the twentieth century legislation."[27]

A more restrained critique of the demotion of economic rights appears in the late Robert McCloskey's classic 1963 article, "Economic Due Process and the Supreme Court: An Exhumation and Reburial."[28] He questions each of the assumptions that give the preferred freedoms—such as speech and religion—higher constitutional status than economic rights of property and contract: Are rights of expression and the other preferred freedoms more important than economic freedom? Are they that much more necessary to self-government? Insofar as the Court's role is to protect legislatively impotent minorities, doesn't this include many economic groups consisting of far-from-affluent people like barmaids or retired railroad workers?[29] Is the Court necessarily more competent in areas of speech or civil rights than in economic matters?

If I understand McCloskey, his reply is: Although there are no satisfactory answers to these questions, the Court has undertaken so many difficult noneconomic matters like equality for minorities and free speech that "judicial economy" counsels letting "the cause of economic rights be left by the Supreme Court to lie in its uneasy grave."[30] That seems unsatisfactory. For one thing, whatever force that answer may have had in 1963, it has that force no longer, for the Court now seems to be withdrawing from the work with civil rights and civil liberties that McCloskey thought would tax its resources and prestige so much. Indeed, just in terms of workload, the 1990–1991 and 1991–1992 terms were the lightest in years, perhaps out of a conscious decision to reduce the role of the Court in American life.

Moreover, although the Court has largely withdrawn from adjudicating economic issues, thereby implicitly demoting the values at issue, it has not done so entirely. It continues, for example, to apply rational basis analysis to economic and social welfare cases, that is, a requirement that there be some reason for a regulation. This is indeed feeble, but it is not nothing. In more than a few cases where economic and social rights such as subsistence, education, medical care, or food were involved, the Court has struck down the regulation under one constitutional rubric or another, such as equal protection, due process, and the right to travel.[31] And in some cases that have sustained economic regulations, three and sometimes four justices have dissented.[32] Even the recent punitive damages case, which rebuffed a due process challenge to high punitive damages, left open the possibility that in some cases the Court might go the other way.[33] In the interstate commerce area, the Court has used the equal protection clause to strike down a discriminatory Alabama tax that was immune to commerce clause treatment because the McCarran-Ferguson Act exempts insurance from restraints of the commerce clause.[34]

It has also been suggested that some of the recent takings cases reinstate property rights to a high value, although this is still unclear. Indisputably, however, the Court has given wealth an enormous political boost by equating political expenditure with speech, making such expenditures almost uncontrollable by Congress.[35]

Society's Choices. None of this amounts to a true resurrection, however, and there are good reasons for refusing to do so. I do not mean to denigrate the importance of economic rights. It is difficult to exercise political rights fully or to experience much spiritual benefit from freedom of expression or association if one is hungry or without a job, as shown by the apathy of poor people toward politics and voting.

But there is a great deal of sense in what Lord Radcliffe, a wise English judge, wrote in a little book in 1960 about the proper place of public policy in the common law, an English analogue to our constitutional law. First deploring the English courts' "mistak[ing] a fashion in economic thinking or social philosophy for the basic faith

143

to which they are committed . . . [which is protection for] the complex of liberties which are needed to preserve the freedom of the human spirit," he went on to say:

> We all feel that there are relationships arising out of human institutions which deserve special protection from outside invasion or even voluntary relinquishment: marital and parental relationships, freedom of religious worship, freedom of association, freedom of labor, and freedom of artistic and productive expression.[36]

Moreover, as more than a few have pointed out, the law of property and contract is not something given on Mount Sinai but a human construct. To give great protection to contracts against state regulation, to protect real property against government zoning or other laws, to strike down wages or hours legislation—all this is to protect legal or other arrangements that were created by society in the first place and that depend on society's protection. A contract is of value only because society chooses to enforce the contracting parties' agreements; some contracts will not be enforced, for they are against public morals or too unfair. As Laurence Tribe has written in his chapter on takings and the contract clause, in these cases the law protects "settled expectations," but these expectations are settled only because of a socially created set of legal arrangements that could well have been created differently and sometimes have been.[37] Indeed, the Court has said in contract clause cases that where an industry is subject to established government regulation, the expectations are not settled and are therefore not entitled to protection under the contract clause.[38]

The issue here is really this: Is it good for the society for this unaccountable countermajoritarian institution to overrule the elected branches in economic matters? That it is sometimes appropriate is now a closed question. The question is when, and that turns on the questions McCloskey asked: When is it needed? When is it workable? And if both questions are answered positively, how much will it cost, in whatever currency is relevant, that is, prestige, moral authority, weakening of the other branches, and frustration of the democratic will?

I tried to answer some of these questions a few years ago, and I would like simply to incorporate some of those responses with some additional remarks. And I would like to concentrate my response not on all legislation affecting property rights but on the kinds of enactments that Epstein, Siegan, and their colleagues would like to strike down.

In the first place, in many of these cases, the legislature is preferring one person's or group's property to another. In *Hawaii Housing Authority v. Midkiff,* a case upholding Hawaiian land reform law and sharply criticized by Professor Epstein, the Court was clearly favoring one economic group while disadvantaging another; in wage-hour legislation, entry barriers, price controls, and similar matters—all measures that the advocates of economic rights would strike down—the Court is disadvantaging one group of property holders and favoring another.[39]

Why should the Court step in on behalf of one economic group to reverse a legislative judgment in favor of another? Epstein considers the National Labor Relations Act unconstitutional,[40] but why should courts overrule legislatures to favor the owners of property in capital over the owners of property in labor? After all, Locke himself said that labor justified property rights in the first place.[41] In the Hawaiian land reform case, why favor the owners of the lands to be broken up over the existing lessees, who were to be allowed to buy the land? Where rent control is concerned, why favor the landlord over the tenant? All have property rights of one kind or another.

To protect economic rights at the expense of the democratic process is usually to favor the status quo. But not always, for the economic rights at issue may be for the benefit of a dynamic economic entity against some other, more established one. In America today, however, most economic rights seeking constitutional protection are likely to be those of the haves against the have-nots.

And that is what the Epstein-Siegan view almost explicitly seeks. Professor Epstein wants the Court consistently to favor the haves, those who own or possess property or things, for his primary goal is to prevent redistribution of wealth that is intended to enhance equality or to make up for unequal bargaining power.[42] Apart from the merits of such a preference, few things would aggravate class conflict more than the perception that the Court is explicitly allied with the few who have wealth and power against the many who have neither. The bitter fights in 1801 over John Adams's effort to pack the federal courts to create a Federalist rear guard against Jeffersonian democracy and the turmoil in the early 1930s are vivid historical examples of the trouble such judicial favoritism can produce.

Economic Factionalism. The economic civil rights view also plunges the Court into the center of economic struggle, into the pit of economic factionalism. As long ago as *Federalist* 10, Madison stressed the bitterness of economic strife:

> [T]he most common and durable source of factions has been the various and unequal distribution of property. Those who hold and those who are without property have ever formed

distinct interests in society. Those who are creditors, and those who are debtors, fall under a like discrimination. A landed interest, a manufacturing interest, a mercantile interest, a moneyed interest, with many lesser interests, grow up of necessity in civilized nations, and divide them into different classes, actuated by different sentiments and views. *The regulation of these various and interfering interests forms the principal task of modern legislation, and involves the spirit of party and faction in the necessary and ordinary operations of the government* [emphasis added].[43]

He thought that the wealthy minority would always be at the mercy of the less affluent majority, but that certainly does not seem to be true today.

In contrast with Madison's statement, which stresses the inextricable link between property rights and politics, consider the pronouncement about basic First Amendment freedoms by Justice Robert H. Jackson in the West Virginia flag salute cases: "The very purpose of the Bill of Rights was to withdraw certain subjects from the vicissitudes of political controversy, to place them *beyond the reach of majorities and officials* and to establish them as legal principles to be applied by the courts."[44] Thomas Jefferson thought the same, as he wrote to Madison when explaining that a bill of rights was necessary so that the courts could protect them as a matter of law.[45]

There may also be historical support for giving much more judicial protection for speech and other First Amendment rights, such as religion and the press. Contrary to the Nedelsky view, William Nelson has suggested that where moral questions were concerned, the absence of police, bureaucracies, and armies made consensus necessary for enforcement. Where economic matters were at issue, the colonists lived and accepted continuing controversy.[46]

Admittedly, the "subjects" of these "legal principles" do not always stay "withdraw[n] . . . from the vicissitudes of political controversy," as the abortion issue shows. But flag burning is a good illustration of the point. After a relatively brief and intense political flurry as the administration tried to make political capital from the initial outrage of many Americans at the Court's decision,[47] sober second thought reasserted itself. A consensus developed that the First Amendment right of expression was involved and that it is too dangerous to tamper with it. The issue went away. It is hard to believe that that would be the outcome of an economic struggle.

Judicial Activism. Economic struggle has always been the stuff of politics. Such an insistence on creating economic civil rights to veto outcomes of the legislative struggle—primarily state and local struggles that are varied, complex, difficult to understand without knowing local conditions, and often intensely partisan—makes the federal courts the arbiters in these essentially political matters. The results severely damage the federal courts' authority, on which their role in our system depends. The great "self-inflicted wounds"[48] suffered by the Supreme Court— *Dred Scott*, the legal tender cases, and the decision striking down the income tax[49]—were all explicitly connected with property rights, as were the pre–New Deal decisions (although *Dred Scott* was also a race case), and are precisely the kind (except perhaps again for *Dred Scott*) that would be necessary for the Court to protect property rights vigorously.

We depend on judicial review, but it fits somewhat uneasily into a democratic system. If the pre–New Deal period teaches anything, it is that the nation does not want judicial review to be a frequently exercised constitutional veto of democratically created measures to deal with complex economic and social problems.

And that is one of the most important considerations of all: there is no indication that the nation wants this kind of judicial activism. During the bicentennial celebrations, the praise lavished everywhere on our Constitution was not primarily for the original 1787 text itself but really for the freedom of speech, press, and religion in the Bill of Rights. Protecting those rights is what the country wants from the Court. By contrast, the Court's activities in protecting property rights in this century aroused great resentment once before, and might well do so again.

There is another factor to consider when urging equality of property rights with rights such as speech, press, and religion. In that situation the federal courts and ultimately the Supreme Court would be forced to deal with an enormous mass of litigation. There are volumes and volumes of economic and social legislation. Close review of this legislation would overload the federal courts and make them activist beyond anything we now know.

The proponents of economic rights face another serious problem, workability. The current presumption in favor of legislative action that adversely affects those rights is great.[50] Epstein and Siegan would change that, not by swinging all the way over to strict scrutiny of any public economic control, which would defeat virtually every effort at control—a result even the *Wall Street Journal* probably would not welcome—but by using an intermediate level of review of the kind we currently employ for scrutiny of classifications based on gender or illegitimacy: the classification "must serve important governmental objectives and must be substantially related to achievement of those objectives."[51]

Such an intermediate level of scrutiny for regulation of property rights would add methodological misery to the political thicket because it is the hardest of all standards to apply and to make consistent. What an "important" objective is and who should determine whether an objective is sufficiently important are highly disputable questions. And when is a measure "substantially related to" that objective, as opposed to a weaker link? As then-Justice William Rehnquist noted in his dissenting opinion in *Craig v. Boren*, the addition of an intermediate level of review creates an opportunity for excessive subjectivity on the part of judges.[52] The gender and illegitimacy cases illustrate the indeterminacy of intermediate review—not only are the decisions sharply divided, but it is difficult to find any real consistency among them.[53]

The problems with intermediate review are particularly acute in economic matters. Many of the economic regulatory, tax, and other legislative and administrative acts that adversely affect one group's property rights grow out of complex economic and social contexts.[54] The determination of the substantiality of the link between means and ends calls for a detailed knowledge of the background and an experienced judgment as to what will, or perhaps only may, work. The means-end link is simply too fact-specific for an outsider like a distant judge to assess substantiality, a task obviated by the rational basis test.

Other examples of the difficulties the Court would face were it to undertake an intermediate analysis of property rights appear from Epstein's own analysis of some decisions.[55] He severely criticizes, for example, *Midkiff*, the Hawaiian land reform case, for adopting the wrong solution to a "market failure problem." He writes: "The better place to look for land shortages and high prices is in the extensive network of state land use regulations that is today beyond constitutional challenge, even though it facilitates the very oligopolist practices that land reform statutes are said to counteract."[56] That is surely a matter on which experts can reasonably differ. How, therefore, can courts sensibly decide such a question?

Professor Siegan also suggests that the government must show that "a similar result cannot be achieved by less drastic means." As Judge Bork commented about this, the test "is loaded with ambiguities and disguised tradeoffs. . . . A court undertaking such matters will have no guidance other than its own sense of legislative prudence" about whether a different measure will in fact produce a sufficiently "similar" result.[57] All in all, there is too little to gain and too much to lose for the Court to abandon its currently restrained enthusiasm for judicial protection for economic rights.[58]

Statutory Construction

The second matter I want to cover is statutory construction and the relevance of legislative history in construing statutes. A recent great controversy concerned the relevance of the original intent of constitutional provisions. Those who sought to narrow and to limit constitutional protection for individual rights, such as Edwin Meese, the former attorney general, and Judge Bork, argued that the only way to control judicial arbitrariness and adventurism was to restrict constitutional interpretation to the original intent of the framers.[59] In practice, "judicial arbitrariness" meant judicial recognition of a right to use contraception or to have an abortion,[60] the incorporation of the Bill of Rights into the Fourteenth Amendment so that it binds state and local officials as well as federal,[61] and the raising of a high wall of separation between church and state.[62]

That issue seems to have faded. The primary arguments against it included the concern that unless the courts went beyond original intent, we would straitjacket the Constitution in knee breeches and wigs and prevent it from growing; also the historical record is usually so obscure that ascertaining the original intent is often almost impossible.[63]

With respect to statutes, however, it is paradoxical that conservative jurists have all but abandoned the concept of "intent." In the past fifty to sixty years there has not been much dispute over the proposition that, as former Chief Judge Patricia M. Wald recently put it, "it is the business of the courts to try and enforce . . . [statutes] as Congress meant them to be enforced."[64] It is not that difficult to amend statutes, to respond to changing needs, and it is often not difficult to ascertain the legislative intent from the legislative history if the statute is not clear, as is so often the case.

Lately, however, some conservative judges, most notably Justice Antonin Scalia and Judge Alex Kozinski, have tired of the judicial restraint that they originally found so useful. Instead, they have called for vigorous judicial activism where one would least expect it: statutory construction. While not calling for the application of public policy considerations to the construction of statutes—that would be a bit too blatant—Justice Scalia has urged judges to ignore legislative history as "irrelevant." Instead, they should focus on "rationalizing the law," "making a harmonious whole out of the system of laws." In earlier speeches reported at his confirmation hearing in 1986, he said, "Asking what the legislators intended . . . is quite the wrong question." Resort to committee reports, congressional debates, and other standard methods of learning what Congress wanted to achieve is wrong, for they do not reflect the views of the "full Congress." They are staff products, not read by members of Congress, and not intended to inform them but to influence the courts or to satisfy lobbyists. The fact that the planned and agreed-upon legislative history avoids the need for a specific legislative amendment is also a bad thing for Justice Scalia. The fact that Congress approved one judicial interpretation of an

149

unclear provision rather than another should be ignored by courts. Instead, all ambiguities should be left to the administrative agencies and the courts. A statute should be read, according to Justice Scalia, not in keeping with what most members understood but with the meaning that is "most in accord with context and ordinary usage, . . . [and] with the surrounding body of law"—all of which judges of course decide. The goal of the judge is to "rationalize," to "harmonize" the corpus juris of the law.[65]

Obviously, this is an invitation to freewheeling judicial control over statutes. It also misconstrues and misunderstands the nature of the legislative process. The "full Congress" rarely does anything, for there are too many matters for any individual member to cover. Party discipline, the existence of party whips and floor leaders, committee chairmanships—all these emphasize that on most issues, members of Congress must rely on their leaders. This does not justify judges ignoring what legislators have accepted through this delegation.

Moreover, Justice Scalia and Judge Kozinski misrepresent how committee reports and other authoritative legislative history are put together and treated. Although some legislative history is indeed manufactured, committee reports are taken seriously by Congress. They are often the subject of lengthy negotiation, for everyone expects them to be studied closely as the authoritative interpretation of the law. Even floor exchanges can be highly reliable indicators of legislative intent, for they are sometimes used by floor managers to assure colleagues that certain interpretations are either to be made or to be avoided; at least one such crucial exchange in the debate on the Civil Rights Restoration Act of 1988 avoided an irrelevant but intractable controversy over certain religious matters. And Justice Scalia is wrong in assuming that congressmen and senators do not read the reports— they are more likely to read the committee report, the official interpretation of a bill written in ordinary prose, than the bill itself, which is often technical and difficult. Of course much legislative history is worthless, but judges know this and are not fooled.

The Scalia approach intrudes the judge's own vision of public policy over that of the legislature even in areas that all are agreed are in the legislative domain. Preventing such intrusion is one reason why, as Justice Scalia has noted, critics of the pre–New Deal Court urged reliance on legislative history. For nowhere in the Constitution is a commission given to judges to assert their own views of the meaning of statutes—*Congress* has the legislative powers under Article I of our Constitution; that does not mean just enacting a group of words for judges to interpret and to apply as they see fit. It means deliberately setting norms, and the duty of judges is to apply those norms as

Congress intended them to be applied.

Justice Scalia and Judge Kozinski naturally stress that where the meaning is plain, judges should follow it; Judge Kozinski even goes so far as to suggest that reliance on legislative history encourages sloppiness and ambiguity. Only someone who has not tried to hammer out an agreement on language among people of sharply conflicting views can think sloppiness is the key problem. As a technical matter, it is not hard to write a relatively nonsloppy statute—the House and Senate Office of Legislative Counsel do it all the time, as well as is humanly possible. The problem is to reconcile often sharply conflicting views and to anticipate what cannot be foreseen, which creates the ambiguities.

But Justice Scalia is not so eager to follow even the apparent meaning, for as noted, his goal is to "harmonize," to "rationalize" the law. In one of his speeches, he rejects the view that "interpretative doubts . . . are to be resolved by judicial resort to an intention entertained by the lawmaking body at the time of enactment."[66] Instead, interpretive doubts are to be resolved by assessing the meaning that would reasonably have been conveyed to a citizen at the time the law was enacted, as modified by the relationship of the statute to later enactments, similarly interpreted. Rarely has there been so blatant an appeal to what Judge Kozinski condemns as "judicial subjectivism."

Judicial Interpretation in Practice. How this works in practice can be seen in two recent cases. In *Patterson v. McLean Credit Union*,[67] one of the 1989 civil rights decisions, a black teller sued her employer under the 1866 Civil Rights Act for racial harassment. The Court's conservative majority concluded that not only did the act not apply to on-the-job harassment, but they went out of their way to add that it also did not cover a promotion unless it involved "an opportunity for a new and distinct relationship between the employer and employee" (whatever that means). For this interpretation, Justice Anthony Kennedy, writing for the five-four majority, relied on his own reading of the statutory phrase "make and enforce" a contract and his conception of how the 1866 act "harmonized" with the 1964 Civil Rights Act, despite the one-hundred-year difference between them. No precedent or other authority whatsoever was relied on, and a great deal of legislative history showing that Congress intended that this post–Civil War law be given a broad scope was simply ignored. The Civil Rights Bill of 1991 corrected much of this problem.

Another recent illustration is a little-noticed social security case. Congress had made it clear that the government should forget about any erroneous overpayment if the recipient was not at fault and was

151

needy. Emil Zwiezen and his wife had been overpaid a few years and underpaid several others, and they applied for the amount of under-payment. In their late seventies and totally dependent on their monthly checks, they were almost certain to have the overpayment forgiven. The Department of Health and Human Services, however, had adopted a regulation reducing the underpayment amounts by what was over-paid, and the Zwiezens wound up with nothing. They could not pay their water bill, fell behind on house payments, and feared a loss of medical care. The Zwiezens and others sued and initially won, but in a five-to-four decision, the Supreme Court, in an opinion by Justice Antonin Scalia, upheld the HHS policy as "not at all unreasonable."[68] The dissenters angrily pointed out that this undermined the "clear congressional intent" to forgive overpayment to the needy, but the majority hardly bothered to respond.[69]

While much more could be said about Justice Scalia's theories of statutory construction, one comment may be sufficient although some may find it cynical. It seems curious that this radical approach to legislative interpretation generally seems to produce conservative out-comes. Is it no more than coincidence that the application of this approach, which weakens legislative power, appears when conserva-tives have come to dominate the bench and the White House, and liberalism's sole recourse is to Congress?

Public policy is indeed an unruly horse. But courts, and particularly the Supreme Court, cannot escape riding it. The real questions are how and where. The likelihood is that the Court will fully accept neither the invitation to adopt a vigorous notion of public policy from the proponents of economic civil rights nor Justice Scalia's theory of freewheeling statutory construction. Some movement in both directions has already taken place, however, and for those of us who were unhappy with how that horse was ridden before 1954, more unhap-piness seems likely.

9

Judicial Review
in the Era of the Founding

Gordon S. Wood

Recent historical writings make clear that the origins of the modern practice of judicial review can best be found in the post–Civil War era. During the last part of the nineteenth and the beginning of the twentieth centuries, the Americans' understanding of judicial power had dramatically changed, and the myth of the Marshall Court was created, climaxing with Albert J. Beveridge's four-volume biography of John Marshall completed in 1916. The term "judicial review" itself was apparently coined by Edward Corwin only in 1910. From then on, the power of the Supreme Court grew, but perhaps not until the past generation has the Court's authority expanded to the remarkable extent that we see today.[1]

Yet to conclude from the new historical literature that the American Revolution and the Founding Fathers had little or nothing to do with the beginnings of judicial review would be a mistake. Quite the contrary. However important the post–Civil War period and past forty years have been in the development of judicial review, the essential foundations of the practice were laid in the late eighteenth and early nineteenth centuries. It may be true that only in the twentieth century has the Supreme Court become the all-encompassing guardian of the Constitution, but the crucial decisions, the significant changes, that led to this modern conclusion were made in the founding era. The extraordinary reputation of the Marshall Court may be largely an invention of the late nineteenth and early twentieth centuries, but it is by no means a false or undeserved reputation. Although members of the founding generation could not have anticipated the enlarged role the courts now play in American life, they did create the sources out of which that enlarged role eventually emerged. Not only did the Founding Fathers radically transform the character of the judiciary in America and give it a significance it had never had before in Anglo-American culture, but they gave American judges the legal weapons that eventually made modern judicial review possible.

The Judiciary at the Time of the Revolution

Today we find it difficult to recapture the insignificance of the colonial judiciary in the decades before the American Revolution. Perhaps that is why, despite our institutional studies of the colonial governors and the colonial assemblies, we have not yet a single book-length work on the colonial judiciary. Judges in colonial America were regarded essentially as appendages or extensions of royal authority embodied in the governors or chief magistrates. Unlike their counterparts in the mother country, who as a consequence of the Glorious Revolution had won tenure during good behavior, the colonial judges continued to hold office at the pleasure of the Crown. Consequently, many colonists identified the judges, or magistrates, as they were often called, with the governors. Indeed, some concluded that there were really "no more than two powers in any government, viz. the power to make laws, and the power to execute them; for the judicial power is only a branch of the executive, the CHIEF of every country being the first magistrate."[2] Even John Adams in 1766 regarded "the first grand division of constitutional powers" as "those of legislation and those of execution," with "the administration of justice" resting in "the executive part of the constitution."[3] The colonial judges therefore bore much of the opprobrium attached to the royal governors and were often circumscribed by the power of popular juries to an extent not found in England itself.

Since Americans had become convinced that the dependence of the judges on executive caprice was "dangerous to liberty and property of the subject," they sought to end that dependence at the Revolution.[4] Most of the revolutionary state constitutions of 1776–1777 took away from the governors their traditional power to appoint judges and gave it to the legislatures. The judges' tenure clearly no longer depended on the pleasure of the chief magistrate. These changes in the judiciary's status were often justified by reference to the doctrine of separation of powers made famous in the eighteenth century by Montesquieu— that, as the Virginia Constitution of 1776 asserted, "the legislative, executive, and judiciary departments shall be separate and distinct, so that neither exercise the powers properly belonging to the other."

This separation of the judges from their customary magisterial connection made them independent of the governors, but they were not yet independent of the people or their representatives in the legislatures. Although Americans in 1776 may have talked of the separation of executive, legislative, and judicial powers and invoked Montesquieu's maxim, they meant only to isolate the executive from the other two departments and to prevent the chief magistrates from tampering with the assemblies and the judges. The legislative and judicial powers were scarcely separated from each other at all. In fact, the Revolution tended to reverse what had been a growing mid-eighteenth century distinction between legislative and judicial responsibilities. Consequently, during the 1770s and 1780s the assemblies became increasingly involved in controlling the courts and in making what were essentially private law judgments. While the Revolution therefore eliminated the courts' earlier dependence on the governors, it brought them more and more under the dominion of the legislatures. Not only did the legislatures in some of the states elect the judges for a prescribed number of years—annually in Rhode Island, Connecticut, and Vermont—but even those states granting tenure during good behavior gave the legislatures control of the judges' salaries and fees and the power of their removal, including by simple address of the legislature.

Because judges had been so identified with the much-hated magisterial power, many American revolutionaries in 1776 sought not to strengthen the judiciary but to weaken it. They especially feared the seemingly arbitrary discretionary authority that colonial judges had exercised. Indeed, because of the confusion flowing from the different metropolitan and provincial sources of American law, the discretionary authority of colonial judges had been far greater than that exercised by judges in England itself.

The result, as Thomas Jefferson put it in 1776, was that Americans had come to view judicial activity as "the eccentric impulses of whimsical, capricious designing man" and had come to believe that their legislatures, because they represented the people and had been the guardians of their liberties against royal encroachment, could be trusted to dispense justice "equally and impartially to every description of men." By having the new state legislatures write down the laws in black and white, the revolutionaries aimed to circumscribe the much-resented former judicial discretion and to turn the judge into what Jefferson hoped would be "a mere machine."[5] Consequently, nearly all the revolutionary states to one degree or another attempted to weed out archaic English laws and legal technicalities and to simplify and codify parts of the common law. Society, it was said, often with ample quotations from the Italian legal reformer Beccaria, needed "but few laws, and these simple, clear, sensible, and easy in their application to the actions of men."[6] Only through scientific codification and strict judicial observance of what William Henry Drayton of South Carolina called in 1778, quoting Beccaria, "the letter of the law" could the people be protected from becoming "slaves to the magistrates."[7]

Never entirely lost, the Enlightenment promise of codification continued as part of radical thinking into the nineteenth century. By the 1780s, however, many revolutionaries had already begun to realize that precise legislative enactment was not working out as they had hoped. Many statutes were enacted, and many laws were printed but rarely in the way reformers like Thomas Jefferson and James Madison had expected. Unstable, annually elected, and log-rolling democratic legislatures broke apart plans for comprehensive legal codes and passed statutes in such confused and piecemeal ways that the purpose of simplicity and clarity was defeated: "For every new law . . . acts as rubbish, under which we bury the former."[8] More laws were passed than anyone could keep up with; in fact, said a disgruntled Madison in 1786, more laws were passed in the ten years following the Declaration of Independence than in the entire colonial period. This proliferation of statutes meant that judicial discretion, far from diminishing, became more prevalent than it had been before the Revolution, as judges tried to pick their way through the legal mazes.

Reforming the Reforms

By the 1780s many Americans, already having serious second thoughts about their earlier confidence in their popularly elected legislatures, were beginning to reevaluate their former hostility to judicial power and discretion. When particular statutes had to be enacted for every circumstance, said Connecticut clergyman Moses Mather as early as 1781, the laws proliferated, resulting in a confusion that wicked men turned to their private advantage. All the legislatures should really do was enact a few plain general rules of equity and leave their interpretation to the courts. "Indeed," said Mather, "where civil justice is to be administered not by particular statutes, but by the application of general rules of equity, much will depend upon the wisdom and integrity of the judges."[9] A far cry from the Beccarian reformist sentiments of 1776, this statement represented the extent to which experience had changed American thinking since the Declaration of Independence.

By the 1780s many Americans concluded that their popular state assemblies "(*the very fountain from whence justice must necessarily flow*)"[10] not only were incapable of simplifying and codifying the law but, more alarming, had become the greatest threat to minority rights and individual liberties and the principal source of injustice in the society. At the same time more and more American leaders began looking to the once-feared judiciary as a primary means of restraining these rampaging popular legislatures. In 1786 William Plummer, a future U.S. senator and governor of New Hampshire, concluded that the very "existence" of America's elective governments had come to depend upon the judiciary: "That is the only body of men who will have an effective check upon a numerous Assembly."[11]

In the massive rethinking that took place in the 1780s nearly all parts of America's governments were reformed and reconstituted—reforms and reconstitutions that were often justified by ingenious manipulations of Montesquieu's doctrine of the separation of powers. But the part of government that benefited most from the rethinking and remodeling of the 1780s was the judiciary. In the decade following the Declaration of Independence the position of the judiciary in American life began to be transformed—from the much scorned and insignificant appendage of Crown authority into what Americans increasingly called one of "the three capital powers of Government," from minor magistrates identified with the colonial executives into an equal and independent part of a modern tripartite government.[12]

It was a remarkable transformation, taking place as it did in such a relatively short period of time, and, surprisingly, its history has never been written. For all our studies of the Supreme Court and its great decisions, for all our recent investigations in legal history, we still have no history of the emergence of what Americans called an "independent judiciary" at the end of the eighteenth century and the beginning of the nineteenth century—perhaps because we take a strong independent judiciary so much for granted. The development of an independent judiciary is all the more remarkable because it flew in the face of much conventional eighteenth-century wisdom. Convincing Americans that judges appointed for life were an integral and independent part of their democratic governments—equal in status and authority to the popularly elected executives and legislatures—was no mean accomplishment. Such a change in thinking was a measure of how severe the crisis of the 1780s really was and how deep the disillusionment with popular legislative government had become since the idealistic confidence of 1776.

By the 1780s judges in several states were gingerly and ambiguously moving in isolated but important decisions to impose restraints on what the legislatures were enacting as law, attempting in effect to say to the legislatures, as Judge George Wythe of Virginia did in 1782, "Here is the limit of your authority, and, hither, shall you go, but no further."[13] Yet cautious and tentative as they were, such attempts by the judiciary "to declare the nullity of a law passed in its forms by the legislative power, without exercising the power of that branch," were not readily justified, for they raised, in the words of Judge Edmund Pendleton of Virginia, "a deep, and important, and . . . a tremendous question, the decision of which might involve consequences to which gentlemen may not have extended their ideas."[14]

Even those who agreed that many of the laws passed by the state legislatures in the 1780s were unjust and even unconstitutional nevertheless could not agree that judges ought to have the authority to declare such legislation void. For judges to declare laws enacted by popularly elected legislatures as unconstitutional and invalid seemed flagrantly inconsistent with free popular government. Such judicial usurpation, said Richard Spraight of North Carolina, was "absurd" and "operated as an absolute negative on the proceedings of the Legislature, which no judiciary ought ever to possess." Instead of being governed by their representatives in the assembly, the people would be subject to the will of a few individuals in the court, "who united in their own persons the legislative and judiciary powers"—a despotism more insufferable than that of the Roman decemvirate or of any monarchy in Europe.[15]

Most Americans, even those deeply concerned with the legislative abuses of the 1780s, were too fully aware of the modern positivist conception of law (made famous by Blackstone in his *Commentaries of the Laws of England*), too deeply committed to consent as the basis for law, and from their colonial experience too apprehensive of the possible arbitrariness and uncertainties of judicial discretion to permit judges to set aside laws made by the elected representatives of the people. "This," said a perplexed Madison in 1788, "makes the Judiciary Department paramount in fact to the Legislature, which was never intended and can never be proper."[16]

Yet we know that judicial review of some form did develop in these early decades of the new republic. What was it, and how did it arise? Given the founders' confused view of judicial review as improper and dangerous or, at best, as an exceptional and awesome political act, simply adding up, as we are apt to do, the several examples during the 1780s and 1790s in which the courts set aside legislative acts as unconstitutional can never explain its origins.

The sources of something as significant and forbidding as judicial review could never lie in the accumulation of a few sporadic judicial precedents but had to flow from fundamental changes taking place

in Americans' ideas of government and law. As a result of the heavy
criticism of their revolutionary actions in the 1770s and 1780s, the
legislatures were rapidly losing their exclusive authority as the representatives of the people, and legal sovereignty, even as Blackstone
understood it, was being located not in any legislative body but in
the people at large. Many Americans were coming to regard the state
legislatures as simply another kind of magistracy, and the supposed
lawmaking of the legislatures as simply the promulgation of decrees
to which the people, standing outside the entire government, had
never given their full and unqualified assent. Therefore it was possible
now to argue, as one Rhode Islander did in 1787, that all acts of a
legislature were still "liable to examination and scrutiny by the people,
that is, by the Supreme Judiciary, their servants for this purpose; and
those [acts] that militate with the fundamental laws, or impugn the
principles of the constitution, are to be judicially set aside as void,
and of no effect."[17]

It was left to Alexander Hamilton in *Federalist* 78, however, to
draw out most fully the logic of this argument. The so-called representatives of the people in the state legislatures did not really embody
the people, as Parliament, for example, presumably embodied the
people of Britain. On the contrary, the state legislatures were really
only one kind of servant of the people with a limited delegated
authority to act on their behalf. Americans, said Hamilton, had no
intention of allowing "the representatives of the people to substitute
their *will* to that of their constituents." In fact it was "far more rational
to suppose, that the courts were designed to be an intermediate body
between the people and the legislature, in order, among other things,
to keep the latter within the limits assigned their authority." Judges
were just another kind of servant of the sovereign people. Therefore,
said Hamilton in summarizing a commonly emerging view, the authority of the judges to set aside acts of the legislatures lay in the fact
that in America real and ultimate sovereignty rested with the people
themselves, not with their representatives in the legislatures. Judicial
review did not

> by any means suppose a superiority of the judicial to the
> legislative power. It only supposes that the power of the
> people is superior to both; and that where the will of the
> legislature declared in its statutes, stands in opposition to
> that of the people, declared in the constitution, the
> judges . . . ought to regulate their decisions by the funda-
> mental laws, rather than by those which are not fundamental.

Although establishing the judiciary as a separate and equal agent or servant of the people alongside the legislatures and executives may have been crucial in justifying judicial independence and in granting judges the authority to void legislative acts, by itself it did not create what came to be called judicial review. The idea of fundamental law and its embodiment in a written constitution were also important.

Fundamental Law

Almost all eighteenth-century Englishmen on both sides of the Atlantic had recognized something called fundamental law as a guide to the moral rightness and constitutionality of ordinary law and politics. Nearly everyone repeatedly invoked the Magna Carta and other fundamental laws of the English constitution. Theorists as different as John Locke and Bolingbroke referred equally to the basic principles of the constitution as fundamental law. Even the rise of legislative sovereignty in eighteenth-century England did not displace this prevalent notion of fundamental law. Blackstone himself, despite his commitment to legislative sovereignty, believed that Parliament was limited by what he called an overriding natural law. Yet all these theoretical references to the principles of the constitution and fundamental law had little day-to-day practical importance. At best this fundamental or natural law of the English constitution was seen as a kind of moral inhibition or conscience existing in the minds of legislators and others. It was so basic and primal, so imposing and political, that it was really enforceable only by the popular elective process or ultimately by the people's right of revolution. Eighteenth-century Englishmen talked about fundamental or natural law, invoked it constantly in their rhetoric, but had great difficulty conceiving of it as something they could call upon in their everyday political and legal business.[18]

The written constitutions of 1776–1777, however, gave revolutionary Americans a handle with which to grasp this otherwise insubstantial fundamental law. Suddenly the fundamental law and the first principles that Englishmen had referred to for generations had a degree of explicitness and reality that they had never before quite had. The Constitution in America, said James Iredell of North Carolina, was not therefore "a mere imaginary thing, about which ten thousand different opinions may be formed, but a written document to which all may have recourse, and to which, therefore, the judges cannot witfully blind themselves."[19]

But were the judges to have an exclusive authority to determine what was constitutional and what was not? All Americans agreed that the written constitution, as Edmund Pendleton conceded in 1782, "must be considered as a rule obligatory upon every department, not to be departed from on any occasion."[20] But it was not immediately evident to Pendleton or to others that the judiciary had any special or unique power to invoke this obligatory rule to limit the other departments of the government, particularly the legislatures. In other words, it was clear by the 1780s that legislatures in America were bound by explicitly written constitutions in ways that the English Parliament was not. It was not yet clear, however, that the courts by themselves were able to enforce those boundaries upon the legislatures. "The great argument is," said Iredell in 1786 in summarizing the position of those opposed to judicial review,

> that the Assembly have not a *right* to violate the constitution, yet if they *in fact* do so, the only remedy is, either by a humble petition that the law may be repealed, or a universal resistance of the people. But that in the mean time, their act, whatever it is, is to be obeyed as a law; for the judicial power is not to presume to question the power of an act of Assembly.[21]

While both Jefferson and Madison thought that judges might act as the guardians of popular rights and might resist encroachments on these rights, they never believed that judges had any special or unique power to interpret the Constitution. In fact, they remained convinced to the end of their lives that all parts of America's governments had the authority to interpret the fundamental law of the Constitution—all departments had what Madison called "a *concurrent* right to expound the constitution."[22] And when the several departments disagreed in their understanding of the fundamental law, wrote Madison in *Federalist* 49, only "an appeal to the people themselves, . . . can alone declare its true meaning, and enforce its observance." Written constitutions, including the Bill of Rights, remained for Jefferson and Madison a set of great first principles to which the several governmental departments, including the judiciary, could appeal in those extraordinary occasions of violation. Since none of these departments could "pretend to an exclusive or superior right of settling the boundaries between their respective powers," however, the ultimate appeal in these quasi-revolutionary situations had to be to the people.[23] This was *not* judicial review as we have come to know it.

In other words, many revolutionaries still thought that fundamental law, even when expressed in a written constitution, was so fundamental, so different in kind from ordinary law, that its invocation had to be essentially an exceptional and awesomely delicate political exercise. The courts might on occasion set aside legislation that violated fundamental law, but such an act could not be a part of routine judicial business; it necessarily had to be an extraordinary expression of public authority, the kind of extreme and remarkable action the people themselves would take if they could. This kind of judicial review was, as it has been aptly described, a "substitute for revolution."[24]

This is why many of the delegates to the Philadelphia Convention in 1787 still regarded judicial nullification of legislation with a sense of awe and wonder, impressed, as Elbridge Gerry was, that "in some States, the Judges had actually set aside laws as being against the Constitution." This is also why many others in the convention, including James Wilson and George Mason, wanted to join the judges with the executive in a council of revision and thus give the judiciary a double negative over the laws. They considered that the power of the judges by themselves to declare unconstitutional laws void was too extreme, too exceptional, and too fearful an act to be used against all those ordinary unjust, unwise, and dangerous laws that were nevertheless not "so unconstitutional as to justify the Judges in refusing to give them effect."[25] Such remarks suggest that most of the founders, even when they conceded the power of judges to void unconstitutional legislation in very clear cases, scarcely conceived of such a power in modern terms. They simply could not yet imagine the courts' having the authority to expound constitutions in a routine judicial manner.[26] For many of them judicial review remained an extraordinary and solemn political action, akin to the interposition of the states suggested by Jefferson and Madison in the Kentucky and Virginia Resolutions of 1798—something to be invoked only on the rare occasions of flagrant and unequivocal violations of the Constitution. It was not to be exercised in doubtful cases of unconstitutionality and thus could not yet be an aspect of ordinary judicial activity.[27]

The idea of fundamental written law, important as it was, therefore could not by itself have led to the development of America's judicial review. Other countries since the eighteenth century have had formal rigid and written constitutions—Belgium and France, for example— without regularly allowing their courts to set aside legislative acts that conflict with these written constitutions, not to mention construing these constitutions in order to do justice. Written constitutions by themselves did not create the peculiarly American process of judicial review in the early republic. Judicial review, as it has come to be practiced in the United States, is so pervasive, so powerful, and so much a part of our everyday judicial proceedings that the presence of a written fundamental law can scarcely explain its development.

It cannot explain it because what gives significance to our conception of a constitution as written fundamental law is not that it is written or that it is fundamental but rather that it runs in our ordinary court system. Although America's constitutions may be higher laws, they are just like all our other lowly laws in that they are implemented through our normal practice of adversarial justice in the regular courts.

Some countries with written constitutions—Brazil, for example—permit their supreme courts to pass on the constitutionality of legislation before it is enacted into law. But exercising superpublic or superjudicial authority in this way is not how most American courts operate. Judicial review results from two litigants contesting an issue using routine legal processes in the regular court system. The fact that our written fundamental constitutions, our public laws, are interpreted and construed in a routine fashion in our ordinary court system, and not in some superpublic supreme court, is at the heart of our peculiar practice of judicial review.

Thus the source of judicial review as we understand it today lies not in the idea of fundamental law or in written constitutions but in the transformation of this written fundamental law into the kind of law that could be expounded and construed in the ordinary court system.

The Legalization of Fundamental Law

We cannot appreciate what opening the Constitution to routine judicial construction really signified unless we understand how important judicial interpretation was to the workings of the common law. The eighteenth-century English constitution was essentially a judge-made constitution. The common law that underlay the constitution remained largely unwritten and was really an accumulation of judicial decisions, precedents, and interpretations that went back centuries. Of course, by the eighteenth century parliamentary statutes had added considerably to the common law and could and did amend it at will. The English judges, however, still had to fit these statutes into the whole system of law and to make sense of the written law in particular cases. Thus the English common law judges, despite having to bow to the sovereignty of Parliament, were left with an extraordinary amount of room for statutory and common law interpretation and construction for the purpose of doing justice. And, as Blackstone pointed out, there were well-worked out rules for judges to follow in construing and interpreting the law—rules that Hamilton in *Federalist* 83 called "rules of *common sense*, adopted by the courts in the construction of the laws."

What many of the founders did, culminating in the developments and decisions of the Marshall Court, was to collapse the earlier distinction between fundamental and ordinary law. They brought the higher law of the Constitution within the rubric of ordinary law and subjected it to the long-standing rules of legal exposition and construction as if it were no different from a lowly statute. In effect, all the wide-ranging power of explication and interpretation traditionally wielded by common law judges over ordinary statutes in relation to the law was now applied to the Constitution itself. American judges could now construe the all-too-brief words of the Constitution in relation to subject matter, intention, context, and reasonableness as if they were the words of an ordinary statute. The result was the beginning of the creation of a special body of textual exegeses and legal expositions and precedents that we have come to call constitutional law. This accumulative body of constitutional law in America is now nearly 200 years old; there is nothing quite like it anywhere else in the world.

This process of equating constitutional and ordinary law has aptly been called "the legalization of fundamental law."[28] It might equally be called the domestication of the Constitution, for it tamed what had hitherto been an object of fearful significance and wonder to the point where it could routinely run in the ordinary court system. Considering the Constitution, in Gerald Gunther's words, as "a species of law and accordingly cognizable in courts of law" permitted judges not only to expound and construct the Constitution as if it were an ordinary statute but also to expect regular enforcement of the Constitution as if it were a simple statute.[29] The momentous implications of this transformation cannot be exaggerated. Because, in Marshall's words, it was "emphatically the province and duty of the judicial department to say what the law is," treating the Constitution as mere law that had to be expounded and interpreted and applied to particular cases gave special constitutional authority to American judges not shared by judges elsewhere in the world; it was what made American judicial review possible.[30]

Although this legalization of fundamental law has been attributed to the "deliberate design" of Marshall, it developed over too many years and became too widely acceptable to be the consequence of a single person's intentions, however crucially important they may have been.[31] In fact, from the Revolution to the early years of the nineteenth century we can see the gradual but fitful steps by which the transformation took place. The initial identification of fundamental law with a written constitution, followed by the need to compare this written constitution with other laws, then the lodging in the judiciary of the power of determining which law was superior, which in turn led to the blurring of constitutional and ordinary law in the regular court system that resulted finally in the legal interpretation of fundamental law in accord with what Hamilton in his argument for the constitutionality of the Bank of the United States called "the usual and established rules of construction" applied to statutory and other ordinary law—all these halting steps can be traced in the arguments and decisions of the period.[32]

This legalization of fundamental law and the development of judicial review went hand in hand with the demarcation of an exclusive sphere of legal activity for judges. If determining constitutional law were to be simply a routine act of legal interpretation and not an earth-shaking political exercise, then the entire process of adjudication had to be removed from politics and from legislative tampering. After 1800, judges shed their traditional broad and ill-defined political and magisterial roles that had previously identified them with the executive branch and adopted roles that were much more exclusively legal. The behavior of Samuel Chase in politically haranguing juries from the bench and of John Jay and Oliver Ellsworth in performing diplomatic missions while sitting as justices of the Supreme Court was not duplicated. Moreover, as early as Hayburn's case in 1792 several justices of the Supreme Court protested against the Congress's assigning administrative and magisterial duties to them on the grounds that it violated the separation of powers. Judges withdrew from politics, promoted the development of law as a science known best by trained experts, and limited their activities to the regular courts, which became increasingly professional and less burdened by popular juries.

The legalization or domestication of constitutional law meant that the courts now tended to avoid the most explosive and partisan political issues. Certainly the Marshall Court succeeded as well as it did because it retreated from the advanced and exposed political positions, including enlarged definitions of treason and of federal jurisdiction over the common law of crimes, that the Federalists had tried to stake out for the national judiciary in the 1790s. As the judges pulled back from politics, however, the courts attempted at the same time to designate other important issues as particular issues of law that were within their exclusive jurisdiction. Men began to draw lines around what was political or legislative and what was legal or judicial and to justify the distinctions by the doctrine of separation of powers. As early as 1787 Hamilton argued in the New York Assembly that the state constitution prevented anyone from being deprived of his rights except "by the law of the land" or, as a recent act of the assembly had put it, "by due process of law," which, said Hamilton in an astonishing and novel twist, had "a precise technical import": these words were now "only applicable to the process and proceedings of the courts of justice; they can never be referred to an act of legislature," even though the legislature had written them.[33] As Marshall said in his *Marbury* decision, which was crucial in defining this newly reduced but exclusive role for the courts, some questions were political: "They respect the nation, not individual rights," and thus were "only politically examinable." But questions involving the vested rights of individuals were different; they were in their "nature, judicial, and must be tried by the judicial authority."[34]

Placing legal boundaries around issues such as property rights and contracts had the effect of isolating these issues from popular tampering, partisan debate, and the clashes of interest-group politics. The power to interpret constitutions became a matter not of political interest to be determined by legislatures but of the "fixed principles" of a domesticated constitutional law to be determined only by judges. Without the protection of the courts and the intricacies of the common law, it was even argued in Pennsylvania in 1805, "rights would remain forever without remedies and wrongs without redress." Americans could no longer count on their popularly elected legislatures to solve many of the problems of their lives: "For the varying exigencies of social life, for the complicated interests of an enterprising nation, the positive acts of the legislature can provide little."[35]

It is hard to imagine a more severe indictment of popular democracy. Many apparently had come to believe that a society as unruly and as democratic as America's needed the moderating influence of an aristocracy. Outside of the South, however, aristocracy in America was hard to come by; but necessity invented one. As Alexis de Tocqueville pointed out, lawyers in the early nineteenth century had come to constitute whatever aristocracy America possessed, at least in the North. Through their influence on the judiciary they tempered America's turbulent majoritarian governments and promoted the rights of individuals and minorities. "The courts of justice," Tocqueville said, "are the visible organs by which the legal profession is enabled to control the democracy."[36] It is still a shrewd judgment.

Notes

CHAPTER 1: INTRODUCTION, *Robert A. Licht*

1. *Federalist* 78.
2. See Christopher Wolfe, *The Rise of Modern Judicial Review: From Constitutional Interpretation to Judge-Made Law* (New York: Basic Books, 1986).
3. See Allan Bloom, ed., *Confronting the Constitution: The Challenge to Locke, Montesquieu, Jefferson, and the Federalists from Unitarianism, Historicism, Marxism, Freudianism, Pragmatism, Existentialism* (Washington, D.C.: AEI Press, 1990).
4. See Robert A. Licht, "Introduction," in *The Framers and Fundamental Rights,* ed. Robert A. Licht (Washington, D.C.: AEI Press, 1992), p. 1.
5. Planned Parenthood of SE Pennsylvania v. Casey, majority opinion, p. 22.
6. Ibid., p. 23.
7. Ibid., p. 24.
8. Ibid., p. 25.
9. Ibid., p. 26.
10. Ibid., p. 20.
11. Ibid., p. 23.
12. Ibid., p. 25.

CHAPTER 2: INDEED A COURT, *George Anastaplo*

1. The United States Supreme Court first met, pursuant to the Judiciary Act of 1789, in February 1790. See, on Congress's supervision of the national courts with respect to their existence, jurisdiction, and processes, George Anastaplo, *The Constitution of 1787: A Commentary* (Baltimore: Johns Hopkins University Press, 1989), lect. 10, sec. 2, and lect. 2, sec. 3; George Anastaplo, "The Amendments to the Constitution," *Loyola University of Chicago Law Journal*, vol. 23 (1992), lect. 8, sec. 5, p. 631. These two commentaries on the Constitution of the United States will be cited hereafter as *Commentaries 1* and *Commentaries 2*.
2. This bears on how the litigation in *Barron v. Baltimore*, 7 Pet. (32 U.S.) 243 (1833), is to be understood. See Anastaplo, *Commentaries 2*, lect. 6, secs. 6–7.
3. The lamentable decline of Dizzy Dean is instructive here. See Anastaplo, *Commentaries 1*, p. xvii.
4. I mean by "Anglo-American" those things shared by the English-speaking peoples in Great Britain and North America. The Anglo-Americans share a constitutional heritage that goes back to Magna Carta, if not before.
5. The Supreme Court is given the delicate assignment of resolving legal disputes between those "individuals" known as states. See, for example, George Anastaplo, "On Freedom: Explorations," *Oklahoma City University Law Journal*, vol. 17, pt. 2 (1992).
6. See, for example, Swift v. Tyson, 41 U.S. (16 Pet.) 1 (1842). Compare the ill-conceived case of Erie Railroad Co. v. Tompkins, 304 U.S. 64 (1938). See, for discussions of these matters, William T. Braithwaite, "The Common Law and the

Judicial Power: An Introduction to *Swift-Erie*," in John A. Murley, Robert L. Stone, and William T. Braithwaite, eds., *Law and Philosophy: The Practice of Theory* (Athens, Ohio: Ohio University Press, 1992), p. 774; Michael Conant, *The Constitution and the Economy* (Norman: Oklahoma University Press, 1991); Anastaplo, *Commentaries 1*, lect. 10, secs. 5–9, lect. 11, sec. 1.

7. William W. Crosskey has argued that the few genuine precedents for judicial review before 1787 were limited to special circumstances. See Crosskey, *Politics and the Constitution in the History of the United States* (Chicago: University of Chicago Press, 1953), pp. 938–1046. It is a different question to ask what the executive and the courts may do to protect their constitutional prerogatives from congressional invasions. In the long run they can probably do little unless the people are prepared to intervene.

8. See Anastaplo, *Commentaries 1*, lect. 4, secs. 6–7.

9. The courts *are* expected to be guided by the Constitution in the way they conduct treason trials. See Anastaplo, *Commentaries 1*, lect. 11, sec. 9; also, n. 22, below. They are guided by the Bill of Rights in the way they are to conduct judicial proceedings. See Anastaplo, *Commentaries 2*, lect. 7. The restraints upon ex post facto laws and bills of attainder also provide guidance for the courts.

10. Dred Scott v. Sandford, 60 U.S. (19 How.) 393 (1857). I return to Dred Scott in "Consequences of the Dred Scott Decision." See also n. 26, below. Marbury v. Madison, 5 U.S. (1 Cranch) 137 (1803), the other recognized exercise of judicial review of acts of Congress before the Civil War, was far more important for what was done with it later than for what it did then. In any event, most of our personal rights and the powers-allocation principles were recognized and developed in England long before judicial review could be counted upon to protect such rights or to implement such principles. See, on Marbury, Crosskey, *Politics and the Constitution*, pp. 1035–46. See, also, n. 21, below.

11. The British judges exercise "judicial review" only in this sense. If Congress intends to proceed otherwise than the "interpreting" court suggests, it can then run the political risk of disregarding (or overruling) what the court has done. That is, Congress could say, or seem to say, that it does not want to respect the Constitution as commonly understood.

12. A salutary pronouncement here, aside from the judicial review issue, is Justice Black's opinion for the Court in the Steel Seizure Case, 343 U.S. 572 (1952). The principles drawn upon here by Justice Black could be of help in our distinguishing between two sets of executive actions during the recent Persian Gulf encounter: the Desert Shield defensive response (emergency in character) and the Desert Storm offensive phase (to which the president shifted in November 1990, without congressional authorization). The Iran arms–contra aid debacle also comes to mind here. See Anastaplo, *Commentaries 1*, pp. 317–18; also n. 20, below. See, as well, George Anastaplo, *The American Moralist: On Ethics, Law and Government* (Athens: Ohio University Press, 1992), pp. xvi–xix, 225.

13. Brown v. Board of Education, 347 U.S. 483 (1954). But Brown is not an instance of the judicial review of an act of Congress. Compare Bolling v. Sharpe, 347 U.S. 497 (1954). The Brown Court would have done even better if it had relied also on the Declaration of Independence.

14. See, for example, the Civil Rights Cases, 109 U.S. 3 (1883). What Congress tried to do here reminds me of the recognition of rights by Parliament over centuries. One scholar has observed, "What finally turned the tide [against racial discrimination] were a series of legislative enactments: the Civil Rights Act of 1964 [78 Stat. 241], the Voting Rights Act of 1965 [79 Stat. 437], and the Fair Housing Act of 1968 [82 Stat. 437]. The struggle against racial discrimination required the conscientious effort of all three branches." Louis Fisher, "The Curious Belief in Judicial Supremacy," *Suffolk University Law Review*, vol. 25 (1991), pp. 85, 113–14. See, also, Anastaplo, *Commentaries 2*, lect. 3. Are not additional civil rights, sometimes in the form of entitlements, being recognized by congressional legislation in our time?

15. See, for example, Plessy v. Ferguson, 163 U.S. 537 (1896).

16. See, for example, Gibbons v. Ogden, 22 U.S. (9 Wheat.) 1 (1824); and Wickard v. Filburn, 317 U.S. 111 (1942). See, also, Crosskey, *Politics and the Constitution*, pp. 250–80; and Anastaplo, *Commentaries 1*, lect. 5.

17. United States v. Kahriger, 345 U.S. 22, 38 (1952) (Justice Frankfurter, dissenting). Justice Frankfurter quotes here from the opinion for the Court by Chief Justice Taft, in the Child Labor Tax Case, 259 U.S. 20, 38 (1922).

18. Somewhat more plausible are the arguments for state "interposition" found in the Virginia Resolutions of 1798. See George Anastaplo, *The Constitutionalist: Notes on the First Amendment* (Dallas: Southern Methodist University Press, 1971), p. 822.

19. The people of the United States, in their collective capacity, do not immediately control either the national courts or the governments of the various states to the degree or in the way that they control the Congress and president of the United States. See, on the critical element of control in these matters, McCulloch v. Maryland, 4 Wheat. (17 U.S.) 316, 428–29 (1819).

20. Consider, for example, the attempts made from time to time to get the courts to rule on whether the president has usurped the power of Congress to declare war. Conversely, Congress, if so minded, can use its appropriation powers to keep the president in line here. See n. 12, above.

21. The same can be said, in a minor mode, about the original-jurisdiction issue dealt with in Marbury v. Madison.

22. It is easier to distinguish *political* from *constitutional* in those instances where traditional rights are involved. It is harder to do so where the issue is the extent of legislative power. Are not the courts expected to respect traditional rights in their own proceedings? See n. 9, above.

23. See Anastaplo, *Commentaries 1*, lects. 10 and 11. See, also, n 6.

24. See, for example, Baker v. Carr, 369 U.S. 186 (1962), and Reynolds v. Sims, 377 U.S. 533 (1964). Congress should, pursuant to the Republican Form of Government Guarantee, have acted much earlier (and perhaps more sensibly) with respect to these matters. See Anastaplo, *Commentaries 1*, lect. 13, sec. 5.

25. Gerald Gunther, *Constitutional Law* (Westbury, N.Y.: Foundation Press, 1991) 12th ed., p. 212.

26. It does not seem to be generally appreciated that these interventions by the Supreme Court may have had their origins *not* in a desire to protect the

integrity and powers of Congress and of the states but rather in a desire, fueled by proslavery concerns, to cut down (in a roundabout way) the range of the congressional commerce power. Here, too, William Crosskey's work is instructive. See, for example, George Anastaplo, "Mr. Crosskey, the American Constitution, and the Natures of Things," *Loyola University of Chicago Law Journal*, vol. 15 (1984), pp. 181, 224, n. 46. See, also, Anastaplo, "Slavery and the Constitution: Explorations," *Texas Tech Law Review*, vol. 20 (1989), p. 677.

CHAPTER 3: PRESERVING A LIVING CONSTITUTION, *Walter Berns*

1. "Brutus," 15, March 20, 1788, in Phillip B. Kurland and Ralph Lerner, eds., *The Founders' Constitution* (Chicago: University of Chicago Press, 1987), vol. 4, pp. 238-39.

2. Calder v. Bull, 3 Dallas 386, 387-88 (1798).

3. Ibid., pp. 398-99. Concurring opinion.

4. Fletcher v. Peck, 6 Cranch 87, 139 (1810).

5. Ibid., p. 143. Concurring opinion.

6. Savings and Loan Association v. Topeka, 20 Wall. 655 (1875); L.Ed. At pp. 455, 461.

7. Ibid., p. 463. It should be pointed out that this case was decided long before the "takings" clause of the Fifth Amendment (or any other provision of the Bill of Rights) had been incorporated into the Fourteenth Amendment, which means that at that time the Constitution of the United States imposed no restrictions on state "takings." Thus, in effect, the Court held that the *state* constitution did not permit the state to do this; in line with this, the cases cited in support of the judgment were all state cases. But, of course, the Court had no authority to expound the meaning of state constitutions.

8. James Madison to Spencer Roane, September 2, 1819, in Marvin Meyers, ed., *The Mind of the Founder: Sources of the Political Thought of James Madison*, rev. ed. (Hanover, Mass.: Brandeis University Press, by University Press of New England, 1981), pp. 361-62.

9. James Madison to Henry Lee, June 25, 1824, in Gaillard Hunt, ed., *The Writings of James Madison*, vol. 9 (New York: G. P. Putnam's Sons, 1900-1910), p. 191. Emphasis not in the original. The passage cited in the text begins as follows: "I entirely concur in the propriety of resorting to the sense in which the Constitution was accepted and ratified by the nation. In that sense alone it is the legitimate Constitution."

10. Marbury v. Madison, I Cranch 137, 176, 178 (1803).

11. Thomas Jefferson to Wilson Cary Nicholas, September 7, 1803, in Jefferson, *Writings* (New York: Library of America, 1984), p. 1140.

12. *Federalist* 78.

13. William Cranch, "Preface," 1 Cranch iii (1804), in Phillip B. Kurland and Ralph Lerner, eds., *The Founders' Constitution* (Chicago: University of Chicago Press, 1977), vol. 4, p. 188.

14. Robert P. Kraynak, "Tocqueville's Constitutionalism," *American Political Science Review*, vol. 81, no. 4 (December 1987), p. 1191.

15. William J. Brennan, Jr., "The Constitution of the United States: Contempo-

rary Ratification," *South Texas Law Review*, vol. 27 (1986), pp. 433, 434.

16. Lochner v. New York, 198 U.S. 45 (1905).

17. See, for example, Griswold v. Connecticut, 381 U.S. 479 (1965).

18. Buck v. Bell, 274 U.S. 200 (1927). See Walter Berns, "Buck v. Bell: Due Process of Law?" *Western Political Quarterly*, vol. 6 (December 1953).

19. Jacobson v. Massachusetts, 197 U.S. 11 (1905).

20. *Eugenical News*, vol. 19 (November–December 1934), pp. 140–41.

21. Lochner v. New York, p. 75. Dissenting opinion.

22. McCulloch v. Maryland, 4 Wheat. 316, 407, 415 (1819).

23. See Walter Berns, *Taking the Constitution Seriously* (New York: Simon and Schuster, 1987), pp. 207–8. The statement has been misquoted many times, beginning in Chief Justice Charles Evans Hughes's opinion for the Court in Home Building & Loan Assoc. v. Blaisdell, 290 U.S. 398, 443 (1934).

24. Harper v. Virginia State Board of Elections, 383 U.S. 663, 669 (1966).

25. Ibid., p. 676. Dissenting opinion.

26. The idea of natural law rests on the following presuppositions. 1. A last and profound unity of mankind, a unity of conscience in the last and least of human beings. However darkened or enlightened by primitive civilizations and progressive cultures, by deleterious habits become traditions and by lack of serious efforts to live up to the demand of critical consciousness, there exists a unity and community of human conscience, of human nature through all the epochs, in all races, in all nations. 2. The ability of the human intellect to perceive the essential and the unchangeable nature of things, in other words, the actual objective reality. The measure of our knowledge is the thing in its essence; it is not the categorical forms of the subjective mind, induced by the phenomena of the things that produce order out of the chaos of the phenomena. . . 3. Granted that the human mind recognizes the nature of things, this nature is for the existing thing at the same time its end and perfection. It is the degree of realized idea in an existing thing that determines the degree of its goodness. 4. Superiority of the intellect. The intellect recognizes the nature of things and presents to the will the concrete thing as a good that ought to be striven after (Heinrich A. Rommen, *The State in Catholic Thought: A Treatise in Political Philosophy* [St. Louis: B. Herder Book Co., 1945], pp. 169–70).

27. Carl L. Becker, *The Declaration of Independence: A Study in the History of Political Ideas* (New York: Vintage Books, 1942), p. 277.

28. "The enumeration in the Constitution of certain rights, shall not be construed to deny or disparage others retained by the people."

29. Roscoe Pound, "Introduction," Russell B. Patterson, *The Forgotten Ninth Amendment* (Indianapolis: Bobbs-Merrill Co., Inc., 1955), pp. ii, iv.

30. See Berns, *Taking the Constitution Seriously*, p. 23.

31. Leo Strauss, *Natural Right and History* (Chicago: University of Chicago Press, 1953), pp. 1–2.

32. Sanford Levinson, *Constitutional Faith* (Princeton: Princeton University Press, 1988), p. 172.

33. Ibid., pp. 64–65.

34. Thomas L. Pangle, "Post-Modernist Thought," *Wall Street Journal*, January 5, 1989.

35. Levinson, *Constitutional Faith*, p. 191.

36. Michael J. Perry, *Morality, Politics, and Law: A Bicentennial Essay* (New York: Oxford University Press, 1988), pp. 148, 149, 150.

37. Ibid., p. 162.

38. Three of these clauses are to be found in the Fifth Amendment (grand jury indictment, double jeopardy, and due process), one in the Fourteenth Amendment (due process), and one in Article I, section 2 (where the president is given the power to grant reprieves).

39. Johnson v. Transportation Agency, Santa Clara County, 480 U.S. 616, 647 (1987). Concurring opinion.

40. Fred Baumann, "Historicism and the Constitution," in Allan Bloom, ed., *Confronting the Constitution* (Washington, D.C.: AEI Press, 1990), p. 286.

41. Joseph L. Rauh, Jr., "The Supreme Court: A Body Politic," *Washington Post*, March 5, 1980.

CHAPTER 4: GUARDING FROM LEGISLATIVE TYRANNY, *Joseph M. Bessette*

1. See, for example, Alexander Hamilton, James Madison, and John Jay, *Federalist 37, The Federalist Papers*, ed. Clinton Rossiter (New York: New American Library, 1961), pp. 226–27.

2. *Federalist 47*, p. 301.

3. Ibid.

4. *The Portable Thomas Jefferson*, ed. Merrill D. Peterson (New York: Viking Press, 1975), p. 164, emphasis in the original.

5. *Federalist 48*, p. 309, emphasis added.

6. Ibid.

7. For the first three points, see *Federalist 48*, p. 310.

8. *Federalist 63*, p. 389.

9. *Federalist 49*, p. 316.

10. *Federalist 71*, p. 433.

11. *Federalist 51*, p. 320.

12. Ibid., p. 321.

13. Ibid., pp. 321–22.

14. Ibid., p. 321.

15. Ibid., p. 322.

16. *Federalist 78*, p. 470.

17. Ibid., pp. 465–66.

18. Ibid., p. 466.

19. Ibid., p. 441. The phrase "stern virtue" is from Publius's discussion in *Federalist 73* of the likelihood that a president, whose salary was controlled by the legislature, would act on his independent judgment against legislative inclinations.

20. *Federalist 71*, p. 433.

21. Ibid., pp. 432, 434–35.

22. Letter to Edmund Pendleton, June 21, 1789 in *Letters and Other Writings of James Madison*, 4 vols. (New York: R. Worthington, 1884), vol. 1, p. 478, emphasis added.

23. Andrew Jackson, "Veto Message, July 10, 1832" in *A Compilation of the Messages and Papers of the Presidents, 1789–1897*, 10 vols., ed. James D. Richardson (Washington, D.C.: Government Printing Office, 1896), vol. 2, p. 582.

24. *Federalist* 63, p. 389.

CHAPTER 5: EDUCATION AND THE CONSTITUTION, *Eva T. H. Brann*

1. James Madison, *Notes of the Debates in the Federal Convention of 1787* (New York: W. W. Norton, 1966), pp. 477–78, 639.

2. *The Annals of America* (Chicago: Encyclopaedia Britannica), vol. 3, p. 314.

3. Wilson Smith, ed., *Theories of Education in Early America 1655–1819* (Indianapolis: Bobbs-Merrill, 1973), p. 244.

4. Ibid., pp. 292–305.

5. *Annals*, vol. 3, pp. 604–5.

6. *Annals*, vol. 4, p. 117.

7. Gordon C. Lee, ed., *Crusade against Ignorance: Thomas Jefferson on Education* (New York: Columbia University, 1964), p. 75.

8. Ibid., p. 79.

9. Ibid., p. 136

10. *Annals*, vol. 3, p. 610.

11. Gordon S. Wood, *The Creation of the American Republic 1776–1787* (Chapel Hill: University of North Carolina Press, 1969), pp. 426–27.

12. Frederick Rudolph, *The American College and University* (New York: Random House, 1962), pp. 209–10.

13. Staff, Social Sciences I, eds., *The People Shall Judge* (Chicago: University of Chicago Press, 1949), vol. 1, pp. 458–63.

14. David Fellman, *The Supreme Court and Education* (New York: Columbia University, 1976), p. 117.

15. E. Edmund Reutter, Jr., *The Supreme Court's Impact on Public Education* (Phi Delta Kappa and National Organization of Legal Problems of Education, 1982), pp. 5–9.

16. Fellman, *The Supreme Court and Education*, p. 89.

17. Lee, *Crusade against Ignorance*, p. 117.

18. Ibid., pp. 133–34.

19. Lawrence A. Cremin, *The Republic and the School: Horace Mann on the Education of Free Men* (New York: Columbia University, 1957), p. 93.

20. Ibid., p. 97.

21. John Dewey, *Democracy and Education* (New York: Free Press, 1944), pp. 120–21.

22. John J. Patrick, *James Madison and the Federal Papers* (Bloomington: ERIC, 1990), p. 10.

23. Ibid., p. 1.

24. Ibid., pp. 2–4.

25. Ibid., p. 2.

26. Alexis de Tocqueville, *Democracy in America* (New York: Vintage Books, 1958), vol. 1, p. 172.

27. Nathan Glazer and Daniel Patrick Moynihan, *Beyond the Melting Pot* (Cambridge: MIT Press, 1963), p. v.

28. Alexander Hamilton, John Jay, and James Madison, *The Federalist* (New York: Modern Library, n.d.), p. 54.

29. Diane Ravitch, "Multiculturalism: E Pluribus Plures," *Key Reporter*, vol. 56, no. 1 (Autumn 1990), p. 2.

30. Ibid., p. 2.

CHAPTER 6: ONE OF THE GUARDIANS, SOMETIMES, *Louis Fisher*

1. Max Farrand, ed., *The Records of the Federal Convention*, vol. 2 (New Haven: Yale University Press, 1937), pp. 46, 132–33, 146, 172, 186, 430; Jonathan Elliot, ed., *The Debates in the Several State Conventions on the Adoption of the Federal Constitution*, vol. 3 (Washington, D.C.: 1836–1845), p. 532; Benjamin Wright, ed., *The Federalist*, p. 503 (Hamilton's 80).

2. Farrand, vol. 2, p. 92.

3. Ibid., p. 93.

4. Gaillard Hunt, ed., *The Writings of James Madison*, vol. 5 (New York: G. P. Putnam's, 1904), p. 294.

5. *Collected Legal Papers* (New York: Harcourt, Brace and Howe, 1920), pp. 295–96.

6. *Annals of Congress*, 1st Congress, 1st session, June 8, 1789, p. 439.

7. Ibid., June 17, 1789, p. 500.

8. Hylton v. United States, 3 Dall. 171, 175 (1796).

9. Cooper v. Telfair, 4 Dall. 14, 19 (1800).

10. *The Writings of Thomas Jefferson*, memorial ed., vol. 10 (Washington, D.C.: 1903–1904), p. 61.

11. 8 *Annals of Congress*, 5th Congress, 2nd & 3rd sessions, 1798, p. 2152.

12. *Writings of Thomas Jefferson*, vol. 11, pp. 43–44.

13. Ibid., p. 51.

14. 6 Stat. 802, c. 45 (1840).

15. U.S. Congress, House, Committee on the Judiciary, "Matthew Lyon–Heirs of," House Report 86, 26th Congress, 1st session, 1840, p. 2, reproduced in part in Louis Fisher, *American Constitutional Law* (New York: McGraw-Hill, 1990), pp. 642–43.

16. New York Times Co. v. Sullivan, 376 U.S. 254, 276 (1964).

17. Marbury v. Madison, 5 U.S. (1 Cr.) 137, 177 (1803).

18. Warren E. Burger, "The Doctrine of Judicial Review: Mr. Marshall, Mr. Jefferson, and Mr. Marbury," in Mark Cannon and David O'Brien, eds., *Views from the Bench* (Chatham, N.J.: Chatham House publishers, 1985), p. 14.

19. Albert Beveridge, *The Life of John Marshall*, vol. 3 (Boston: Houghton Mifflin, 1919), p. 177.

20. Benjamin Wright, ed., *The Federalist* (Cambridge: Harvard University Press, 1961), pp. 508–9.

21. Walter Murphy, "Why *Marbury* Matters," *Constitution*, vol. 1 (1989), p. 62.

22. U.S. Congress, Senate, Committee on the Judiciary, "Reorganization of the Federal Judiciary," S. Rept. No. 711, 75th Congress, 1st session, 1937, p. 3.

23. Ibid., p. 14.

24. Ibid., p. 19.

25. Ibid., p. 20.

26. Ibid., pp. 20–22.

27. Ibid., p. 23.

28. Henry W. Edgerton, "The Incidence of Judicial Control over Congress," *Cornell Law Quarterly*, vol. 22, no. 3 (April 1937), pp. 299–348.

29. Ibid., p. 300.

30. Ibid., p. 301.

31. Charles Warren, *Congress, the Constitution and the Supreme Court* (Boston: Little, Brown, 1925). A second edition appeared in 1935.

32. Edgerton, "Judicial Control over Congress," p. 311.

33. Ibid.

34. Warren, *Congress, the Constitution, and the Supreme Court*, p. 135.

35. J. Moore, ed., *The Works of James Buchanan*, vol. 10 (Philadelphia: J. B. Lippincott, 1910), p. 106. Emphasis in original.

36. James D. Richardson, ed., *A Compilation of the Messages and Papers of the Presidents*, vol. 7 (New York: Bureau of National Literature, 1897–1925), p. 2962.

37. Roy Basler, ed., *Collected Works of Abraham Lincoln*, vol. 2 (New Brunswick: Rutgers University Press, 1953), p. 516.

38. Richardson, *Messages and Papers of the Presidents*, vol. 7, p. 3210.

39. 12 Stat. 432, c. 111 (1862).

40. 10 Op. Att'y Gen. 382, 387 (1862).

41. Ibid., p. 397.

42. Ibid., p. 398. Emphasis in original.

43. Ibid., p. 409.

44. Ibid., p.412.

45. Ibid., p. 413. Emphasis in original.

46. 109 U.S. 3 (1883).

47. Warren, *Congress, the Constitution, and the Supreme Court*, p. 134. These civil rights cases appear in Warren's list on p. 282.

48. Edgerton, "Judicial Control over Congress," p. 325.

49. Bradwell v. State, 16 Wall. (83 U.S.) 130 (1873).

50. *Congressional Record*, 45th Congress, 2nd session, 1878, p. 1821.

51. *Congressional Record*, 46th Congress, 1st session, 1879, p. 1084; 20 Stat. 292 (1879).

52. In re Lockwood, 154 U.S. 116 (1894).

53. Reed v. Reed, 404 U.S. 71 (1971).

54. John D. Johnston, Jr., and Charles L. Knapp, "Sex Discrimination by Law: A Study in Judicial Perspective," *New York University Law Review*, vol. 46 (1971), p. 676.

55. Edgerton, "Judicial Control over Congress," p. 325.

56. Ibid., pp. 332–36.

57. Ibid., pp. 337–44.

58. Ibid., pp. 344–46.
59. Ibid., p. 347.
60. Ibid., p. 348.
61. Ibid.
62. Ibid.
63. West Virginia State Board of Education v. Barnette, 319 U.S. 624 (1943).
64. Minersville School District v. Gobitis, 310 U.S. 586 (1940).
65. David R. Manwaring, *Render unto Caesar: The Flag-Salute Controversy* (Chicago: University of Chicago Press, 1962); Francis H. Heller, "A Turning Point for Religious Liberty," *Virginia Law Review*, vol. 29 (1943), p. 440.
66. Jones v. Opelika, 316 U.S. 584, 624 (1942).
67. William Howard Taft, "Criticisms of the Federal Judiciary," *American Law Review*, vol. 29 (1895), p. 643.
68. Hirabayashi v. United States, 320 U.S. 81 (1943).
69. Korematsu v. United States, 323 U.S. 214 (1944).
70. Ibid., p. 242.
71. Ibid., p. 246.
72. Earl Warren, "The Bill of Rights and the Military," *New York University Law Review*, vol. 37 (1962), p. 193.
73. Ibid., p. 202.
74. Ibid.
75. Ibid.
76. U.S. Congress, Commission on Wartime Relocation and Internment of Civilians, *Personal Justice Denied: Report of the Commission on Wartime Relocation and Internment of Civilians* (December 1982), p. 18.
77. Ibid., p. 238.
78. 102 Stat. 903, § 1(1).
79. Ibid., p. 904, § 2(a).
80. "Delayed Reparations and an Apology," *Washington Post*, October 10, 1990, p. A1.
81. Griffin v. School Bd., 377 U.S. 218, 229 (1964).
82. Zurcher v. Stanford Daily, 436 U.S. 547 (1978).
83. 94 Stat. 1879 (1980). For further details on this debate, see Fisher, *American Constitutional Law*, pp. 868–69, 890–92.
84. Goldman v. Weinberger, 475 U.S. 503 (1986).
85. 101 Stat. 1086–87, § 508 (1987).
86. Fisher, *American Constitutional Law*, pp. 740–46.
87. Ibid., pp. 545–46, 633, 712, 791, 873, 888, 1067–68, 1149–50.
88. Washington v. Chrisman, 455 U.S. 1 (1982).
89. State v. Chrisman, 676 P.2d 419 (Wash. 1984).
90. 448 U.S. 297 (1980).
91. See, for example, Right to Choose v. Byrne, 450 A.2d 925 (N.J. 1982); Committee to Defend Reprod. Rights v. Myers, 625 P.2d 779 (Cal. 1981); Moe v. Secretary of Administration, 417 N.E.2d 387 (Mass. 1981).
92. In re T.W., 551 So.2d 1186, 1191 (Fla. 1989).
93. Ibid., p. 1202 (J. Grimes, concurring in part, dissenting in part).

CHAPTER 7: REPUBLICAN SCHOOLMASTER, *Ralph Lerner*

1. The vast secondary literature that has been spawned by this issue gives no sign of abating. This is to be expected, since the proper relation between judicial power and public opinion remains a problem, live and urgent, if mocking of final formulations.

2. Alexis de Tocqueville, *Democracy in America*, trans. George Lawrence (New York, 1966), vol. 1, pp. 137, 247–48, 252–54 (pt. 1, chap. 8; pt. 2, chap. 8).

3. See, above all, Charles Warren, "New Light on the History of the Federal Judiciary Act of 1789," *Harvard Law Review*, vol. 37 (1923), pp. 49–132.

4. *Register of Debates in Congress*, 19th Congress, 1st session, vol. 2, pt. 1, p. 1101 (Kerr), hereafter cited as *Congressional Debates;* Felix Frankfurter and James M. Landis, *The Business of the Supreme Court* (New York, 1927), pp. 12–13; Peter Archer, *The Queen's Courts* (Harmondsworth, England, 1956), pp. 250–51; Roscoe Pound, *Organization of Courts* (Boston, 1940), p. 107; and "A Democratic Federalist" (October 17, 1787), in Herbert J. Storing, ed., *The Complete Anti-Federalist* (Chicago, 1981), vol. 3, p. 61. But see *Congressional Debates*, 19th Congress, 1st session, vol. 2, pt. 1, pp. 873–74 (Webster).

5. The story of complaints, recommendations, and responses is summarized, along with much relevant historical background, in Frankfurter and Landis, *Business of the Supreme Court*, pp. 4–30. See also Leonard D. White, *The Federalists* (New York, 1948), pp. 483–84; Charles Warren, *The Supreme Court in United States History* (Boston, 1923), vol. 1, pp. 85–90; *Congressional Debates*, 19th Congress, 1st session, vol. 2, pt. 1, p. 977 (Powell).

6. Alexander Addison, *Reports of Cases in the County Courts of the Fifth Circuit . . . of Pennsylvania. And Charges to Grand Juries of those County Courts* (Washington, D.C., 1800), pt. 2, pp. 75–76 (June 1793).

7. Grand jury charge of South Carolina judge William Henry Drayton (November 1774), in Peter Force, comp., *American Archives*, 4th ser. (Washington, D.C., 1837–1846), vol. 1, pp. 959–60; John Dickinson, "President of the State of Pennsylvania, to the Chief Justice and other Judges of the Pennsylvania Supreme Court," October 8, 1785, in Samuel Hazard, ed., *Pennsylvania Archives*, 1st ser. (Philadelphia, 1852–1856), vol. 10, pp. 523–24.

8. Griffith J. McRee, ed., *Life and Correspondence of James Iredell* (Cambridge, Mass., 1857–1858), vol. 1, pp. 387–88 (May 1, 1778); grand jury charge of Judge Samuel Ashe (June 11, 1778), in Walter Clark, ed., *The State Records of North Carolina* (Winston, N.C., 1896), vol. 13, pp. 443, 441, 444.

9. Henry P. Johnston, ed., *The Correspondence and Public Papers of John Jay* (New York, 1890–1893), vol. 3, p. 390 (April–May 1790); grand jury charge of District Judge John Sitgreaves, *Gazette of the United States* (Philadelphia), May 4, 1791.

On occasion, Pennsylvania Judge Alexander Addison gave clear signs of knowing that his use of the charge went beyond his official capacity; Addison, *Reports of Cases*, pt. 2, pp. 165–66 (September 1795), p. 187 (September 1796). But his was a case where self-awareness was not always accompanied by moderation.

10. For Chief Justice Thomas Hutchinson, see Josiah Quincy, Jr., comp., *Reports of Cases . . . of the Province of Massachusetts Bay, between 1761 and 1772* (Boston,

1865), pp. 262–70, 309. For Chief Justice Frederick Smyth, see Richard S. Field, *The Provincial Courts of New Jersey, with Sketches of the Bench and Bar* (New York: New Jersey Historical Society, *Collections,* 1849), vol. 3, pp. 175, 180–81. For postwar resentment, see Richard D. Younger, *The People's Panel: The Grand Jury in the United States, 1634–1941* (Providence, R.I., 1963), p. 41.

11. Grand jury charge of Virginia judge Richard Parker, *Palladium* (Frankfort, Ky.), October 23, 1798; Addison, *Reports of Cases,* pt. 2, pp. iii–iv.

12. Descriptions of those occasions may be found in Frank Monaghan, *John Jay* (New York, 1935), p. 314; McRee, *Life of Iredell,* vol. 2, p. 435; George Van Santvoord, *Sketches of the Lives and Judicial Services of the Chief-Justices of the Supreme Court of the United States* (New York, 1854), pp. 262–63; William Garrott Brown, *The Life of Oliver Ellsworth* (New York, 1905), p. 245; Frankfurter and Landis, *Business of the Supreme Court,* p. 20; Warren, *Supreme Court in United States History,* vol. 1, p. 59, n 1.

13. Johnston, *Correspondence of Jay,* vol. 3, pp. 387–89 (April–May 1790); see also grand jury charges of district judges in New Hampshire and Maine printed in *Columbian Centinel* (Boston), July 31, 1790 (John Sullivan), and August 25, 1790 (David Sewall).

14. McRee, *Life of Iredell,* vol. 2, p. 394 (May 1793), p. 484 (May 1796); Brown, *Life of Ellsworth,* p. 247 (April 1796); Johnston, *Correspondence of Jay,* vol. 3, pp. 389–90 (April–May 1790). Compare Thomas Jefferson, First Inaugural Address, March 4, 1801, in James D. Richardson, ed., *A Compilation of the Messages and Papers of the Presidents, 1789–1897* (Washington, D.C., 1896–1899), vol. 1, p. 322.

15. Johnston, *Correspondence of Jay,* vol. 3, pp. 394–95.

16. Ibid., p. 395 (April–May 1790); see also *Pennsylvania Gazette* (Philadelphia), April 14, 1790 (Wilson), and *Columbian Centinel* (Boston), July 28, 1792 (Jay). Justice Wilson was especially insistent on developing a kind of patriotism and law-abidingness that grew out of "rationally beloved" laws: "I mean not . . . to recommend to you an implicit and an understanding approbation of the laws of your country. Admire; but admire with reason on your side"; Robert Green McCloskey, ed., *The Works of James Wilson* (Cambridge, Mass., 1967), vol. 2, p. 823 (May 1791).

17. McRee, *Life of Iredell,* vol. 2, pp. 365–66 (October 12, 1792); see also Johnston, *Correspondence of Jay,* vol. 3, p. 484 (May 23, 1796).

18. Brown, *Life of Ellsworth,* p. 246 (April 1796); *Federalist* 2, p. 9, in Jacob E. Cooke, ed., *The Federalist* (Middletown, Conn., 1961), hereafter cited as *Federalist.* Compare Henry Adams, *History of the United States during the Administrations of Thomas Jefferson and James Madison* (New York, 1889–1892), vol. 1, pp. 1–11, for another view of Jay's providentially blessed land.

19. *Columbian Centinel* (Boston), July 28, 1792 (Jay).

20. McRee, *Life of Iredell,* vol. 2, p. 467 (April 12, 1796), pp. 506–8 (May 22, 1797), pp. 484–85 (May 23, 1976); *Columbian Centinel* (Boston), July 28, 1792 (Jay).

21. McRee, *Life of Iredell,* vol. 2, p. 485 (May 23, 1796); Francis Wharton, ed., *State Trials of the United States during the Administrations of Washington and Adams* (Philadelphia, 1849), p. 57 (Jay); Brown, *Life of Ellsworth,* p. 247 (April 1796).

22. McCloskey, *Works of Wilson,* vol. 2, pp. 822–23 (May 1791). See also

Wharton, *State Trials*, p. 62; Wilson spoke of useful lessons to be taught and learned in the courtroom so that "a practical knowledge and a just sense" of a free people's duties might be "diffused universally among the citizens." This theme of the grand jurors' duty to instruct others "when you blend yourselves again among your neighbors" is well stated by Chief Justice William Henry Drayton of South Carolina in some of his charges to Charleston grand juries; see Hezekiah Niles, ed., *Principles and Acts of the Revolution in America* (New York, 1876), p. 333 (April 23, 1776), pp. 347, 352 (October 21, 1777); see also Addison, *Reports of Cases*, pt. 2, p. 110 (September 1794).

23. There are two texts in print. The original draft is in Johnston, *Correspondence of Jay*, vol. 3, pp. 478–85 (May 22, 1793). The final version, which was delivered and then "printed by the government for the purpose of explaining abroad the position of the United States," appears in Wharton, *State Trials*, pp. 49–59.

24. Wharton, *State Trials*, pp. 49–52, 58–59 (Jay).

25. Ibid., pp. 52–57 (Jay).

26. Ibid., pp. 57–58 (Jay).

27. Ibid., pp. 62–63 (Wilson); Johnston, *Correspondence of Jay*, vol. 3, pp. 481–82 (May 22, 1793). Nothing in Jay's charge runs counter to Hamilton's argument in Pacificus 4 (July 10, 1793), on the limits or inappropriateness of gratitude as a principle of international conduct.

28. Wharton, *State Trials*, p. 62 (Wilson); Johnston, *Correspondence of Jay*, vol. 3, p. 482.

29. Johnston, *Correspondence of Jay*, vol. 3, p. 485; *Columbian Centinel* (Boston), July 28, 1792 (Jay).

30. Wharton, *State Trials*, p. 58 (Jay); Johnston, *Correspondence of Jay*, vol. 3, pp. 389–90 (April–May 1790); Henry Flanders, *The Lives and Times of the Chief Justices of the Supreme Court of the United States*, rev. ed. (New York, 1875), vol. 2, p. 192 (Ellsworth); McRee, *Life of Iredell*, vol. 2, p. 467 (April 12, 1796).

31. The text of Justice Chase's offending grand jury charge of May 2, 1803, is reproduced in Charles Evans, *Report of the Trial of the Hon. Samuel Chase . . .* (Baltimore, 1805), app., exh. 8, pp. 60–62. The Samuel H. Smith–Thomas Lloyd transcription of the Chase impeachment is printed in *Debates and Proceedings in the Congress of the United States, 1789–1824* (Washington, D.C., 1834–1856), 8th Congress, 2nd session, hereafter cited as *Annals of Congress*. The charge appears at pp. 673–76.

32. Marbury v. Madison, 1 Cranch 137 (1803), and Stuart v. Laird, 1 Cranch 299 (1803).

33. Yet such was Justice Chase's hope. See his gloss on this text in Evans, *Report of the Chase Trial*, app., p. 39, and in *Annals of Congress*, 8th Congress, 2nd session, p. 148. Henry Adams comments on this passage of the charge in his *John Randolph* (Boston, 1883), p. 136:

> There was gross absurdity in the idea that the people who, by an immense majority, had decided to carry on their government in one way should be forced by one of their servants to turn about and go in the opposite direction; and the indecorum was greater than the absurdity, for if Judge Chase or any other official held such doctrines,

even though he were right, he was bound not to insult officially the people who employed him.

There was absurdity enough, perhaps, without exaggerating the matter. Chase did not entertain the delusion that the people could "be forced" to adopt contrary principles, but he obviously acted as though he believed that they had been persuaded out of one set of opinions and into another set.

34. Edmund Burke, "Reflections on the Revolution in France," in *The Works of The Right Honourable Edmund Burke* (London: Bohn's British Classics, 1854–1856), vol. 2, pp. 282, 332–34. The earliest published account of Chase's charge found its theorizing repulsive and attacked it for its "unjust reproaches cast upon . . . the fundamental and characteristic principles of the nation itself"; *National Intelligencer and Washington Advertiser* (Washington), May 20, 1803.

35. See the evidence of Maryland aristocrats "exciting the favor of the people they associate with on no other occasion," in Chilton Williamson, *American Suffrage: From Property to Democracy, 1760-1860* (Princeton, N.J., 1960), pp. 140–46. A sufficient explanation of aristocratic acquiescence in suffrage reform is given by Tocqueville, *Democracy in America*, vol. 1, p. 52 (pt. 1, chap. 4).

36. Evans, *Report of the Chase Trial*, pp. 242–44 (Harper), app., pp. 37–38 (Chase); *Annals of Congress*, 8th Congress, 2nd session, pp. 556–58 (Harper), p. 146 (Chase), p. 639 (Rodney).

37. Chief Justice Taney's charge to a grand jury, 30 Federal Cases 998, at 999, Case 18,257 (1836).

38. Learned Hand, *The Bill of Rights* (Cambridge, Mass., 1958), p. 73.

39. Max Farrand, ed., *The Records of the Federal Convention of 1787*, rev. ed. (New Haven, Conn., 1937), vol. 1, p. 84; Noah Webster, "An Examination into the Leading Principles of the Federal Constitution . . .," in Paul Leicester Ford, ed., *Pamphlets on the Constitution of the United States, Published during Its Discussion by the People, 1787-1788* (Brooklyn, 1888), p. 59.

40. Jonathan Elliot, ed., *The Debates in the Several State Conventions on the Adoption of the Federal Constitution . . .*, 2nd ed. (Philadelphia, 1888), vol. 3, pp. 164–65, 232, 536–37.

41. Ibid., vol. 2, pp. 252, 254.

42. Leonard D. White, *The Jeffersonians* (New York, 1951), p. 550. White argues explicitly (pp. 547–50) that the same social class dominated public life throughout the first forty years of the national government and implicitly that the political differences among them were of only secondary importance.

43. *Federalist* 55, p. 378; 76, pp. 513–14; 51, p. 349; 22, p. 142.

44. *Federalist* 27, p. 175; 28, p. 179; 73, pp. 497, 493; 37, p. 239.

45. *Federalist* 71, pp. 482–83. Compare Lincoln's "Young Men's Lyceum Address" on the perpetuation of our political institutions (January 27, 1838) for another analysis of the motivations of those leaders whose *"all was staked"* on demonstrating in practice that the people were capable of self-government; Roy F. Basler et al., eds., *The Collected Works of Abraham Lincoln* (New Brunswick, N.J., 1953–1955), vol. 1, p. 113. Consider, in the light of Lincoln's statement of the problem posed by ambition, Publius's exception of "a few aspiring characters"

(*Federalist* 57, p. 386) and his explicit silence about his own motives (*Federalist* 1, p. 6).

46. *Federalist* 71, p. 482; 35, pp. 218–22; 57, pp. 385–87.

47. *Federalist* 64, p. 433; 63, pp.422–23; 62, p. 419; 58, p. 395.

48. *Federalist* 76, pp. 510–11; 68, pp. 460–61; 75, p. 505; 73, p. 497.

49. *Federalist* 76, p. 511.

50. *Federalist* 49, p. 341; 78, pp. 525, 527–28 (emphasis added); 71, p. 483.

51. A fair, even inevitable, objection would be, Was there in fact, in 1787, any wary distrust of the judiciary on grounds of its "nondemocratic" character? According to Jackson Turner Main, "the argument which developed a hundred years later, that the [Supreme] Court was undemocratic because of its lack of responsibility, and that it was biased against changes desired by the majority, while implied by a few [Anti-Federalist] writers, was never clearly stated"; *The Antifederalists: Critics of the Constitution, 1781–1788* (Chicago, 1964), p. 156. One might also question whether there was much political sensitivity to a judiciary as independent as the one proposed by the Constitutional Convention by recalling that, at the time, a majority of the states (including New York) provided for judicial tenure during good behavior and that all the states filled their highest courts by appointment, not election; William Clarence Webster, "A Comparative Study of the State Constitutions of the American Revolution," *Annals*, vol. 9 (1897), pp. 401–3; James Schouler, *Constitutional Studies, State and Federal* (New York, 1904), pp. 64–65; but see Roscoe Pound, *The Formative Era of American Law* (Boston, 1938), pp. 91–92, on the prevailing distrust of judges. Note, too, the forebodings of Federal Farmer 3 and 15 (October 10, 1787 and January 18, 1788), and of Brutus 11 and 15 (January 31, 1788, and March 20, 1788), in Storing, *Complete Anti-Federalist*, vol. 2, pp. 244, 315–16, 321, 422, 438, 442.

No moderately sensitive reader of *Federalist* 78 can overlook the defensive character of its rhetoric. Publius wrote as though prevailing opinion were hostile to (or uncertain of the wisdom of) the judicial arrangement embodied in the Constitution. What leads a partisan to answer objections the opposition has not yet raised? These three considerations may well be present here: (a) to provide as thorough a defense as he can for what is to him a supremely important cause; (b) to avoid having to dwell on other objections, more or equally important; (c) to defend a position clearly seen by him as vulnerable because of his expectations (in this instance, of the political role of the Supreme Court), though not yet recognized as such by the opposition. I incline to the opinion that the tone and mode of argument of *Federalist* 78 are sufficiently understood by holding that Hamilton's hopes and fears took in a longer futurity than his foes'.

52. *Federalist* 78, pp. 522–23.

53. Farrand, *Records*, vol. 2, p. 34; *Federalist*, 37, p. 235. Publius is not of two minds on this matter; the author of *Federalist* 78 could say in *Federalist* 79, p. 533, "The mensuration of the faculties of the mind has, I believe, no place in the catalogue of known arts." In *Federalist* 51, pp. 348–49, there is a discussion of the will (and, for that matter, of the ambition and interest) of the several departments of government without any exemption of the judiciary.

54. *Federalist* 78, pp. 522–23; 81, p. 545; 65, pp. 441, 443.

55. *Federalist* 51, pp. 347–49.

56. *Federalist* 63, p. 428; 51, p. 348; 57, p. 384.

57. *Federalist* 71, pp. 482–83; 31, p. 195. See Jean-Jacques Rousseau, *De contrat social* (1762), bk. 2, chap. 3.

58. *Federalist* 22, p. 139; 58, p. 397; 71, p. 482.

59. *Federalist* 71, p. 483; 28, p. 178 (cf. *Federalist* 21, pp. 131–32); 63, p. 425. Publius had no difficulty in speaking of "the sense of the people" being operative where that sense is determined by a select body popularly chosen; see the discussion of the electoral college in *Federalist* 68, p. 458.

60. *Federalist* 78, pp. 526–29; 51, p. 348.

61. *Federalist* 78, p. 528; 82, p. 556; Aratus 3, *State Gazette of North-Carolina* (Edenton), June 4, 1789.

62. See Brutus 11 (January 31, 1788), in Storing, *Complete Anti-Federalist,* vol. 2, pp. 418, 420; Elliot, *Debates,* vol. 4, p. 258 (C. Pinckney); *Federalist* 16, p. 102; 22, pp. 143–44; 80, pp. 535, 537–38.

63. Farrand, *Records,* vol. 1, p. 21.

64. Ibid., pp. 138–39; vol. 2, pp. 73–74.

65. Ibid., vol. 2, pp. 73, 75; vol. 1, p. 139; vol. 2, p. 342; *Federalist* 73, p. 499.

66. This need not utterly rule out any judicial activity beyond deciding cases and controversies; see the careful discussion in Russell Wheeler, "The Extrajudicial Activities of the Early Supreme Court," in Philip B. Kurland, ed., *The Supreme Court Review, 1973,* pp. 123–58, esp. pp. 127–31.

67. James Kent, *Commentaries on American Law,* 1st ed. (New York, 1826–1830), lect. 14, vol. 1, pp. 273–74; Aratus 3, *State Gazette of North-Carolina* (Edenton), June 4, 1789.

68. Abraham Lincoln, "Reply to Douglas, Ottawa, Ill." (August 21, 1858), in Basler et al., *Collected Works of Lincoln,* vol. 3, p. 27; John Quincy Adams, *The Jubilee of the Constitution* (New York, 1839), p. 54. See Lincoln, "The Repeal of the Missouri Compromise" (October 16, 1854), in Basler et al., *Collected Works of Lincoln,* vol. 2, p. 255.

69. *Congressional Debates,* 19th Congress, 1st session, vol. 2, pt. 1, p. 554 (Harper), p. 878 (Webster), p. 1100 (Kerr). I have adapted the language of Lord Devlin—"A judge is tethered to the positive law but not shackled to it"—as conveying quite precisely the kind of relation between judge and public opinion that the early Congresses envisioned; Sir Patrick Devlin, *The Enforcement of Morals* (London, 1965), p. 94.

CHAPTER 8: PUBLIC POLICY, *Herman Schwartz*

1. Jacobellis v. Ohio, 378 U.S. 184, 197 (1964).

2. Marbury v. Madison, 5 U.S. 137, 168 (1803).

3. Lord Radcliffe, *The Law and Its Compass* (Evanston, Ill.: Northwestern University Press, 1960), p. 46.

4. Ibid., pp. 48–49.

5. Griswold v. Connecticut, 381 U.S. 479, 527 (1965) (Justice Stewart dissent-

ing); Plyler v. Doe, 457 U.S. 202, 242 (1982) (Chief Justice Burger dissenting); and Lochner v. New York, 198 U.S. 45, 74–76 (1904) (Justice Holmes dissenting). Justice Robert Jackson was unhappy about the school desegregation decision because he thought it was not law but social policy. Richard Kluger, *Simple Justice* (New York: Vintage, 1975), pp. 604–10.

6. For a discussion of some implications of the distinction, see Jennifer Nedelsky, *Private Property and the Limits of American Constitutionalism* (Chicago: University of Chicago Press, 1990), pp. 198–99.

7. Arguably, President Dwight Eisenhower's nominations were an exception to this, as are occasional nominations based on personal friendship, like President Harry Truman's, or the exceptional prestige of a nominee such as Benjamin N. Cardozo. See generally Herman Schwartz, *Packing the Courts* (New York: Chas. Scribner's Sons, 1988).

8. Of course in many cases logic and precedent do have independent force, and the distinction has some justification. See, for example, the recent punitive damages case, Pacific Mutual Life Ins. Co. v. Haslip, 111 S. Ct. 1032 (1991), where most of the Court would probably have gone the other way as a matter of public policy. But these are not usually the hard controversial cases, for which we have created a judiciary with life tenure.

9. Basic Law of the Federal Republic of Germany, Article 93; Constitutional Act of February 27, 1991, Concerning the Constitutional Court of the Czech and Slovak Federal Republic, Article 2. The German abortion decision is translated and excerpted in Donald Kommers, *The Constitutional Jurisprudence of the Federal Republic of Germany* (Durham, N.C.: Duke University Press, 1989), pp. 348–59.

10. Kommers, *Judicial Politics in West Germany* (Sage, 1966).

11. Mauro Cappelletti, *Judicial Review in Comparative Perspective* (Oxford: Oxford University Press, 1989).

12. Baker v. Carr, 369 U.S. 186, 217 (1962).

13. Allen v. Wright, 468 U.S. 737 (1984); Warth v. Seldin, 422 U.S. 490 (1975).

14. See, for example, Duke Power v. Carolina Environmental Study Group, 438 U.S. 59 (1978).

15. Laird v. Tatum, 408 U.S. 1, 15 (1972).

16. Allen v. Wright, 468 U.S. at 791. This reached a ludicrous extreme when the Court held that while a taxpayer has standing to challenge the grant of tax money to a religious institution for religious purposes, he may not challenge a gift of tangible property to that same religious institution for the same religious purposes. Valley Forge College v. Americans United for Separation of Church and State, 454 U.S. 700 (1982).

17. See Laura Underkuffler, "Property: An Essay," *Yale Law Journal*, vol. 100 (1990), p. 127 (summarizing different conceptions of property); Rose, "Property Rights Regimes and the New Takings—An Evolutionary Approach," *Tennessee Law Review*, vol. 57 (1990), p. 577.

18. 198 U.S. 45 (1905).

19. James Madison, *Federalist 10, The Federalist Papers*, ed. Clinton Rossiter (New York: New American Library, 1961), p. 87.

20. See Herman Schwartz, "Property Rights and the Constitution: Will the Ugly Duckling Become a Swan?" *American University Law Review,* vol. 37 (1987), pp. 9, 21.

21. Trustees of Dartmouth College v. Woodward, 17 U.S. (4 Wheat.) 518 (1819); Fletcher v. Peck, 10 U.S. 87 (1810).

22. Fletcher, 10 U.S. at 143–46 (Justice Johnson concurring).

23. Dred Scott v. Sandford, 60 U.S. 393 (1856); United States v. E.C. Knight, 198 U.S. 45 (1905); Hammer v. Dagenhart, 247 U.S. 251 (1918).

24. Compare United States Trust Co. v. New Jersey, 431 U.S. 1 (1977), and Allied Structural Steel v. Spannaus, 438 U.S. 234 (1978), with Energy Reserves Group v. Kansas Power and Light Co., 459 U.S. 400 (1983).

25. Ferguson v. Skrupa, 372 U.S. 726 (1962).

26. C. Peter Magrath, *Yazoo* (New York: Norton, 1966), pp. 114, 115.

27. Richard Epstein, *Takings—Private Property and the Power of Eminent Domain* (Cambridge: Harvard University Press, 1985), p. 281.

28. 1962 Sup. Ct. Rev. 34.

29. Goesaert v. Cleary, 355 U.S. 464 (1948); United States Railroad Retirement Bd. v. Fritz, 449 U.S. 1966 (1980).

30. Robert McCloskey, "Economic Due Process and the Supreme Court: An Exhumation and Reburial" (1963), *Supreme Court Review* (1982 vol.), p. 62.

31. Plyler v. Doe, 457 U.S. 202 (1981) (education); Wohlgemuth v. Williams, 416 U.S. 910 (1974) (welfare); Memorial Hospital v. Maricopa County, 415 U.S. 250 (1974) (health care); U.S. Dept. of Agriculture v. Moreno, 413 U.S. 528 (1973) (food stamps); but see Lyng v. Castillo, 477 U.S. 635 (1986) (food stamps denial allowed).

32. United States Railroad Retirement Bd. v. Fritz, 449 U.S. at 182 (Justices Brennan and Marshall dissenting); Schweiker v. Wilson, 450 U.S. 221, 239 (1981) (Justice Powell dissenting).

33. Pacific Mutual Life Ins. Co. V. Haslip, 111 S. Ct. 1032 (1991).

34. Metro. Life Ins. v. Ward, 470 U.S. 869 (1985).

35. Buckley v. Valeo, 424 U.S. 656 (1975); but see Austin v. Mich. St. Chamber of Commerce, 110 S. Ct. 1391 (1990). Some have also argued that the Supreme Court has been increasing protection for property by invoking the First Amendment's protection for speech. Mark Tushnet, "An Essay on Rights," *Texas Law Review,* vol. 62 (1984), pp. 1363, 1387.

36. Radcliffe, supra n. 3, pp. 64, 66.

37. Laurence Tribe, *American Constitutional Law,* 2nd ed., chap. 9 (Mineola, N.Y.: Foundation Press, 1988), p. 587.

38. Energy Reserves Group Inc. v. Kansas Power and Light Co., 459 U.S. 400 (1983).

39. Hawaii Hous. Auth. v. Midkiff, 467 U.S. 229, 241–43 (1984) (upholding statute transferring land from lessors to lessees to reduce ownership concentration); West Coast Hotel Co. v. Parrish, 300 U.S. 379, 396–97 (1937) (upholding statute establishing minimum wages for women); Morehead v. New York ex rel. Tipaldo, 298 U.S. 587, 618 (1936) (overruling state minimum wage law to benefit adult female employees); Bowman Transp., Inc. v. Arkansas-Best Freight Sys.,

Inc., 419 U.S. 281, 293 (1974) (upholding determination of Interstate Commerce Commission that benefits of new shipper's market entry outweighed adverse effect); Nebbia v. New York, 291 U.S. 502, 521 (1934) (upholding regulation of milk prices charged by dealers to storekeepers); Munn v. Illinois, 94 U.S. 113, 135 (1877) (affirming regulation of grain storage rates charged by warehouse owners).

40. Epstein, *Takings*, p. 280.

41. John Locke, *Second Treatise of Government*, ed. Thomas Cook (New York: Hafner Pub., 1947), p. 134.

42. See Epstein, *Takings*, pp. 252–53.

43. *Federalist* 10, p. 79.

44. West Virginia State Bd. of Educ. v. Barnette, 319 U.S. 624, 638 (1943) (Justice Jackson concurring).

45. Letter, Thomas Jefferson to James Madison (October 17, 1788), in Robert A. Rutland et al., eds., *Papers of James Madison 1788–89*, vol. 11 (Charlottesville: University of Virginia Press, 1977), p. 297.

46. William Nelson, "The Eighteenth Century Constitution as a Basis for Protecting Individual Liberty," in *Liberty and Community: Constitution and Rights in the Early American Republic* (New York: Oceana Press, 1989).

47. The two flag-burning decisions are Texas v. Johnson, 491 U.S. 397 (1989), and United States v. Eichman, 110 S. Ct. 2404 (1990).

48. C. E. Hughes, *The Supreme Court of the United States* (New York: Columbia University Press, 1928), p. 50.

49. Scott v. Sandford, 60 U.S. 393, 404–5 (1857) (denial of citizenship to Negro slaves based on status as property of slaveholders); Hepburn v. Griswold, 75 U.S. 603, 623 (1870) (use of U.S. notes as legal tender for debts considered an unconstitutional impairment of contract obligations); Pollock v. Farmer's Loan & Trust Co., 158 U.S. 601, 637 (1895) (income tax unconstitutional because not apportioned according to representation).

50. See West Coast Hotel v. Parrish, 300 U.S. 379, 397–98 (1937) (every presumption favors validity of legislative enactment and upholding Washington minimum wage law).

51. Epstein, *Takings*, pp. 137-40 (advocating intermediate level of review for both First Amendment and eminent domain cases); Craig v. Boren, 429 U.S. 190, 197 (1976) (emphasis added) (applying intermediate review to classification based on gender); Regents of the University of California v. Bakke, 438 U.S. 265, 359 (1978) (Justice Brennan concurring) (advocating intermediate level of review for some race classifications [quoting Boren, 429 U.S. at 197]).

52. I would think we have had enough difficulty with the two standards of review which our cases have recognized—the norm of "rational basis," and the "compelling state interest" required where a "suspect classification" is involved—so as to counsel weightily against the insertion of still another "standard" between those two. How is this Court to divine [sic] what objectives are important? How is it to determine whether a particular law is "substantially" related to the achievement of such objective, rather than related in some other way

to its achievement? Both of the phrases used are so diaphanous and elastic as to invite subjective judicial preferences or prejudices relating to particular types of legislation, masquerading as judgments whether such legislation is directed at "important" objectives or, whether the relationship to those objectives is "substantial" enough. . . . [T]he introduction of the adverb "substantially" requires courts to make subjective judgments as to operational effects, for which neither their expertise nor their access to data fits them.

429 U.S. at 220–21.

53. Compare, for example, Trimble v. Gordon, 430 U.S. 762 (1977), with Lalli v. Lalli, 439 U.S. 259 (1978); Caban v. Mohammed, 441 U.S. 380 (1979), with Parham v. Hughes, 441 U.S. 347 (1979); Craig v. Boren, 429 U.S. 190 (1976), with Michael M. v. Superior Court of Sonoma County, 450 U.S. 464 (1981).

54. See, for example, Hawaii Hous. Auth. v. Midkiff, 467 U.S. 229, 231–32 (1984) (finding State of Hawaii's reason for taking real property from lessors and transferring it to lessees was to reduce concentration of fee simple ownerships in state).

55. Epstein, *Takings*, pp. 180–81.

56. Ibid., pp. 181, 184.

57. See Robert Bork, "The Constitution, Original Intent and Economic Rights," *San Diego Law Review*, vol. 23 (1986), pp. 823, 831 ("In the case of most laws about which there is likely to be controversy, the social sciences are simply not up to the task assigned.").

58. Recent takings cases show some indications that the Court may be ready to embark on a more vigorous protection for economic rights, but it is still too early to tell. See First English Evangelical Lutheran Church of Glendale v. County of Los Angeles, 107 S. Ct. 2378 (1987); Nollen v. California Coastal Comm., 107 S. Ct. 31141 (1987).

59. Robert Bork, *Tradition and Morality in Constitutional Law* (Washington, D.C.: American Enterprise Institute, 1984), p. 10.

60. U.S. Congress, Senate, *Hearings before the Committee on the Judiciary, United States Senate, on the Nomination of Robert H. Bork to be Associate Justice of the Supreme Court of the United States*, 100th Congress, 2d session, 1987, passim.

61. Edwin Meese, Address to the American Bar Association, July 9, 1985, pp. 13–14.

62. See Wallace v. Jaffree, 472 U.S. 38, 113 (Justice Rehnquist dissenting).

63. See Schwartz, *Packing the Courts*, pp. 34–38.

64. Patricia M. Wald, "The Sizzling Sleeper: The Use of Legislative History in Construction Statutes in the 1988–89 Term of the Supreme Court," *American University Law Review*, vol. 39 (1990), p. 277.

65. The Scalia statements appear in "Statements before U.S. Senate Judiciary Committee on Nomination of Antonin Scalia to Supreme Court," *Daily Labor Report*, August 7, 1986, and Green v. Bock Laundry Mach. Co., 490 U.S. 504, 528 (1989) (Justice Scalia dissenting).

66. The language quoted by Justice Scalia is from Harry Jones, "Statutory Doubts and Legislative Intention," *Columbia Law Review*, vol. 40 (1940), pp. 957, 965.

67. Patterson v. McLean Credit Union, 491 U.S. 164 (1989).
68. Sullivan v. Everhart, 494 U.S. 83, 93 (1990).
69. Ibid. at 102 (Justice Stevens dissenting).

CHAPTER 9: JUDICIAL REVIEW AT THE FOUNDING, *Gordon S. Wood*

1. For recent revisionist studies of the history of judicial review, and particularly the history of Marbury v. Madison, see Christopher Wolfe, *The Rise of Modern Judicial Review: From Constitutional Interpretation to Judge-Made Law* (New York, 1986); J. M. Sosin, *The Aristocracy of the Long Robe: The Origins of Judicial Review in America* (Westport, Conn., 1989); and Robert Lowry Clinton, *Marbury v. Madison and Judicial Review* (Lawrence, Kan., 1989).

2. [Anon.], *Four Letters on Interesting Subjects* (Philadelphia, 1776), p. 21.

3. [John Adams], *Boston Gazette*, January 27, 1766, in Charles F. Adams, ed., *Works of John Adams* . . . (Boston, 1850–1856), vol. 3, pp. 480–82.

4. [William Henry Drayton], *A Letter from Freeman of South-Carolina* . . . (Charleston, 1774).

5. Thomas Jefferson to Edmund Pendleton, August 26, 1776, in Julian P. Boyd et al., eds., *Papers of Thomas Jefferson* (Princeton, 1950–), vol. 1, p. 505.

6. "On the Present States of America," October 10, 1776, Peter Force, ed., *American Archives* . . . , 5th ser. (Washington, D.C., 1837–1846), vol. 2, p. 969.

7. William Henry Drayton, Speech to General Assembly of South Carolina, January 20, 1778, in Hezekiah Niles, ed., *Principles and Acts of the Revolution in America* (New York, 1876), p. 359. For a discussion of the confused state of colonial law and the prevalence of judicial discretion, see Gordon S. Wood, *The Creation of the American Republic, 1776–1787* (Chapel Hill, N.C., 1969), pp. 291–305.

8. [Anon.], *Rudiments of Law and Government, Deduced from the Law of Nature* (Charleston, S.C., 1783), pp. 35–37.

9. Moses Mather, *Sermon, Preached in the Audience of the General Assembly . . . on the Day of Their Anniversary Election, May 10, 1781* (New London, 1781), pp. 7–8.

10. Charleston, *State Gazette of South Carolina*, September 8, 1784.

11. Lynn W. Turner, *William Plumer of New Hampshire, 1759–1850* (Chapel Hill, N.C., 1962), pp. 34–35.

12. Address of Massachusetts Convention (1780), in Oscar Handlin and Mary Handlin, eds., *The Popular Sources of Political Authority: Documents on the Massachusetts Constitution of 1780* (Cambridge, Mass., 1966), p. 437.

13. Commonwealth of Va. v. Caton and others (November 1782), in Peter Call, ed., *Reports of Cases Argued and Decided in the Court of Appeals of Virginia* (Richmond, 1833), vol. 4, p. 8.

14. Ibid., pp. 17–18.

15. Richard Spraight to James Iredell, August 12, 1787, in Griffith J. McRee, *Life and Correspondence of James Iredell* (New York, 1857–1858), vol. 2, pp. 169–70.

16. James Madison's "Observations on Jefferson's Draft of a Constitution for Virginia," 1788, in Boyd et al., eds., *Papers of Jefferson*, vol. 6, p. 315.

17. *Providence Gazette*, May 12, 1787.

18. See especially J. W. Gough, *Fundamental Law in English Constitutional*

History (Oxford, 1955, 1961), pp. 186–90, 206, 214.

19. James Iredell to Richard Spraight, August 26, 1787, in McRee, *Life of Iredell,* vol. 2, pp. 172–76.

20. Commonwealth of Va. v. Caton, in Call, ed., *Reports,* vol. 4, p. 17.

21. James Iredell, "To the Public," August 17, 1786, in McRee, *Life of Iredell,* vol. 2, p. 147.

22. James Madison, "Helvidius No. II," 1793, in Gaillard Hunt, ed., *The Writings of James Madison* (New York, 1900–1910), vol. 4, p. 155.

23. *Federalist* 49.

24. Sylvia Snowiss, *Judicial Review and the Law of the Constitution* (New Haven, Conn., 1990), p. 74. Snowiss's recent book is by far the best single work we have on the origins of judicial review. Her argument that constitutional law became legalized in the early republic, though overly schematic and precious at times, elevates the discussion to a new plane, and I have relied on it extensively. Her book, unlike so many of the other recent studies of judicial review, has the added virtue of not seeming to have a political ax to grind.

25. Max Farrand, ed., *The Records of the Federal Convention of 1787* (New Haven, Conn., 1937), vol. 1, pp. 97, 73.

26. For this reason some congressmen in 1792 debated establishing a regular procedure for federal judges to notify Congress officially when a law was declared unconstitutional—so nervous were they over the gravity of such an action. Joseph Gales, comp., *Annals of the Congress of the United States* (Washington, D.C., 1834), vol. 3, p. 557.

27. As Justice Samuel Chase said in Hylton v. United States (1796), if the constitutionality of Congress's law had been *"doubtful,"* he would have been bound "to receive the construction of the legislature" (3 Dallas 172–73). As late as 1800 in Cooper v. Telfair Justices Bushrod Washington and William Paterson agreed that judicial review was an extraordinary act, to be only infrequently exercised. "The presumption . . . must always be in favour of the validity of laws, if the contrary is not clearly demonstrated," declared Washington. For the Supreme Court "to pronounce any law void," said Paterson, there "must be a clear and unequivocal breach of the constitution, not a doubtful and argumentative implication" (4 Dallas 18–19). This had to be the position of judges as long as judicial review seemed to resemble the momentousness of, say, Jefferson's 1798 idea of state nullification.

28. Snowiss, *Judicial Review,* p. 64.

29. Gerald Gunther, "Judicial Review," in Leonard W. Levy et al., eds., *Encyclopedia of the American Constitution* (New York, 1986), p. 1055.

30. Marbury v. Madison (1803), William Cranch, ed., *U.S. Supreme Court Reports* (Washington, 1804), p. 177. Robert Clinton seems to believe that treating the Constitution as law, as the framers did, formed no basis for modern judicial review; statutory construction of the Constitution, he says, does not "inexorably" lead to modern judicial activism. Perhaps not "inexorably," but legalizing the Constitution was surely the most important and requisite initial step in making possible judicial review, including modern judicial activism. Clinton, moreover, does not seem to appreciate the extraordinary degree of interpretive power

wielded by the English common law judges within their restricted domain of "statutory construction." Knowing the words of a statute in English jurisprudence is not the same as knowing the law; in a like manner knowing the words of the Constitution is not the same as knowing constitutional law. In both cases judicial interpretation of texts requires extensive knowledge of whole legal systems and involves the continual creation of new legal meanings; indeed, English judges have been accused of making the law as a legislator does almost as much as American judges. Thus for American judges to treat the federal Constitution and the state constitutions as a species of law to be brought within the domain of "statutory construction" was no minor achievement. Clinton, Marbury v. Madison, p. 23.

31. Snowiss, *Judicial Review*, p. 172.

32. Alexander Hamilton, quoted in Wolfe, *Modern Judicial Review*, p. 30.

33. Alexander Hamilton, "Remarks in New York Assembly," February 6, 1787, in Harold C. Syrett et al., eds., *The Papers of Alexander Hamilton* (New York, 1961–), vol. 4, p. 35. The view expressed by Hamilton did not of course immediately take hold. The attorney general of North Carolina, for example, argued in 1794 that the clauses of the state constitution referring to due process and the law of the land were not limitations on the legislature; they were "declarations the people thought proper to make of their rights, not against a power they supposed their own representatives might usurp, but against oppression and usurpation in general . . . , by a pretended prerogative against or without the authority of law." Thus the phrase that no one could be deprived of his property except by the law of the land meant simply "a law for the people of North Carolina, made or adopted by themselves by the intervention of their own legislature." Edward S. Corwin, "The Doctrine of Due Process of Law before the Civil War," *Harvard Law Review*, vol. 24 (1911), pp. 371–72. Blackstone had written that one of the absolute rights of individuals was "the right of property: which consists in the free use, enjoyment and disposal of all his acquisitions, without any control or diminution, *save only by the laws of the land*"—which of course for Blackstone included those laws enacted by Parliament. Corwin, "Basic Doctrine of American Constitutional Law," *Michigan Law Review*, vol. 12 (1914), p. 254.

34. Marbury v. Madison (1803), in Cranch, ed., *U.S. Supreme Court Reports*, pp. 166, 167.

35. Alexander J. Dallas, quoted in Richard E. Ellis, *The Jeffersonian Crisis: Courts and Politics in the Young Republic* (New York, 1971), p. 179; Michael Les Benedict, "Laissez-Faire and Liberty: A Re-Evaluation of the Meaning and Origins of Laissez-Faire Constitutionalism," *Law and History Review*, vol. 3 (1985), pp. 323–26.

36. Alexis de Tocqueville, *Democracy in America*, ed. Phillip Bradley (New York, 1956), vol. 1, p. 278.

Index

legalization of, 164–65
written, 160–63
See also Constitution; Natural
law

Gerry, Elbridge, 132, 162
Gorham, Nathaniel, 132
Grand jury
Supreme Court justices' role in,
100–101
as vehicle for political
instruction, 101–4, 108–9
Gunther, Gerald, 164

Hamilton, Alexander, 1, 5
on checks and balances, 86
on judicial review, 159
on kind of administration,
120–21
on power of written state
constitution, 165
on will and confidence of the
people, 120–21
Harris v. McRae, 97
Haskins, George, 137
Hawaii Housing Authority v. Midkiff,
144–45, 148
Hayburn's case, 165
Henry, Patrick, 8, 119–20
Hirabayashi v. United States, 94
Holmes, Oliver Wendell
opinion in *Buck v. Bell*, 39
on Supreme Court's role in
public policy, 137
on Supreme Court's power, 83
House of Representatives, 54–56

Independent counsel provisions, 56–57
Individual rights
criticism of Supreme Court
decisions affecting, 92
protection under Alien and
Sedition Laws, 84
Iredell, James, 19, 104
on the Constitution as written
document, 160
on judicial power, 161
political instruction by, 101–2
Jackson, Andrew, 57–58

Jackson, Robert, 92–93, 146
Jay, John
on foreign policy, 109
on strategy for judicial
instruction, 105–6
on Supreme Court circuit
riding, 7
on use of political charge, 102
use of political charge by,
104–6, 117
Jefferson, Thomas, 10
on balance of powers, 48
on Constitution and its
guardians, 37
on education and the
Constitution, 68–69
on judicial activity, 155
on natural rights philosophy, 41
on necessity of a bill of rights,
146
on proposals for university,
63–64
on role of judge, 155
Johnson, Andrew, 56
Johnson, William, 35–36, 141
Judges
authority of, 38–40, 44–45
development of legal activity
of, 163–66
legislative branch in selection
of, 154–55
perceived separateness of,
132–33
provision in Constitution for,
24–25, 83
See also Judiciary
Judicial activism
in economic rights cases, 146–48
from failure of Congress, 40–42
source of, 20
in statutory construction, 149
Judicial branch
provisions in Constitution for, 83
requirement for discretion by,
156
separation from the people of,
128–29
states' post-Revolution reaction
to, 154–60
See also Judiciary

A Note on the Book

This book was edited by
Ann Petty, Dana Lane, and Cheryl Weissman
of the staff of the AEI Press.
The index was prepared by Shirley Kessel.
The text was set in Palatino, a typeface designed by
the twentieth-century Swiss designer Hermann Zapf.
Publication Technology Corporation of Fairfax, Virginia,
set the type, and Edwards Brothers Incorporated,
of Ann Arbor, Michigan, printed and bound the book,
using permanent acid-free paper.

The AEI Press is the publisher for the American Enterprise Institute for Public Policy Research, 1150 17th Street, N.W., Washington, D.C. 20036; *Christopher C. DeMuth*, publisher; *Edward Styles*, director; *Dana Lane*, assistant director; *Ann Petty*, editor; *Cheryl Weissman*, editor; *Mary Cristina Delaney*, editorial assistant (rights and permissions). Books published by the AEI Press are distributed by arrangement with the University Press of America, 4720 Boston Way, Lanham, Md. 20706.

www.ingramcontent.com/pod-product-compliance
Lightning Source LLC
Jackson TN
JSHW011935131224
75386JS00041B/1404